Raising Boys in a New Kind of World

RAISING BOYS in a NEW KIND of WORLD

MICHAEL REIST

DUNDURN
TORONTO

Editor: Allister Thompson
Design: Jesse Hooper
Printer: Webcom

Library and Archives Canada Cataloguing in Publication

Reist, Michael
    Raising boys in a new kind of world / by Michael Reist.

Includes bibliographical references and index.
Issued also in electronic formats.
ISBN 978-1-4597-0043-7

    1. Boys. 2. Parenting. 3. Child rearing. I. Title.

HQ775.R45 2011   649'.132   C2011-903837-4

2   3   4   5   15   14   13   12

Conseil des Arts   Canada Council
du Canada   for the Arts

Canada

ONTARIO ARTS COUNCIL
CONSEIL DES ARTS DE L'ONTARIO

We acknowledge the support of the **Canada Council for the Arts** and the **Ontario Arts Council** for our publishing program. We also acknowledge the financial support of the **Government of Canada** through the **Canada Book Fund** and **Livres Canada Books**, and the **Government of Ontario** through the **Ontario Book Publishing Tax Credit** and the **Ontario Media Development Corporation**.

Care has been taken to trace the ownership of copyright material used in this book. The author and the publisher welcome any information enabling them to rectify any references or credits in subsequent editions.

J. Kirk Howard, President

Printed and bound in Canada.
www.dundurn.com

Dundurn	Gazelle Book Services Limited	Dundurn
3 Church Street, Suite 500	White Cross Mills	2250 Military Road
Toronto, Ontario, Canada	High Town, Lancaster, England	Tonawanda, NY
M5E 1M2	LA1 4XS	U.S.A. 14150

MIX
Paper from
responsible sources
FSC
www.fsc.org   FSC® C004071

To Thomas, Rachel, Justin, and Luke

CONTENTS

Acknowledgements   9

PART ONE: A New Kind of World   **11**
A World of Change   13
The World of School   23

PART TWO: A Not So New Kind of Boy   **45**
The Unique Nature of Boys   47
Understanding Normal Boy Behaviour   73
ADD or Normal Boy Behaviour?   87
Practical Strategies That Work with All Boys   103
Boys, Reading, and Writing   117
The Emotional Lives of Boys   131
Boys and Sports   153
Bullying   157

PART THREE: The Electronic World of Boys   **177**
The World of Video Games   179
The World of Social Networking   195
The World of Movies and Television   201
How to Deal with the Electronic World   205

PART FOUR: A New Kind of Parent   **209**
Parenting in a New Kind of World   211
The Will to Power   233

Anger   241
Communication   245
Self-Esteem   251
Discipline   257

PART FIVE: Raising Boys with Character   **263**
What Media Teaches About Character   265
What is Character?   269
Can Character be Taught?   273
The Nature of Character   283
On Being a "Good Parent"   295
Advice to Fathers   297

Bibliography   299
Index   305

ACKNOWLEDGEMENTS

For detailed advice and expert editing, I would like to thank Allister Thompson, senior editor at Dundurn Press, as well as freelance editor Christina Attard.

I am grateful to the staff of the Caledon Public Library, particularly Penny Ridler, for their moral support and the quiet space they provide in an over-stimulating world.

The administration of Dufferin-Peel Catholic District School Board, particularly my superintendents, Cathy Saytar and Paul McMorrow, and my principal, Ed McMahon, have supported my work outside of the classroom for many years.

I have learned much from my colleagues at Robert F. Hall Catholic Secondary School, where I owe a particular debt of gratitude to my friends, Cecilia Kennedy and Brenda Holtkamp.

My most important influences in educational administration and teaching have been Lorne Howcroft, Sr. Lucille Corrigan, and Sr. Grace Martin, my first mentor and kind ear, as well as Oliva Tersigni, who showed me it was possible to "change with the times" without losing one's integrity.

Many of my most important mentors I have only met through their written words. The greatest of these is A.S. Neill, who completely changed the way I thought about education and child-rearing. Alice Miller, Neil Postman, Robert Bly, James Hollis, Jean Vanier, William Pollack, Michael Gurian, and Leonard Sax have also had a profound and liberating influence on my thinking about raising children, being male, and the special needs of boys.

I am particularly indebted to my personal mentor and dear friend, Graham Jackson, a leading thinker in the area of male gender issues.

Of course, my greatest debt lies with the hundreds of students (and their parents) I have taught, counselled, and mentored over thirty years in the classroom. Much of the information in this book comes directly from them.

My wife, Linda, has been my main collaborator and wise guide in all my work. My children, Thomas, Rachel, Justin, and Luke, continue to teach me new things every day about this new kind of world!

PART ONE

A NEW KIND of WORLD

A WORLD of CHANGE

What's New About the World and What's Not?

The more things change, the more they stay the same. One thing that has remained the same over the centuries is parental disdain for the new kind of world they see around them. This world is only new to us, and it's the only one our children know. They haven't lived long enough to see the kind of social change that has taken place in the last twenty or thirty years. For them, what they see around them is "normal," and they have nothing to compare it with until they start to learn about history. It has always been this way. Parents feel the changes in the world; kids don't. Parents often react defensively, and children do not understand what all the fuss is about. Negative parental reactions often originate in hostility toward change. Most adults tend to see their own formative years as normal and what comes afterward as a decline. The only constant is change, and parents and their children experience this in fundamentally different ways.

In the parent-child dynamic, one question is often: Which of us is going to change? Another is: Are we going to move forward or backward? We can assume a conservative attitude toward the modern world, holding on to those things we value, or a progressive one, embracing positive change. In the end, both are necessary. Many things about the past are worth keeping, and many things about the present and future are worth embracing. The adult who changes with the times is a positive image, but there is a danger of being swept away. Change is inevitable, but some is for the better, some for the worse.

T.H. White said, "The old exist for the benefit of the young, not vice versa." Adults have a guiding role to play in managing the impact of social change as children negotiate their way through the world. The dragons that lurk on the periphery are real. One of the most powerful examples today is corporate capitalism, its marketing to children, and the creation of a shallow popular culture that stands ready to claim our children as unconscious full-time citizens.

This leaves parents facing their own worries, another constant in parental history. Will my child be happy? Will he be successful? Am I doing the right thing? Am I screwing my kid up? Am I being too lenient? Am I being too strict? What is normal? This book attempts to help parents answer these questions, as well as others, such as: What should we hold on to and what should we let go of? What are the new rules? Do any of the old ones still apply? In a world of moral relativism, these questions are more important than ever before.

Jesus Meets *Family Guy*: The Postmodern Crisis

Every period in history is dominated by a school of philosophy or system of thought. The school that dominates our time is called post-modernism. It began with a very important message, the need to move beyond the cultural dominance of "dead white males" and beyond a Euro-centric, patriarchal culture to one that includes the voice of the so-called "Other." This was an all-encompassing term for those voices that had never been included in any systems of power — women and cultural minorities most of all. Postmodernism blew the whistle on gender, race, and class structures and the way only a few players were deciding what was "true" and "normal."

Postmodernism has done the world a great service. It has opened our collective minds to the possibility that we may not have the complete truth and that we should include a whole new range of people in the discussion. In the transition from a universal truth to a "democracy of ideas," postmodernism made us question our assumptions about everything.

This radical questioning has led to the postmodern crisis. The impulse to question all structures of power did not stop at politics, religion, and culture. It moved into all areas of life. One of the most problematic is morality. Before postmodernism, there were certain "sacred cows," areas of morality and behaviour that were not questioned. Some truths were conceived of as objective, universal, and therefore irrefutable. That world is now gone. Postmodernism states that all truths become relative. They can be held by sub-groups only.

This has had profound implications for parents and kids in a postmodern world without metaphysical reference points. If there is one thing that young people seek, it is truth. In adolescence in particular, when they are re-creating themselves, they ask who they are, what the world is, and most importantly, what the truth is. When they look to their culture, they don't see clear answers. When in 2005 a Danish cartoonist was attacked for depicting Muhammad in a cartoon (Islam considers images of the prophet sacrilegious), his response was a postmodern one: It may be sacrilegious to you, but it's not to me. I am under no compulsion to adhere to your conceptions of truth. This logic might not be so bad if the next line of reasoning didn't follow: I am under no obligation to respect your version of the truth.

In an episode of *Family Guy*, there is a scene where Jesus is in the workshop with Joseph and they are fighting about something. Jesus calls God on his cellphone. "Dad, this isn't working out. You need to come and get me." The scene switches to Heaven, where God is in bed with a woman. "Sorry, Son, I can't make it. Besides, it's not my weekend." And he hangs up. Then God turns to the woman and pleads with her that he not have to wear a condom because it's his birthday. This episode was shown all over North America in the six p.m. time slot. This is the postmodern world. Nothing is sacred, everything can be mocked, and nothing is more important than anything else.

Anyone who questions this phenomenon and uses an example from religion is thought to be a reactionary zealot, a closed-minded conservative who cannot tolerate any kind of change and has no sense of humour. Even in our secular, liberal society, we still need immutable core values. Perhaps respect for the views of others might be one of those values. Depicting God in bed with a woman talking about condoms shows no regard for those who have strong religious feelings. We don't need to defend belief in God, but we could defend the notion of respect for those who do.

I feel that one of the reasons why there are such high incidences of depression, substance abuse, apathy, and high-risk behaviour among adolescents is the moral vacuum they live in. If everything is stupid and nothing is important, why would I devote myself to anything? What's the point?

All humans seek transcendent values. As individuals and as cultural groups, we live by certain ideals. What becomes of us when these transcendent ideals are mocked and ridiculed? We end up living in this moral vacuum where sensual pleasure and distraction from anything "inner" becomes the norm. It is a sad norm, because it does not satisfy one of the deepest needs we have: a meaning to life.

Romeo and Juliet Are Back: The Disappearance of Childhood

When Neil Postman wrote his classic work, *The Disappearance of Childhood*, the Internet had not yet been invented — or at least had not entered the public consciousness. Postman's thesis was that an age of literacy had been ushered in with the invention of the printing press, extending the length of childhood beyond puberty. With the mass production of books came mass literacy. Children had to become literate and then acquire the knowledge that it brought. This took time. Now, in the post-literate, visual age, childhood has become shortened once again; some would argue it ends with puberty. Once kids reach the age of sexual awareness, they quickly know what adults know.

For those who grew up in the final years of the age of literacy, there was still a distinction between adult and child knowledge. Becoming an adult meant becoming proficient in the processing of text and being initiated into adult knowledge. Today, especially since the advent of the Internet, the distinctions between child and adult knowledge, experience, behaviour, tastes, and interests are becoming blurred. Increasingly, we have a kind of adolescent society in which children become little adults at thirteen and adults remain big adolescents until fifty or later.

Becoming an adult at thirteen is not without precedent; we need only look back to *Romeo and Juliet*. Juliet was that age. As Paris reminds Juliet's father while coaxing him to approve their marriage, "Younger than she are happy mothers made." Romeo is thought to have been around sixteen. These were common ages for marriage in a world where sexual maturity was the main marker for adulthood. We seem to be returning to that kind of society. There are few "adult secrets" that my grade nines don't know. Because of changing standards in the mass media, they have seen many things that I never have or certainly hadn't when I was fourteen.

Increasingly, teenagers see themselves as equals to the adults in their lives. The kind of deference to age common in the previous generation is slowly disappearing. Respect for age and authority is no longer an automatic social convention; respect is something that has to be earned. This may not necessarily be a bad thing. Earlier generations were taught to unquestioningly respect and obey many authority figures who perhaps did not really deserve it. Perhaps respect and obedience *should* be earned.

If there is one change I have noticed over the years, it is a growing unwillingness to automatically respect roles. More and more, the attitude of teenagers is: "I will respect you if you show me by your actions (not just your words) that you deserve it," and, most importantly, "I will respect you to the same extent that you show respect for me." This is especially true for today's adolescents, who sometimes have more intelligence, common sense, maturity, and even wisdom than some of their elders. As a teacher, I have known many bright and gifted teenagers who have chafed under authorities who were adults in years only.

This demand for respect and the earning of authority could be seen as a very positive trend, but it is going to be difficult for those adults who were raised in a "do what you're told because I said so" kind of world and still believe in it.

New Kinds of Families

Since young people will sometimes find a parental figure in a teacher, it could be said generally that many people are finding family member substitutes elsewhere. Men find sisters in female friends, women find brothers in male friends, and kids find aunts and uncles in a whole range of new connections. Where once we were born into families, many people today are, in a sense, choosing theirs. In the past, the biological nuclear and extended family was an unquestioned norm. Today, with the breakdown of the nuclear family, we often see electrons choosing different nuclei to revolve around.

Over the years I have played the role of father to many kids. I have a female friend I consider a sister. My wife has an elderly female friend who has been a mother figure to her. We could all name relationships that have the quality of a family tie. This is a good thing. In our fast-paced, disjointed world, where families dissolve and then reconstruct every few years, where geographic distance can lead to long gaps in relationships, it is good that we find others to love, to love us, and to fulfill roles previously played by nuclear and extended family. It does take a village to raise a child, and many people are constructing their own little villages in the networks of relationships they create.

A New Kind of God

There are two god images that no longer work for the majority of people in the post-Christian West: the angry, punishing "sky God" and the sensitive "best friend Jesus." God images work when they are invested with the psychic energy of a group. This energy has been largely withdrawn. These images will never die out completely, because there are still many people for whom they make sense.

It is important to distinguish between our images of God and the reality — which is ultimately a great mystery. The prevailing images are anthropocentric ones, of a God made in our own image and likeness. God is depicted as an old man with a white beard who lives up above the clouds. Because Jesus was an historical figure who lived in the Middle East two thousand years ago, our images of him are a little more bound to external reality. However, though there are clearer human parameters dictating an image, we have still remade him into a soft, white, long-haired man, ignoring any relationship to his actual appearance. Most people who were introduced to this superficial God at a young age keep these images in their minds, and they have the same understanding of God as they did when they were children. They have done no inner work in this area.

Images of God have particular relevance to males because of the historical tendency to see the deity as male. This tendency was a by-product of patriarchal social structures. When it came to picturing God in a world ruled by men, the logical choice was a kind of alpha-male God who would be the ultimate king, warrior, disciplinarian, and autocrat. Does this patriarchal view still resonate? For many males, the Old Testament God is more appealing than Jesus. He is a kind of Zeus figure who gets things done and doesn't let anyone stand in his way. He is no-nonsense and virile and has no time for the feelings of others. His own feelings are limited to anger and frustration at those who thwart his will. The Yahweh-Zeus-Sky God is quite commonly found in fantasy role-playing video games and reality TV shows like *The Apprentice* or *Dragon's Den*. The ethos of patriarchy is still strong in business, government, and religion.

The resilience of the Old Testament God image is a reaction to the rise of feminism. As women have gained greater power in society, men seem to experience a feeling of insecurity about their own place in the power structure. In 1991, Susan Faludi published a book titled *Backlash: The Undeclared War Against American Women*, in which she argued, "the last decade has seen a powerful counterassault on women's rights, a backlash, an attempt to retract the handful of small and hard-won victories that the feminist movement did manage to win for women."

One of the forms this backlash has taken is the reassertion of hyper-masculine heroes in popular culture. From Arnold Schwarzenegger (*Terminator* I–IV, 1984–2009) to Sylvester Stallone (*Rocky* I–VI, 1976–2006), the angry, violent male reasserted himself with a vengeance. This image continues apace in movies, video games, and UFC (Ultimate Fighting Championship). There seems to be a desire on the part of many males to reassert their own power or ascendancy, if only in the realm of fantasy. The Old Testament God fits in with this alpha-male hero image. In contrast, the image of the suffering, defeated Jesus is a hard sell today. With his emaciated countenance, crown of thorns, and long white robe, he has become an object of ridicule, even scorn. Videos abound on websites like YouTube that mock and satirize this image of Jesus.

God the Father and our Sons

The other fact that makes the God image particularly problematic for males today is the metaphor of God as father. For many boys, the content of "father" has become damaged or tainted either by their own experience or the image of fatherhood presented in popular culture. Many boys are living without a father physically or emotionally present in the home. Many fathers have "left," even when they are there "in body," and the relationship can range from weak to non-existent. While it is true that there are many fathers who remain actively connected to their sons, the number seems to be shrinking. Men have largely abdicated the parenting role to the mother.

The other source of information about fatherhood comes from popular culture, where the two main images of males are the violent man and the stupid one. The violent man is seldom if ever depicted as a father. He is independent in the extreme, and a family would just hold him back. The stupid man is often portrayed as a father, and this almost seems to be part of his problem. He is shown trapped in a family with a nagging wife and whining kids.

The metaphor of God as father figure is a confusing one for boys, because the content of what "father" means has become so complex. Our images of God give concrete form to an abstract reality. While the image may be worn out, problematic, or obsolete, the reality is as important as it has ever been. Boys experience transcendent reality from a very young age. They wonder about the ultimate questions: Why are we here? Who or what made all this? What is right and wrong? What is true? Kids, like adults, are looking for spiritual paths and wisdom. Boys need a god in the same way they need a father, both the image of a strong positive male and the wisdom and transcendence that such a being might be able to bestow.

Why the Pews are Empty

As traditional organized religions teeter under the pressures created by a new culture, they have tended to retreat and set themselves up over and against it. They no longer see themselves as agents of change within the culture or in dialogue with it. They see it as an enemy, something to protect themselves from, and this often means withdrawing and creating a kind of alternative culture that takes its forms from the past — a simpler time. The complexities of the modern world are simply ignored. This kind of religion will not suffice for most kids, nor should it. They need voices of wisdom helping them discern what's good and bad, what's right and wrong, what's real and unreal about the world in which they find themselves. Organized religion increasingly comes to resemble a kind of "package deal" — an all-inclusive permanent holiday from the complexity of modern life.

The American Jungian analyst, James Hollis, has said we are living between dispensations, that in the West we need a new revelation. To say that psychic energy has been withdrawn from the old forms is not to be understood as trivializing — as though religion was a psychological phenomenon or a balm for the soul.

The word "psyche" is an ancient Greek word meaning "soul." The soul has its own imperatives; it must be fed. The souls of

Western people are starving, but this state of affairs cannot go on forever. The soul will achieve what it needs both on the individual and collective levels.

At the end of the Roman Empire, the pantheon of gods suffered the same withdrawal of psychic energy on the part of the masses. As the current empire crumbles, the same kind of withdrawal seems to be happening around our mythologies, which are the forms that psychic energy takes. That energy will go somewhere else. Right now it has gone into materialism — we worship what we own, and the accumulation of money and objects is equated with virtue. Other quasi-religions are fame (the stars are our saints and being famous makes one virtuous) and physical fitness (we will achieve salvation through our own efforts, and health is virtue). Perhaps the new dispensation will arise out of the environmental crisis. Maybe the Gaia Hypothesis or ecotheology will lead to a new vision of religion and what it means to be religious.

The WORLD of SCHOOL

Mass Media and School

When we were growing up, school had one main competitor: television. Before television, school provided the first curriculum. It offered teachers, books, and resources of all kinds, and this was an information environment kids could not access at home. As Neil Postman has pointed out, after the arrival of television, mass media became the first curriculum. School could not compete with its colourful content, its ability to mesmerize, its hours of operation, or its budget. As television became the most important learning environment, people began to question the relevance of school. With the introduction of the personal computer and the Internet, this question has been magnified a hundred-fold. And now cyberspace has extended itself into the small cellphones that almost all students carry. If television made school "boring," imagine how it must increasingly seem to young people growing up perpetually online.

For years people asked me, "Mike, do you see any difference in kids today from when we were growing up?" During my first twenty years of teaching, I would kind of grope for an answer, but in the past five years or so I have definitely noticed a change. The Internet went public sometime around 1993. Kids born after that are now moving through our high schools, and they are a different breed. Whether or not they are heavy screen users, they are growing up in a world very much influenced by the Internet. The influence is seen in four main areas: attitudes toward authority, attention span, processing of text, and social skills.

The Computer is the New Printing Press

Some time around 1450, Gutenberg perfected the printing press and began the mass production of books. For centuries, books were only in the hands of an elite caste of the literate, the wealthy, and the holy. With the increase in the production of books came an increase in literacy rates. Now anyone could own a book. With the printing press, we entered the age of print, which, Marshall McLuhan told us, came to an end with the invention of television. In the 1950s, print culture was replaced by a visual one. McLuhan did not live long enough to see the Internet. Now, instead of holding books, each person can hold a screen.

Historians have shown us how the invention of the printing press led to the fall of two power structures: the Roman Catholic Church and the monarchy. By 1517, the fragmentation of Christendom had begun with Martin Luther famously posting his ninety-five theses on the church door in Wittenberg. A monolithic Catholic Church, which effectively ruled all of Europe, was fragmented into myriad denominations. Books led to the questioning of church authority and the introduction of the idea of participatory forms of religion. The other structure to fall under the influence of the printed book's ability to disseminate new ideas was the monarchy.

By 1649 in England and 1793 in France, monarchs had been beheaded by the decree of citizen assemblies. An invention, a machine, had led to the birth of democracy, which was about individual agency, the idea that I as an individual have some control over my life and my immediate culture. I do not need to bow to external authority.

The Internet takes this idea of individual agency to a new level. It has introduced the possibility of a kind of radical democracy never before seen. I believe the Internet will have as radical an effect on our culture as the printing press did on its. Though we are too close to see it, the revolution is happening all around us. The two pyramids that still appear to be standing are the family and the school. Some would argue that the nuclear family has already crumbled, but it still seems to persist as an ideal, if not a reality.

School is a pyramid currently under enormous external pressure as a result of information technologies. As the Catholic Church and the European monarchies once were, school is a hierarchical behemoth which operates from the top down and demands unquestioning compliance to its dictates.

The Pyramid Meets the Web: New Attitudes Toward Authority

We grew up in a world of pyramids or hierarchies. There were the people at the top who gave the orders, those in the middle who implemented those orders, and the majority at the bottom who followed orders. Government, church, school, the family — all of the institutions that governed our lives — were arranged in a hierarchical manner. The Internet uses a completely different metaphor than the pyramid — the web. The Internet has no head office and is not owned by anyone. If you don't like what's there, there is no one you can complain to. On the Internet, everyone has a voice and everyone is equal.

One day, I witnessed a meeting of the pyramid and the web. I worked in a school where the principal became the subject of an attack on Facebook. This principal was new to the school and had a more authoritarian approach than his predecessor. The senior students did not like his administrative style, so they chose to express their views online. They created a site specifically aimed at criticizing the principal, both for his administrative style and his character. These were not bad kids or rebels. They were not disenfranchised. They were honour-roll students, including the president of the student council. What's interesting about this story is what happened when the kids were "called on the carpet" for their actions.

On Facebook, it is not hard to figure out who is responsible. The creator of the site is listed, as are its administrators and anyone who posts a comment. So it was not difficult to round up the culprits. The day the kids were called into the office, the web met the pyramid.

The attitude of the administration was outrage: "How dare you! What you did was wrong!" The attitude of the web kids was confusion: "What did we do wrong?" They had done this at home in their bedrooms or basements, on the greatest level playing field history has ever known, and now they were about to be punished for it by the pyramid. A number of students received suspensions, some received verbal reprimands. The story made it to evening newscasts across Canada, and a week or two later, one of the main students was the subject of a front-page feature article in the *Toronto Star* in which he continued to express his incredulity at having been reprimanded at school for something he'd done at home or, perhaps more accurately, in cyberspace.

What this episode revealed was the clash of cultures, occurring nowhere more strongly than at school. Attitudes toward authority have undergone a sea change. The Internet has made possible a kind of radical democracy unknown before. Was Barack Obama elected in the United States because of the Democratic Party's fundraising machine or was it the grassroots support rallied in cyberspace that put him over the top? Around the world we see authoritarian regimes teetering as the masses mobilize and agitate in front of flickering screens.

The other question we have to ask ourselves is whether the pyramid was all it was cracked up to be? There is a voice in our collective heads (sometimes heard out there in the real world): What kids need today is *more* discipline and *more* authority! What is really meant by this is "more control" over youth and a return to the pyramid. We grew up in world where you were rewarded for doing what you were told by someone else. When we used even a modicum of critical thinking and asked "Why?" the justification "Because I said so!" was enough to silence us. This world is passing away.

Do kids need structure? Absolutely. Will they allow it to be imposed on them arbitrarily? Increasingly, the answer is no. Kids want choice and freedom; they want a say in how things are done. They have become used to this kind of autonomy from an early age, and they are frustrated when they enter into systems of power, like school, which operate from the top down.

The War of the Worlds:
School Space and Cyberspace

How do I turn the teacher off? The problem is … you can't. In cyberspace, one is completely autonomous. The person holding the mouse controls everything. With video games, it's not called a mouse; it's a controller! As soon as anything becomes boring, just click and it's gone. If things aren't moving fast enough, I open another screen and have two things going at the same time. I can have as many going on simultaneously as I want. On the screen, I am in charge of what I do and where I go. We grew up with television, which was a passive medium. We just sat and received whatever signal was sent out. The extent of our control was our ability to change the channel. The computer is an interactive medium over which the user has much more control.

From this world, the child enters school space, where there is no mouse or controller. I cannot click the teacher away or minimize the screen. Who would look at a single website for seventy-six minutes, the length of a secondary school class? Last night online, I was in complete control of everything. Here I have no control, or at least, in comparison, I feel as though I don't. Viktor Frankl said, "The last of all human freedoms is the freedom to choose your own attitude." This happens so often in the classroom. When students feel they have no power, they call up their one last "weapon"— their attitude, which may range anywhere from apathy or cynicism to outright hostility and anger. The classroom has become the front line of the conflict between the two kinds of worlds that young people live in: one in which they have a feeling of complete autonomy, the other in which they feel impotent.

In classrooms today, students are sitting through lessons that, to them, are like websites they don't want to visit, or bland, slow-moving video games. They are bored and frustrated. Somehow, we are going to have to figure out how to put the mouse or the controller in their hands. It will require more, not less, from them. Schools will feel this change as a loss of power, having always decided what websites get looked at and games get played. The role of schools is going to have to change — the tensions that exist there cannot continue indefinitely.

The issue comes down to one of power and control. Schools respond to this tension by trying to exert more control over students. Some schools are trying to bring back the pyramid with a vengeance. I don't think this is going to work in the long run. The school of the future is going to have to allow students a greater say, more choice, and as a result, will demand more responsibility for those choices. If students are just following orders out of fear of punishment or hope of reward, there is not a lot of responsibility being taken. If students have to decide for themselves if they want something and how they are going to achieve their goals, they are more likely to take responsibility for the outcomes. More freedom and more responsibility — these are both good things.

Pay Attention! Our ADD Culture

If there is one area where I have noticed a change in kids, it's attention span. Most kids cannot sustain attention on one subject for anything near the length of an average class. The Internet is based on the principle of distraction. Every web page contains all kinds of options, and whatever flickers or moves is noticed. Most people don't stay on one page for very long. There is constant choice, novelty, and change. Compare that world to school, where students can feel trapped in a radically slowed down world.

Some say that the normal attention span of a child is their age in minutes. A ten-year-old should be able to focus for ten minutes before being distracted. However, they will also consistently return to the task. Being distracted is natural; we all have our threshold for paying attention, but I think it is getting lower for everyone.

It could be argued that one of the main indicators of future success in school is the ability to pay attention for long periods of time. Contrary to the common stereotype, even kids with Attention Deficit Disorder (ADD/ADHD) can do that, if they find the activity interesting. There's the rub. Let me revise what I just said: the key indicator of future success in school is the ability to pay attention for long periods *to things you're not interested in!* I find kids less and less willing to commit to activities in which they have little or no interest. This could be seen as a positive quality. To use Joseph Campbell's phrase, they follow their bliss. They can be passionate about their own interests. Some kids are capable of "hyperfocusing," being absorbed in a task to the exclusion of all else. We've all heard the comment, "A bomb could go off while he's … and he wouldn't even notice." This is hyperfocusing. Unfortunately, school does not reward this kind of behaviour.

Success in school demands an equal interest in everything. We have a vision of the well-rounded student who has good general knowledge in all areas. This image is becoming harder to maintain. Many kids are just deciding to put their pencils down and zone out or focus on something else. They may appear lazy or distracted or oppositional, but often they just have a deep-seated belief that there is no point in devoting yourself to something you find boring. For kids today (and increasingly for adults, too), all experience can be reduced to two categories: fun and boring. It is a by-product of what Postman called "The Age of Entertainment," in which all social discourse and every activity tries to make itself appear "entertaining." Every teacher secretly curses Robin Williams for his role in *Dead Poets Society*. The teacher as stand-up comic is a hard role to sustain.

Leonard Sax has advocated earlier specialization in school, and I tend to agree with him. Many parents counter this view by saying, "But they're too young to know what they want." Many students in grade twelve still report having no idea what they want to do with their lives. Perhaps this phenomenon is a result of always having to be at least mediocre at many things. Throughout school, they are required to stay on a sight-seeing bus that never stops moving. They have a superficial look at many things, but they are never allowed to get off the bus and really explore one thing in depth — perhaps thereby discovering a passion. As Mark Twain said, "I've never let school interfere with my education." For many young people, the process of school, with its lock-step curriculum, keeps them from becoming truly educated or proficient in at least one area.

The End of Literacy

The other area where I have noticed an even more profound shift is in students' ability to process text — to read and write. I find this is a particular issue with boys during and after puberty. Testosterone tends to inhibit language production and reception. How many mothers have lamented to me, "When he was little, he used to love to read. He read all the time. And now? He never reads. He used to talk all the time. Now all he does is grunt!" This is the natural result of increased levels of testosterone, a hormone that stimulates the spatial brain while inhibiting the language centre. Cyberspace is a visual-spatial world, not a text world. In this post-literate age, more and more people are getting their information from pictures. The typical male brain is spatial and visual. It loves cyberspace, which is a feast of looking and virtual motion. Boys' reading and writing scores are declining every year because they are coming to school from cyberspace.

When I hand out George Orwell's novel *Nineteen Eighty-Four* to my grade twelve class, I give a little lesson on cognitive functioning. Using my old technology of chalk and blackboard, I draw a line across the board representing thought processes while online. The line starts off straight, then a new line branches off that one, another branches from that, and so on until the board is covered with lines representing the free associations that the mind follows online. One logs on to check the weather and ends up twenty web pages later buying something on eBay.

The mind online works by association pushed along its cognitive path by the principle of distraction or free association. And, I go on to explain, this is only happening on one window. You have five or six windows minimized along the bottom between which you switch. It could be argued that this ability to juggle many mental tasks simultaneously is a wonderful skill. Women's brains have always been credited with greater ability to multi-task, but males are developing this skill in cyberspace. Many of our kids will end up working at a screen, and these abilities may serve them well. Dave Crenshaw, the author of *The Myth of Multitasking*, disagrees. For him, multitasking leads to inefficiency.

However, remember we are comparing cyberspace to the old information environment of school. School is very conservative and slow to change. It is not a visual-spatial environment; it is a language environment that is logical, linear, and verbal. School values the ability to process text above all others. This is true whether you're heading for a career in science, computers, or apprenticing as a plumber. The stickers that school gives out are given most generously to those who can read and write well or can speak and listen well. Visual literacy and the ability to multi-task in space are not (yet) rewarded the way language is.

And so back to my lesson on cognitive functioning with my grade twelve class. I erase the lines of association from cyberspace, and I start again. This time, I say, I am going to illustrate how the mind works when "logged on" to that older information format, the book. I put the chalk on the board, and I tell them, "this is page one." Then I move the chalk along the board in a straight line. "After page one, there is only one place you can go — page two. Followed by page three, then page four, then page five, then page six, then page seven — for three hundred pages!" My students look at me in shock (and with laughter) as this reality sinks in. "Hey, that's right!" they exclaim.

I say, "The only reason I am showing you this is to bring it to consciousness. The decision to be print-literate today is just that: a decision. I grew up in a world that supported print literacy, or at least did not undermine it. You are growing up in a visual-spatial world that does not support print literacy. Print is still the number one ability valued in school. So here's the rub, if you want to be successful in school, you're going to have to *decide* to be print-literate, and that means going into your room, turning off the electronics, and practicing the language arts of reading and writing. Someday school may change, but right now, the rewards go to those who can read, write, speak, and listen."

I feel we owe it to our kids to explain this. I imagine the situation might have been similar when Latin was dying out and being replaced throughout Europe by vernacular languages. Even though the "outside" world was changing, schools continued to keep Latin as the language of instruction. Now, amazingly, we have to impress upon kids that reading and writing generally are the prerequisites for success.

The Final Frontier: Social Skills

One of the biggest differences between cyberspace and school space is that school is a social place. It requires the negotiation of a whole host of "inputs." By this I mean managing the information received from interacting with actual flesh-and-blood human beings with thoughts, emotions, body language, tone of voice, moods, a long list of variables to deal with. What mood is the teacher in? How am I coming across to him, to the other students? What is that person "saying" in their tone, body language, or general behaviour? Answering these questions requires a set of complex skills that can only be practised and developed in real-life situations.

The social environment of school is the one in which kids spend most of their day. Teachers notice more and more kids who seem to have a difficult time reading social feedback. They also see a decline in the ability to practise basic social protocols like waiting your turn, waiting for someone to finish speaking before you speak, seeing a situation from another person's point of view, and modifying one's behaviour according to the situation, to name a few. A growing percentage of teachers' time is spent imparting social skills.

In cyberspace, very few social skills are required; communication is mostly one-way. Cyberspace is a solitary landscape where it is always your turn and your voice is the only one that matters. Social networks like MSN, Facebook, email, and text messaging require some back-and-forth, but the mode of communication is quite simplistic. There is no tone of voice and no body language (emoticons are used for this purpose). Communication takes the form of lines of text, often using acronyms and abbreviations. Compared to prose writing, there are no stylistic nuances. There is very little to infer because nothing is implied. Statements are often quite blunt and superficial. There is little need to read between the lines, because there's usually nothing there.

Sit Still! The Need for Movement

Finally, cyberspace is a place in which one can move around. The movement is only virtual, but it is perceived by the mind as real. This is especially true in video games, where the movement is usually through a landscape or, in the case of sports video games, a playing field. The bodily-kinaesthetic boy, who needs to move around, derives some degree of satisfaction from this virtual movement. When he comes to school, this freedom to move is often forbidden. Elementary schools are still relatively tolerant of movement, although this seems to be changing as I hear more about the primary division, where some boys are increasingly considered problematic. The bodily-kinaesthetic boy who comes to high school may be faced with three seventy-six-minute periods before he has a lunch break. In most high school classrooms, there is little opportunity for movement, and sitting still is one of the most valued behaviours a student can demonstrate. Fidgeting, moving around in one's seat, walking around in class, or asking to go to the washroom are seen as annoyances and treated as disruptions.

A Word About the History of School

Schools as we know them today are a product of the post-war period. The Baby Boom created such growth in enrolments that education had to reorganize itself and retool to function on a mass scale. Boards amalgamated and schools became bigger. Education, which had been administered on a more human scale before the war, now turned into an effort of mass production. Schools were built on a factory model, a single process applied uniformly to raw materials, creating a value-added product: graduates.

The social experiment of mass schooling up to the age of eighteen is now about sixty years old. The pressures on this institution have never been greater. They are difficult to see from the outside. If you drive by any modern school, you will see neatly-kept buildings with signs out front announcing upcoming events. All appears well. The pressures are more visible inside the classroom, a place few people see. These internal pressures are caused by three assumptions upon which school is based but which are now obsolete. The first is that print literacy is the main way of measuring intelligence or ability. Secondly, that rigid hierarchical structures work best with children and teenagers. Thirdly, that all children will benefit from the imposition of one standardized process.

Before the 1950s, school generally provided an information environment richer than the home. School had educated teachers, books, and other resources. With the advent of television, school had competition as a dispenser of knowledge. In the age of the Internet, school as an information environment has become obsolete. Its main function today is to provide socialization, distraction, and warehousing of large numbers of youth. Schools keep kids out of their parents' busy lives, off the streets, and out of the full-time workforce.

The cinder-block boxes in which children sit do not make sense to the majority of students. They have tolerated this environment and its processes up until now because of the social payoff and because there was no other game in town. They see the social payoff as questionable, and now there is a new game (sometimes literally

penalties are chafing to so many students. Kids need to see the logic
of the structure and, ideally, to have input into the arrangements.
They come from a world where they have so much autonomy and
expect the same kind of "say" at school. What if kids participated
in formulating the rules? Helped form the rules of the classroom?
Participated in deciding the consequences for misbehaviour? What
if they had a say in curriculum design?

The school of the future will have to be more democratic.
We say we are preparing students for citizenship in a democracy,
yet most schools resemble autocratic dictatorships. They have a
top-down management structure in which procedures and rules
are decreed from above. Principals do what they are told by the
board, teachers take orders from the principal, and students are
directed by the teacher. School rewards unquestioning obedience
to authority; you will be safe as long as you do what you are told.
Any kind of questioning of the teacher or the administration is
met with polite indifference at best or hostility at worst. The alienation so many students feel is a result of this disenfranchisement
— having no control over how things are done. If students had a
say in how schools were run, there would be greater variety, and
the forms would more accurately reflect the diversity among the
population.

Parents' voices also should be brought more into schools. They
too have much to say, but because they are not part of the official hierarchy, they are often excluded. Parents' councils are politely tolerated
as long as they stick to fundraising and other "supportive" activities.
If they begin to tread on areas like budgeting or staffing decisions, or
methods of curriculum delivery, they are met with stony silence. It is
a surprising state of affairs that those who literally pay for the running
of the school have so little say in its management.

This leads to the final assumption: the idea that all children will
benefit from one standardized process. The factory model is part of
what Janice Stein has called "the cult of efficiency."

> Efficiency is often a cloak for political agendas.…
> The discussion of efficiency in the delivery of public
> goods, such as education and healthcare has risen
> to prominence in post-industrial society. When it
> [efficiency] becomes an end rather than a means, a
> value often more important than other values, and
> when we no longer ask the questions, 'efficient at
> what?' or 'for whom?' efficiency becomes a cult.

Public education places a very high value on uniformity, standardization, consistency, and accountability, which are code words for compliance with the status quo. The first priority in the political agenda of any institution is self-preservation, even if it means abandoning its own goals. At this point, the institution becomes dysfunctional. It continues to function, as schools in North America do today, but it does not achieve the end it claims to.

Schools like to use the term "fairness." "That's not fair!" is a verdict robustly delivered by kids of all ages. Fairness is a term predicated upon a notion of justice, but fairness has come to have a much more simplistic definition in public schools. Here it means "sameness." What you do for one, you have to do for the other. "It's only fair." Mel Levine challenged this view in his book *A Mind at a Time*, when he said, "To treat everyone the same is to treat them unequally."

The school of the future is going to have to pay far greater attention to differences and learn how to treat individuals as distinct from each other. In his book *The Rights Revolution*, Michael Ignatieff described the process of claiming individual rights as "enhancing our right to be equal and protecting our right to be different." Again, Levine puts it succinctly in *A Mind at a Time*: "It is normal to be different." What will we do with all our standardized tests, all our norm-based references, all our percentile placements when we finally acknowledge the truth of this statement?

The school of the future is going to have to be a much more complex place where many different things will be happening.

Some students will be sitting in classrooms, others might be at home on their computers, and others may be in the workplace. All will be learning in a different way. The penitentiary model where education is thought of as "time served" will have to be replaced, as will the factory model. Age-mixing will become the new norm. There will be greater emphasis on individualized curriculum and independent learning. The school building will be only one of many possible locations where the student might be found. Evaluation of student knowledge and skills will take many different forms, and percentage grades will be replaced with other forms of feedback. A high school diploma will have many different meanings.

University entrance will no longer be the tail that wags the dog. The great funnel of school starts with a wide, inclusive reception in kindergarten, then acts to restrict more and more kids as they move through the system — heading toward the "logical outcome" of university — the small end of the funnel. Those who do not make it are shunted off to the side, or they "drop down" to another academic level. Our current educational system is a class system (perhaps even a caste system). Our secondary schools resemble the *Titanic* with its first- and second-class compartments, and steerage, which is filled with those for whom the system does not work. The numbers there are growing, not because they're stupid, but because the game is rigged against them and they refuse to play any longer.

In North America, we labour under the myth that every child can be a doctor or a lawyer (these professions have become our questionable personifications of success). They just have to work hard enough. Every kindergarten student is at the starting line for a race to academia. We need to re-think our metaphors of school. Is it a race, a prison, a factory, a game, a hot house, a sorting room for the social order? Or is it the *Titanic*, too big to move out of the way of the iceberg?

In my talks to parent groups, I have used the metaphor of the garden. When the crocus blooms in April, we don't call it gifted. When the Michaelmas Daisy blooms in September, we don't call it learning disabled. Why do we have this understanding about flowers, but not children? When it comes to them, organic meta-phors are more helpful than mechanistic ones. It is interesting that our word "kindergarten" comes from two German words meaning *children* and *garden*. If school were seen as a garden, we would know that each plant has its own nature, needs, and blossoming time. Mechanistic metaphors always imply some kind of "outcome" or "product." The outcome expected of a garden is that all the plants in it thrive and come to fruition — whatever that fruit may be.

Jesus said, "You can judge a tree by its fruits." This statement stands as a particular challenge to schools, whose "fruits" are not always what we would expect. The beautiful four-year-old who entered kindergarten so full of promise, curiosity, and enthusiasm emerges from grade twelve full of insecurities, self-doubt, cyni-cism, and lethargy. School has played a part in this "outcome," and we should have the courage to ask what can be changed and how it can be done.

How Will This Change Happen?

There are three methods of institutional change: top down, bottom up, and inside out. Politicians and administrators have the power to change schools from the top down. Students, parent groups, and teacher associations have the power to agitate for change from the bottom up. Parents and teachers can change schools by altering their expectations of school and their assumptions about education. These are all huge undertakings. Most adults prefer the familiar status quo — we just have to try harder at what we are already doing. We need to spend more money on the problem.

This takes us back to that most profound question in educa-tion, originally posed by A.S. Neill in *Summerhill*: do we make the child fit the school or the school fit the child? If we look at attitude and behaviour problems as symptoms and not the disease, then the whole conversation could change. Instead of asking how to change attitudes and behaviour, we need to ask, what is it about the current environment and practices that are causing these things? This leads to an even more profound question: who needs to change — kids or adults?

Adults do not deal well with change, especially in the conservative world of education. When a strategy doesn't work, we often just redouble our efforts or resort to methods of external control to get kids to comply. We are left with the illusion of a functioning system, but scratch the surface and we see that it is only "working" for those willing to comply. As discussed earlier, the new kind of kid feels a sense of empowerment and entitlement unknown in previous generations. More and more students are simply unwilling to comply with systems of control they deem absurd. Students will change the nature of schools through their refusal to participate.

Our methods will not change until our thinking does, and this is very hard to accomplish. Our paradigms are so ingrained, and we take as normal and objectively true so many things that are simply arbitrary social constructs. School is one of the most obvious examples of a social construct that could be re-arranged a hundred different ways. The main yardstick we apply to institutional change is whether it creates order and efficiency. Any change resulting in something that looked messy would quickly be deemed a failure. In fear of this, the system remains intact, so this takes us back to the simpler strategy of changing the way we think.

When teachers read my book *The Dysfunctional School*, a common response is, "Yes, Mike, I agree with what you're saying, but what does the alternative look like? What can I actually *do differently* in my classroom?" Teachers want strategies external to themselves. They want to change student behaviour without changing their own. If teachers examined their ways of thinking about students, school, and their own role, their behaviours — their strategies — would automatically change.

All adults are resistant to change, and those who work in institutional settings are particularly prone to what I have called "the institutional trance." Under this trance, there are just certain things you don't say or do, behaviours that are acceptable, and others that are unacceptable. The people who function best in institutions are those most completely under the trance. We assume our perceptions are accurate, and we are generally unwilling to question those assumptions.

One of our deepest assumptions is related to the three rules of school. They are not found in any ministry of education documents, not printed in any student handbook, nor are they found posted in any school, yet anyone who has ever been to school knows them. "Sit still, be quiet, and do what you're told." If you follow these three rules, you will do very well — no matter what your ability level.

We have unwavering faith in these rules, and if we were to change them to something like, "Get up and move around, tell me what you want, and take responsibility for your own learning," things would get pretty messy. Each of these rules is based on a completely different set of assumptions about what students are capable of, what school is supposed to be, and the teacher's role in learning.

Any questions about educational change will be better answered if we understand the essential nature of children and how they learn. The successful teacher or parent is not so because of particular tips and tricks and strategies (although these can be very helpful). What distinguishes them is their understanding of young people, which leads to empathy and behaviours that promote growth instead of stunting it. Young people can tell when an adult understands them. A.S. Neill said, "We must always be on the side of the child." This is the most important principle for parents and educators. We are sometimes on the side of the institution, and in this way come to represent the power structures that can and do hurt individuals. We must be on the side of the child, and this means understanding their special nature and needs.

That fundamental question, originally posed by Neill, is screaming at us more loudly now than ever: do we make the child fit the school or the school fit the child? If we are going to do the latter, we need to understand children better then act on that understanding. We know so much more about child development, child psychology, and brain function than we did twenty or fifty years ago. Now we must use that knowledge to change schools and our attitudes about children.

PART TWO

A NOT SO NEW KIND of BOY

The UNIQUE NATURE of BOYS

One of the first things we can do is examine our attitudes toward boys. We all have certain "programs" downloaded into our brains that we're not even aware of — personal, family, and cultural biases passed down over time. One of these commonly held biases is that "boys are a problem," or to use William Pollack's term, "toxic." There seems to be a pervasive attitude that boy energy is difficult to manage and innately disruptive. Great sympathy is often expressed for teachers with a high ratio of boys to girls. Mothers with many sons are told, "I don't know how you do it." We must change our thinking about "boy energy" and see it as something positive to be harnessed and channelled rather than something innately disruptive.

Boys are especially seen as disruptive to institutional decorum, which is a fancy name for the three rules of school: sit still, be quiet, and do what you're told. If you follow these, not only you will do very well in school, and there's a good chance you'll become a teacher. Teachers like these rules; they make perfect sense, and, generally, teachers were students who followed them. When they start teaching and meet students who can't follow the rules, they grow very frustrated.

One of the ideas I like to discuss with teachers is the notion of the "perfect classroom." For many teachers (and parents) the image is one in which students are all quietly working on a task, facing the same way, not talking. The teacher is either instructing at the front of the room, circulating among the students, or sitting quietly at her own desk. All is peaceful and orderly. As any teacher will tell you, these moments *do* come, and we relish them (and hope that our principal will walk in at just that moment), but most also know this is an ideal picture. We need to revise our picture of the perfect classroom to include the noisy-busy variety.

There are two kinds of noisy classrooms. The first is the noisy-busy classroom, where students are engaged in a variety of activities alone, in pairs, or in groups. In this classroom students are relaxed, attentive, and learning. There is freedom within boundaries. All the students know and respect those boundaries, and lots is happening within them.

The other kind is the out-of-control classroom where the boundaries are unclear or inconsistently imposed. Here, there is a lot of acting out and a lot of stress. Needless to say, there is not a lot of learning going on. Barbara Coloroso talks about three kinds of families: the Brick Wall family, the Jelly Fish family, and the Backbone family. These three categories can be applied to classrooms as well. The out-of-control classroom is the Jelly Fish variety, and the noisy-busy classroom is the Backbone one. Our concepts about institutional decorum and the need to have all students dutifully on task can lead to what Coloroso might call the Brick Wall classroom. Another name for it is the "tight ship" classroom.

The Brick Wall or tight ship classroom is usually based on fear. These kinds of classrooms may "show" very well, and the Brick Wall teacher is often held up as a model for parents and other teachers, but I would argue that this is not a healthy environment. Fear leads to stress, which leads to the release of cortisol, a hormone produced by the adrenal gland that inhibits brain activity, among other things. Not only are students in such a classroom living in fear, they simply do not learn as well. The three rules of school have been taken to the extreme. It is an environment inhospitable to all children, but especially to boys.

What we will learn in the next two sections of this book is that following these rules comes more easily to the female brain and hormonal system than it does to the male. We will have to change three things in the future to make schools more boy-friendly. We will have to change the environment, the kinds of activities done there, and, most of all, our expectations and attitudes about boy behaviour. To achieve this, we must understand three fundamental facts about boys.

THREE FUNDAMENTAL FACTS ABOUT BOYS

The Year-and-a-Half Difference

The first fact is that there is a year-and-a-half difference in biological and cognitive development between boys and girls.

Girls develop and mature faster. Female babies generally walk and talk sooner. In the primary grades, we see girls with better fine motor skills. Girls can print sooner and better than boys because of this developmental difference. Unfortunately, this is often interpreted as a question of intelligence or ability. This is how what starts out as a simple difference becomes an advantage. The grade two boy looks over at the printing of the girl beside him and sees its superior quality. He does not say to himself, "Oh, she's on a different developmental timeline than I am." Rather, he concludes, "She's smarter than me," and this eventually becomes generalized to, "Girls are smarter than boys." The teacher encourages and comments on the students' printing. At the girl's desk there is praise; at the boy's there might be frustration in her voice.

The teacher coaches the boy on his b's, d's, and p's, but often what registers is not the factual information of how to connect the ball and the stick, but more deeply it is the tone of frustration. For young children, the affective domain trumps the cognitive domain. The child hears the emotional content more deeply than the rational. He interprets his teacher's frustration as disapproval, disappointment, or even dislike. Surrounded by girls who are further along the developmental continuum, he concludes, "I'm stupid." Listening to the strained voices of teachers and parents, he concludes, "My teacher doesn't like me," and "Mom and Dad are disappointed in me."

It is very important to be aware of this developmental difference and allow for it in our assessments of kids' performances. It might be unreasonable to compare the academic performance of girls to boys of the same age. They are on different developmental timelines. As Leonard Sax argues in his book *Boys Adrift*, differences in rate of cognitive and biological development are one of the main rationales for single-sex schools or single-sex classes. In a co-ed classroom, the range of biological and cognitive maturity can be almost double that in a single-sex classroom.

You're Sooo Immature!

Where the year-and-a-half difference can be most destructive, however, is in the general use of the words "mature" and "immature." Boys are often called immature by both adults and girls. Given the developmental difference, this is merely a statement of fact, but it is not said factually, but rather judgmentally. It is as though boys are somehow at fault and could change by a simple act of will. Boys only appear immature in relation to girls. When you have a group of boys, the spectrum of behaviour is much smaller than in a co-ed class, where the developmental spread can be huge. This spread reaches a high point in the intermediate division, grades seven to ten.

Every year it amazes me to see the range among our grade nine students. I remember teaching Jennifer and Matthew. Jennifer was as tall as me, a fully developed young woman who had already had several boyfriends. She could easily have passed for a supply teacher. Sitting right beside her was Matthew, whose feet literally did not touch the floor. His main interest was getting back home to his Lego. Jennifer wrote long, complicated love stories. Matthew struggled to get a few sentences down. Both of these kids were fourteen!

It happens in all grades. Peter and Phil were two grade twelve students in my university prep course who giggled, talked, and distracted others. They were such nice kids, it was hard to get mad at them. They were also extremely immature. I had to keep reining them in, but it would have done no good to shame them. This was where they were. Not surprisingly, they did poorly in their grade twelve year and had to come back to upgrade their marks. I had them both again, and I was amazed at the difference one more year made in their demonstrated level of maturity. They were much more focused and motivated.

In the primary division we talk about the December babies being at a disadvantage, but this issue exists through all the grades. We just stop seeing it, or we simply blame it on the boy, calling him immature. I have taught many boys I think would have fit in better academically as well as socially, with the cohort just behind them. I have also seen girls who would have been much better placed in the cohort ahead.

I think of poor Sarah, who spent four high school years rolling her eyes at the behaviour of her peers and their struggles to understand the curriculum. She flew through it at the top of the class. It was not that she was gifted. She was just moving with the wrong pack. One of the myths we live by is that all fourteen-year-olds are the same. We group students by chronological age, not ability or previous attainment. As a result we end up with groups who only really have one thing in common, their biological age. Cognitively they are all over the map! The range of ability and previous attainment within a class can be huge. I have taught grade nine classes with some kids reading at a grade four level while others were reading post-grade twelve. We keep them together with their age group for social reasons, but even this logic makes no sense.

Again, the range of social maturity within a classroom can be huge. Outside of school, kids will often gravitate toward friends of different ages, but at a similar stage of social development. There should be more opportunities for age-mixing so that kids who are further along the developmental continuum can find stimulation from older kids, and those who are not as far along can spend time with younger kids and get a feeling for what it's like to be older and more capable. Sometimes a student can spend years at the bottom of his class academically and be cast in the perpetual role of the childish class clown — the "baby" who is never taken seriously and never takes himself seriously. If he were to be given the chance, as a reading buddy or a teacher's helper one or two grades back, to experience himself as mature and intelligent, he could begin to assume that attitude about himself.

It is interesting to note that many of our judgments about a child being mature and intelligent are formed in relation to a peer group. Our assessment may not be objective, but relative. He is labelled immature or a "weak" student because that is how he appears in relation to this particular group.

It is no accident that adolescent girls are attracted to boys a year or two older. They feel a greater affinity. They are, in fact, at a similar developmental stage. The problem with labelling boys "immature" is that it can become a self-fulfilling prophecy — people become what they're perceived to be. "You think I'm immature. Okay, I'll show you how immature I am, since that is all you expect from me."

Boys often feel frustrated and at a perpetual disadvantage. No matter how hard they try, they can end up feeling it is impossible to "catch up" or "keep up," and for innate biological reasons, this may be true. I spent the first six years of my teaching career working at an all-girls school. Those classes had their own unique behavioural characteristics. When I moved to a co-ed school, one of the first things I noticed was the higher electrical charge in the classroom created by hormones, but also by the broader range of "maturity." The boys were more verbal and acted out, but their words and actions often had nothing to do with the topic or activities at hand. They saw themselves in competition with the girls (and each other) for the girls' attention. They could not always keep up in areas requiring abstract thought, so they sought attention in other ways — sometimes at odds with classroom decorum!

The Curse of Cursive

One area where this year-and-a-half difference tends to clearly reveal itself in discrepancies in printing and writing. Girls develop fine motor and graphomotor skills sooner than boys, and printing brings the first wave of this issue. The next comes with cursive writing.

Printing is a necessary skill that all literate people need to possess, but I think we are going to have to let cursive writing go. It should be presented to students as an option. Some students prefer it and do quite well with it. For many others, however, it is extremely difficult and just another barrier to academic success. The ability to write in cursive has no bearing on intelligence or general ability. One grade six boy wrote a fantastic story, full of detail and demonstrating vivid imagination. When it was returned, I asked him what grade he got. "Level Three" (on a four level rating system). When I expressed my disbelief, he explained with a sigh of resignation, "You can't get Level Four unless you write in cursive."

This evaluation criterion wrongly equates a motor skill with intelligence. When I mark a set of grade twelve exams, half to three-quarters of them are printed. I don't think there are many high school teachers, college instructors, or university professors who would demand cursive writing. In some ways, it is a bit of an anachronism, a charming practice from the past.

When I meet a boy with poor fine motor skills or poor graphomotor skills, I encourage him to use a word processing program. This accommodation should be available to all students, not just those formally identified with a language-related disability. There is even evidence showing that the brain works better when two hands are engaged, as in word processing — even if it's finger-pecking — as opposed to writing with one hand, which may stimulate one half of the brain more than the other. Anything that uses both hands simultaneously, like piano playing, is more of a whole-brain activity.

Impulse Control

Another area where the year-and-a-half difference becomes problematic is in the development of impulse control. Boys generally develop this ability later. This is not a question of girls being better. It is a difference, and should be understood and anticipated.

I once did a creative exercise with my senior enhanced English class, mostly girls. We were going to try some abstract expressionist painting techniques! This involved moving all the furniture, placing cans of paint on the floor, and splashing the paint around on large sheets of paper. I gave the students a long leash and encouraged artistic risk-taking and experimentation. It went very well. Since the materials were all out, I decided to let my next class, mostly boys, try the same activity. The results were disastrous. There was paint everywhere, mostly on clothes and bodies. If I were to do this activity again with boys, I would have to change some things, create a more structured format for the exercise, or simply be prepared for the mess and allow more time for clean-up!

It was interesting that one of the more impulsive boys (who, by the way, was thrilled that we were finally doing something fun in English class) went to the trouble of finding a garbage bag, cutting out head and arm holes, and putting it over his school clothes. He knew he had poor impulse control, and here he was preparing for it himself!

One of the reasons schools have trouble with impulsive students is because school places such a high premium on order and external control. As John Dewey told us, we learn best from experience. The only real way to learn impulse control is to be given opportunities to practice it. Schools do not deal well with unstructured time or activities (also known as freedom); they much prefer the control paradigm. I have always been amazed at what difficulty some kids have with unstructured time. It is a sure sign that we have taught them too well to be obedient but have not taught them self-regulation.

Pumpkin carving used to be a common class activity at Halloween. Today it has been replaced by pumpkin decorating. No knife is allowed, even if the teacher is holding it. The pumpkin is left intact and is decorated on the surface. Impulse control is learned by being practised, and instead of creating opportunities for practising it, we do everything we can to protect kids from themselves. Impulsivity becomes a self-fulfilling prophecy.

Red Light, Green Light

I taught a grade nine class in which there were three girls and seventeen boys. About half of the boys had been diagnosed with ADD/ADHD or some other learning disability. Needless to say, impulse control, both verbal and physical, was a daily issue. I used the metaphor of the traffic light, but before I explained it, I posted a picture of one in the top right corner of the blackboard — big enough that they could all see it, but I didn't say anything about it. I let them try to figure it out for two or three days. Finally, by the time I was ready, their curiosity had been aroused and they were ready to listen. I reviewed the meanings of the green, yellow, and red lights, and then I explained that we all have a traffic light in our brains called the frontal lobe.

In some kids, boys in particular, this area of the brain either does not function efficiently or develops a little later. I explained that they needed to work on their own inner traffic light, and if it didn't work, then I would be the traffic light for them. If you can't control yourself, then I will control you for you. This was not meant as a threat but as a logical description of what was going to happen. If nothing else, it is reassuring to many boys to know that someone is going to be watching out for them and helping them perform this function. Some boys' lights are perpetually on green, and they are tired of driving through intersections over and over again — hitting peers, teachers, and principals. The metaphor made sense to the kids, and when someone was getting too close to the line, I would simply make eye contact or say their name and point to the yellow light: caution, slow down.

The Game of Life. The Game of School

All kids love games. Boys love sports. One of the things they love about them (whether or not they are aware of it) is the rules. Boys want to know them and they want them enforced fairly and consistently. (Deep down, this is what they would also like from school.) Sports and games provide a container for male energy. You can go "full out," but you have to stay within the rules. It is the perfect forum for the expression of their energy. One of the best analogies to use with impulsive kids is the image of the playing field or hockey rink. We will look at a picture of a soccer field, basketball court, or hockey rink and talk about the various parts and how they relate to real life. The soccer field and basketball court are best for talking about boundaries. (Interestingly, in hockey, there is no territorial out-of-bounds, other than being off-side.) Once the ball goes out of bounds, the play stops and the other team gets it. It's a negative thing to go outside the boundaries. As long as things stay inside, play can continue and everything is fine.

Life has all kinds of boundaries. The most basic are those of personal and emotional space. The rules of the game do not allow you to hit or punch another person, nor do they allow you to criticize or make fun of anyone. Your freedom ends where the rights of others begin, and almost every situation has its boundaries. I ask the students to name some examples of boundaries. You don't laugh in church. You don't drive through a stop sign. You don't wear a bathing suit to go shopping. You don't create such a distraction in class that no one else can learn or the teacher cannot do his job.

Some boundaries are just social convention, but others have a specific purpose. The boundaries in the classroom are there for a good purpose that benefits everyone. The next step is a consideration of who guards those boundaries. Ideally, we should be watching for them ourselves and trying to stay within them. Sometimes, however, a referee is needed to enforce the rules.

I ask the students: Who are the referees in the game of life or of school: parents, teachers, the principal, police? We discuss what the world would be like without these people, how necessary their role is in guarding those boundaries. Then we discuss the issue of penalties: the yellow card (warning) and the red card (sent off) in soccer and the penalty box in hockey (measured in minutes). For all students, but especially those with poor impulse control, these discussions not only make sense but are reassuring. While they may not show it, students who keep getting penalized by the various referees of life get tired of all the negative feedback. They do not want to be in trouble, but some have a harder time holding back. They act first and think later. Putting the issue this way allows kids to see the problem in terms they can relate to. The final part of the analogy to be addressed is the goal. There are two main goals: learning and socialization. In order for these goals to be achieved, the rules have to be observed and the referees respected.

Abstract Thinking

Another difference between boys and girls shows up in the development of abstract thought. As Barbara Strauch so clearly demonstrates in her important study of the teenage brain, *The Primal Teen*, boys' thinking remains at a concrete level longer than it does for girls. One of the hardest literary concepts to teach grade nine boys is theme. The easiest is plot. Boys are very good at remembering what happened and recounting it. When they are asked to explain the *thematic significance* of these events, their minds often go blank. I find by grade eleven (ages sixteen to seventeen) the ability to think abstractly begins to appear in boys. Every year I get the seventeen-year-old newborn philosopher who wants to discuss the meaning of life, the relationship between good and evil, or the nature of reality. All of a sudden they discover the stimulating world of intellectual ideas! In grade nine, no matter what question I ask on the exam, I'm going to get a large number of boys telling me what happened in the story. Knowing this, I always make sure to have plot questions on tests and exams, giving credit to that skill. Themes need to be taught explicitly.

Symbolism is another concept that can drive the concrete thinker crazy. What do you mean the mockingbird represents all innocent victims? It's just a bird. As Homer Simpson, the ultimate concrete thinker, says, "I swore never to read again after *To Kill a Mockingbird* gave me no useful advice on killing mockingbirds!" Teachers should be aware of this difference and take it into account in their teaching and evaluation strategies. Boys are going to need more explicit instruction and coaching in areas of abstract thought.

Standardized Testing

Blanket standardized testing is yet another area where differences in developmental stages can have important implications. Standardized testing, as the name implies, does not take gender differences or developmental differences into account. Despite the possibility of a gap between boys' and girls' ability to perform, the same test is given to both genders concurrently. Boys always come out "behind," and this gives the appearance that they are somehow deficient in these skill areas. There is a current trend toward "rescuing" boys from illiteracy. Boys feel this attitude of alarm, and their suspicions about being stupid or less capable than girls are simply confirmed. Standardized testing highlights the problem of the rigid application of one process to all students, despite what we know about their differences.

The Education Quality and Accountability Office (EQAO) is a government agency in the province of Ontario that oversees mass blanket testing in grades three, six, nine, and ten. The following excerpt was taken from a Q and A page on the EQAO website in the summer of 2009:

Gender-Based and Sub-Group Differences in the Overall Results in EQAO's Grade 3 and Grade 6 Assessments.

Q. 1. Is the gap between the results of boys and girls in the Grade 3 and Grade 6 provincial assessments consistent across reading, writing and mathematics?

A. Yes. Girls outperform boys in reading, writing and mathematics in both the Grade 3 and Grade 6 assessments. The gap is wider in reading and writing than it is in mathematics.

Q. 2. Why is there a difference in performance between girls and boys?

A. Research suggests that differences in reading and writing results between boys and girls may be due to several factors:

- difference in maturity levels

- difference in reading preferences

- leisure reading (of which girls do more) is correlated generally with reading achievement

- certain instructional practices are not as effective with boys as they are with girls

In addition, cultural values play a part. For example, doing well in school may not be as important to the self-image of boys as it is to the self-image of girls. In order to provide more insight into this question, further research is required.

Q. 3. What can be done to reduce the gender gap in the future?

A. More research will most certainly lead to a better understanding of the underlying causes of the gap and provide us with an array of possible solutions. In the meantime, school boards, schools, teachers, and parents would do well to discuss the matter in order to identify possible factors and to suggest short- and long-term strategies.

Q. 4. What do you plan to do about gender differences in achievement?

A. EQAO's reports provide school boards with a reliable method of assessing gender-based differences in achievement. Boards and schools are asked to develop specific strategies to address differences in achievement as part of their improvement plans.

In short, we know there is a problem with our testing procedures, but we don't know what to do about it. We have asked individual school boards and schools to try to figure it out.

One possible strategy would be to test boys a year later. Another would be to take the money spent on blanket testing, which reveals the same 15–20 percent of students who are "at risk" every year, and put the money toward helping them. Ideally, we should get rid of blanket standardized testing or at least anticipate the resulting lower scores for boys and not "pathologize" a perfectly natural state of affairs.

Fact Two: Boys Love Movement and Space

You are walking through the mall with your five-year-old son. You come to a large open area. What will he do? We all know the answer.

He will likely let go of your hand and start running around in the open space. If we had that boy hooked up to a monitor, we would find his brain was releasing pleasure-inducing chemicals. He actually feels happier when he's moving around. Evolutionary biologists tell us that the male brain has evolved over millennia to be particularly good at moving through space. In a hunter-gatherer society, there was a lot of walking. I read one estimate that in prehistoric times the average male walked fifteen kilometres a day. Today, we have created a social institution that requires children and adolescents sit in a chair for five to six hours a day. It is simply not natural.

Elementary schools generally have a higher tolerance for movement. Because kids spend the whole day in one room, it would be unrealistic to expect sitting the whole time. In secondary schools, there is less tolerance. The standard seventy-six minute class is a long time to sit for a fourteen-year-old in grade nine, as well as for many seventeen-year-olds in grade twelve. Secondary schools must find ways of creating more opportunities for movement. In the province of Ontario, only one physical education credit is required, and this only in one semester. Sports used to include house league games for which any student could sign up. Today extra-curricular sports are limited to a tiny fraction of the student body, the most elite athletes. In our high schools, there are few opportunities for teenagers to move around.

In my classroom, the desks are arranged in the shape of a double horseshoe, leaving a big space in the middle. One day my grade twelve class had been writing a test that required we put the desks in rows. I didn't have time to put them back in the horseshoe configuration before my grade nine class came in — seventeen boys and three girls. When the boys came in, the first thing they asked was very telling. It was not, "Why are the desks changed around?" They asked, "Where did the space go?" That loss was the real issue for them.

When boys come into a classroom, they are more likely to choose seats near the window, the door, or the back, because these areas either have more space or open out onto it. Sitting by the window, a boy can at least see space, even if he can't get to it. By the door, he knows he has an escape route. The back usually has more floor space than the front. If the front does have lots of floor space, there is still a downside — the boy cannot *see* the whole room when he sits there. For males, being able to see a space is very important. At the front, there is too much going on behind him that he can't see. This will raise his anxiety level and cause him to repeatedly turn around or act out his nervousness in other ways. Because space is so important for the male brain, I often recommend that the acting-out boy be seated at the back, where he can see everything and has less of an audience.

I taught English during the last period in the day to a grade nine boy, Jakob, who was highly bodily-kinaesthetic. By this time, he was like a caged bear. He lived quite far from the school, so his bus picked him up in the morning around 6:45 a.m. He rode the bus for an hour, then sat through three long periods, had forty minutes for lunch and then my class. I felt for this kid! He had a habit of getting up every ten minutes or so and just standing up or walking to the door or looking at the bulletin boards. He wasn't disruptive, but he had a huge need for movement and space. I never said a word about him getting up; I allowed it because I understood it. Whenever there was a message to be sent or a box to be carried, I always asked Jakob to do it — anything to give him the chance to move.

One year I taught Massimo, who also could not sit still. My portable classroom sat right beside the cinder running track, and at least once during the class, I had him run around the track. He was a happier, calmer kid for it!

Apparently, some elementary schools are experimenting with "sitting optional" classrooms. Many boys, given the choice, would prefer to work standing up at their desks. Some schools are even ordering a combination of benches and desks. One can purchase "wiggle cushions" filled with air or jell that allow kids to wiggle and squirm as they sit.

High school English classes can be hard places to incorporate movement. Reading and writing are not bodily-kinaesthetic activities. I encourage drama and debating (where the debaters stand and are encouraged to walk around as they make their points) as a way of trying to get some movement into the class.

The issue of movement is related to two other key points: impulse control and attention span. One of the best tips I ever learned was that a child's attention span is roughly their age in minutes, before they become naturally distracted, or to put it in a more positive way, their attention moves on to something else. We all have these natural attention spans. Most of us are unaware of our own. Most people, as they age, develop the ability to maintain focus beyond this natural threshold. In other words, being an adult means you are able to pretend you're interested in things when you're really not. In their book, *Delivered From Distraction*, Edward Hallowell and John Ratey talk about attention deficit disorder as a gift, and express sympathy for the rest of the population who suffer from "attention surplus disorder" — paying too much attention to things that don't matter!

Let's imagine Mark. He is seven and is dutifully working on his math worksheet. At the end of seven minutes, he has reached the limit of his attention span, and he has not yet learned the fine art of "staying on task," even when the task is boring or there are more interesting things to do. Right beside him is the class list of rules that everyone voted on during the first day. One of the rules states, "I will not leave my seat without asking." Mark voted for that rule on the first day because he believes in the importance of order and structure. Now, when he reaches his threshold of attention, does he refer to the list of rules? No, he is the product of hundreds of thousands of years of evolution, during which the ability to move through space was the number one valued and developed skill.

When Mark gets up and starts walking around, he is not being defiant or oppositional. He does not suffer from ADD, nor is he impulsive. He is a perfectly normal seven-year-old boy. His behaviour needs to be understood, allowed, and, at most, managed. Is it disruptive? If not, let it be. He will come back to his seat eventually. If it causes a distraction for others or he is unable to return to the task, he can be shepherded back to his seat. We should guard against turning these natural behaviours into "behavioural issues" or, worse, moral issues about being good or bad. We will talk more about this in the chapter on ADD.

Fact Three: Boys Prefer Action Over Words

Do actions speak louder than words? For the female brain, the preferred mode of expression is words. For the male, it is action. This can sound confusing to the female. "How can you 'express' things through action?" For women, to "express" automatically implies to talk.

James was a former student of mine who lost his father around Christmas time and his mother a few months later. James became the ward of his older sister and finished his grade twelve year in my English class. I used to sit with him for long periods, and he would say almost nothing. "I know I should be talking, sir, but I just don't know what to say. I don't have the words." James eventually found the weight room, where he began to work out. He worked out every day; that was how he grieved. By doing something, through action, he got his feelings out, and for him, it was a perfectly legitimate method.

Another student, Peter, lost his mother. A couple of weeks later, I asked how he and his dad were doing. He said, "Dad came home from the funeral, and he's been down in the basement renovating ever since." Some might call this avoidance or an unhealthy way of dealing with feelings. For many men, it is the preferred, natural way. We say actions speak louder than words, but do we really believe it?

Talking and Skipping: Language Processing

Men are often made to feel inadequate because they do not verbalize as freely and as often as women. I remember discussing this issue with a group of teachers-in-training at York University. After my talk, a young man came up and said, "Thank you for pointing out that fact about men and talking. I often feel totally inadequate in this class of mostly women. The professor will ask a question, and all these hands go up, and so much is said, and I'm still formulating my response to the first question. By the time I figure out what I want to say, the class has moved on to another topic."

I looked at him, smiled, and said, "We need people like you in education. Boys need people like you."

Boys need to see language models of all kinds, not just those who process quickly. There is a fundamental myth that men are not very good at talking. It is more that talking is not their preferred mode of expression and, very often, their rate of language processing is much slower. I compare men talking to skipping. There is a slow, regular rhythm, and men know when they can jump in. From a male point of view, women conversing is like skipping Double Dutch! The rate of flow is just so much faster. Watch a group of men. You will see little eye contact and there are many gaps of silence. Men are comfortable with that, and the whole conversation has a rhythm that is simply different from that of female conversation.

There are at least three stages to verbal language processing: receptive language (taking in what is being said), cognitive processing (thinking about what was said and of something to say in response), and expressive language (saying what you think in a way that others will understand). In my teaching experience, I have found males in general move more slowly through these stages. The delay may be in all three steps or just one. This is sometimes very hard to distinguish, but think of the boy who says, "I know what I want to say, I just don't know how to say it."

When the Thimble Meets Niagara Falls: Receptive and Expressive Language

Going back to receptive verbal language, I like to use a metaphor to explain a common problem in communication. Some kids have very poor receptive language ability. I would compare their capacity for receiving language to a thimble. They need smaller, shorter "inputs," and they need time to process these before new inputs can be given.

Now imagine the child with a thimble for receptive language meeting an adult whose expressive language ability we will compare to Niagara Falls — at least that's how it feels to the thimble-holding child. Very often, such an adult is unable (or unwilling) to understand the mismatch between the talker and the listener. The child whose thimble is full or overflowing has become saturated by language and stops listening. This child will appear to be distracted. "Listen to me when I'm talking to you!" But this is impossible.

Now the conversation moves from the cognitive to the affective level. Feelings become more important than ideas. The child does not hear the content, but "hears" loud and clear on his emotional register that the adult is angry and draws the conclusion, "I am bad." It is so important for teachers and parents to be aware of the multi-dimensional character of communication and to understand the problems that can occur when there is a weakness in one area or a mismatch between the abilities of the speaker and the listener.

As I was packing up after one of my talks, an exasperated elementary school principal declared confidentially, "You know, Mike, everything you said was true, but there *are* some boys who just don't listen!" She had missed the point entirely. There are some boys who find listening difficult, need to see it written down, need to have it delivered in small bits, or need to have instructions repeated or simplified. Maybe she was talking about selective hearing, taking in what we want to hear and blocking out what we don't, or only taking in those ideas that agree with our pre-conceived notions. Is this what the principal was doing during my talk? Perhaps there are some adults who just don't listen! Again, the issue comes back to understanding and acceptance.

What Do You Do When You See a Snake: Talking and Stress

In *Boys and Girls Learn Differently*, Michael Gurian explains how synaptic paths differ in the male and female brains. The differences in the communication styles show up well in the context of a stressful situation. Let's take the simple situation of seeing a snake. If we hook up electrodes to the female brain, we will see the synapses going immediately to the frontal lobe, the language centre. "Look! A snake! There's a snake here!" The default mode of the female brain, when stressed (positively or negatively) is to talk. Hook up the male brain and watch where the synapses go: to the amygdala, the "fight-or-flight" centre. I'm either going to grab the snake or I'm going to run away. From the male point of view, there is no sense talking about it! The default mode of his brain when stressed is to *do* something.

Now, let's apply this to another stressful situation, the lover's quarrel. It's one o'clock in the morning. You have just gotten home from a party. Something was said. There is tension in the air. The female brain's response: "We're going to talk about this right now! We're not going to bed until we've gotten to the bottom of this!" The male response is to run away. Fight or flight! Fight — domestic violence. Flight — the male either leaves the room or runs where many men have learned to run — inside — into silence or what John Gray calls the "male cave."

When I go silent, my wife says, "You're in your cave, aren't you?"

"Yes," I reply.

"That's okay. I'll wait till you come out," she says.

Women prefer words. Men prefer action. Women want to hear, "I love you." Men find these words difficult to say partly because they seem silly. From a male point of view, doing something for another sends a far more powerful message. "What do you mean I don't love you? I changed the tires on your car! I built a bathroom in the basement!" William Pollack calls this "action love."

Use Your Words!

I attended an orientation session with my oldest son for students planning to enter first-year engineering at the University of Toronto. Convocation Hall holds approximately 1,500 people. It was filled mostly with males who, since they were math-physics experts, we might expect to be at the non-verbal, spatial end of the brain spectrum. What I found fascinating about this gathering was how little conversation was taking place as we sat waiting for the session to begin. The majority of these high school seniors were non-verbal males who excelled in spatial thinking. It was perfectly natural that there was so little conversation! These guys were not socially deficient — they just had a different way of being and being together. We should understand this difference in verbal facility and not denigrate those for whom speaking is not their preferred mode of expression.

We are all familiar with the admonition, "Use your words," usually spoken to a young boy who is overwhelmed by emotions and is acting them out in ways deemed inappropriate. His acting out is, in fact, *his* way of communicating. All behaviour is logical. It is up to the wise adult to discern what the behaviour is communicating. "I'm bored. I'm nervous. I'm happy. I'm excited. I don't want to leave." The line, "Use your words" is often spoken condescendingly — as though words are superior to actions. To the adult mind, particularly the female one, this is true, but for the developing mind of a small child, actions are felt to be much more effective. Hitting or biting means more than "Please don't take my toy truck from me."

It is essential for adults to coach kids through the developmental stages to become more adept at articulating their feelings and thoughts, but we must never forget the legitimacy of action. While we would like kids to become more verbally literate, maybe we also must become more behaviourally literate. Even into adolescence, teenagers communicate volumes through their behaviour. Smoking, skipping class, missing curfew — these are all ways of saying "I'm not a little kid any more" or "I want to be more independent."

The Strong, Silent Male: Testosterone and Language

"He used to be such a nice boy! We would sit and talk. He would tell me everything that was going on. And he used to read all the time. He read all the Harry Potter books. Now all he does is grunt and mumble. When I ask him how his day went, all he can say is 'Fine.' When I ask him what he's doing in school, all he says is 'Nothing.' And reading — no way! His English marks are low and he would never pick up a book."

I have heard these lines from countless mothers of adolescent boys. The stereotype of the silent, sullen teenager has a basis in biology. Testosterone inhibits language. During puberty, when testosterone levels in males rise dramatically, verbal language proficiency declines. Part of his silence is caused by his emotional and psychological need to break from Mother (no more long talks and confidences), but what should be kept in mind is that this phase is not chosen. The boy doesn't deliberately decide to stop talking. Those who were very verbal in childhood can find this change just as frustrating as the adults in his life. He used to "get a lot out" through talking. It provided that "discharging of affect" for him. How is he to "get it out" now? Very often, he will revert to action, that more basic form of communication. And since testosterone feeds aggression, not to mention muscle mass, aggressive behaviour can become one of the ways he might resort to for "getting it out."

Disciplining a Boy or Communicating with a Stressed Male

Testosterone is probably the most influential hormone in male behaviour. It fuels aggression, competition, self-assertion, self-reliance, movement, concreteness, and spatial awareness. All of these things are positive. One of them has a dark side, however: aggression. While it may be good to be an aggressive salesman or athlete, the dark side is violence. Negative aggressive behaviour is most commonly fuelled by feelings of anger, frustration, powerlessness, or threat.

"Sit Down!"

Let's apply some of what we've talked about to the issue of disciplining a boy or communicating with a stressed male. One of the first things we will likely do is ask or require him to sit down. We feel a greater sense of control in this arrangement, and that he will listen better. We have inhibited one of his most fundamental needs, movement. He feels trapped, and his testosterone level rises. I remember a sixteen-year-old who was brought into the office. He had been caught wearing his baseball cap, which was not allowed. He came to the office willingly, resigned to the fact that he had been caught. The teacher who had brought him asked him to sit down. "I don't want to sit down," was the boy's reply. The teacher persisted. "Sit down!" The boy again replied, "I don't want to sit down." It ended up with the police. What started out as a routine discipline situation quickly escalated because of this restriction of movement. The boy's testosterone level rose as he felt threatened.

Boys feel more relaxed, think better, and speak better if they are moving around or have the freedom to do so. If they are moving, it doesn't mean they are not concentrating. A twelve-year-old came in one evening furious at his mother about restrictions she wanted to place on his video game playing. He took a rubber ball and circled the table, walking fairly quickly and bouncing the ball at the same time. As he did this, I sat calmly while he poured out his feelings — in words! The movement acted as a catalyst, and he was able to articulate his thoughts and feelings much better than had he been sitting facing me. I have seen this phenomenon time and time again, where boys with strong feelings, when allowed movement, were much more likely to express themselves. When disciplining a boy or talking to a stressed male, do not demand sitting.

Move in Close

Our second common behaviour when we discipline kids is moving in close. In addition to the need for movement, males have a huge need for space (which movement requires). When we move in on a male's space, again, his testosterone level rises. He feels threatened by the violation of his territory, even if it is his own personal bubble. Standing one's ground. Not backing down. Crossing the line. All of these expressions are metaphorical, showing the importance of space and spatial awareness to males.

Stand back and give him space. I have conversed with angry boys who chose to stand on the other side of the room. This maximized their space and allowed for the possibility of movement. The expression, "Back off!" is a powerful one and means exactly what it says. Give me space! Another expression, "Get out of my face!" expresses this very graphically. Personal space has to do with feelings of power and control. When it shrinks, our anxiety level rises. People who live in densely populated high rises with limited personal space are less likely to talk to their neighbours. Talking implies an overlapping of personal space, and when that space is at a premium, less conversation occurs. The stereotype of the talkative, neighbourly country dweller has some truth to it. He has lots of space to retreat back into. He does not feel the same sense of "surrender" around communication as people in confined spaces. What's true of where we live is also true of the personal bubble in which we all live. The more space we have, the more relaxed we are.

"Look at Me When I'm Talking to You!"

The third thing we often do when disciplining boys is demand eye contact. "Look at me when I'm talking to you!" Females prefer eye contact because they feel it creates a greater connection and therefore better communication. Males can find it invasive and threatening. They look then look away. Their main goal is to determine if someone or something is a threat. When forced to make eye contact with an angry or stressed adult, the boy feels a great sense of threat. His testosterone level rises, as does his potential for aggressive behaviour. Eye contact is not a requirement for effective communication. Just because a boy is not looking at you doesn't mean he isn't listening.

"Talk!"

After we've pushed this boy's testosterone levels through the roof, the final thing we do is ask for words — those things he has trouble formulating at the best of times. "What did you think you were doing?" Not only are we requiring language processing, which testosterone inhibits, but the question is a very strange one. We didn't ask "What happened?" which would simply require a narrative re-telling. The question has several levels: What were your intentions? Do you realize how wrong you are? Do you realize how wrong *I* think you are? It's more of a shaming comment than an actual question. At any rate, the child is still being asked to come up with words. As we learned earlier with the snake, the boy will fight or take flight. He will have an aggressive reaction, physically or verbally, or he will flee by running away or going silent.

The alternative is to give him time. "We will talk about this later, when you're not so upset." (Or sometimes even better, "We'll talk about this later, when I'm not so upset.") In most cases, the issue does not have to be dealt with in the heat of the moment. If it can wait, let it. You will get much further with a male who is not stressed.

UNDERSTANDING NORMAL BOY BEHAVIOUR

Zoning Out

"Zoning out" is a behaviour found more commonly in males and has important implications for the classroom. If we measure female brain activity over a twenty-four-hour period, we find that their brains are more consistently active. Some would say that women's brains are always "on," that they are always thinking. It's been shown that women think in their sleep. Who is the first to hear the baby crying in the night? Women are also more likely to report going to bed with a problem and waking up with a solution.

If we measure male brain activity over time, we find that it has natural zoning-out periods. These occur naturally and are regularly spaced, if the brain is not externally stimulated to engage in some activity. As Michael Gurian points out in *Boys and Girls Learn Differently*, evolutionary biologists trace this back to our primal roots, when women were the main caregivers, living socially with other women, sharing information, watching out for children, on guard for external threats. In short, women from earliest times have had to be "on." Men, on the other hand, engaged in activities that involved much more solitude and "down time." Hunting and gathering were not always social activities and involved a lot of moving, waiting, and watching. We still see modern-day equivalents in men who are able to sit in ice-fishing huts or hunting blinds for hours. They do not sit thinking and ruminating over things. If they are with others, they don't discuss much. They certainly do not talk about their feelings! They go into a kind of suspended mode in which mental activity is reduced.

If we want to understand the male brain, a good place to start might be the personal computer. Many of the standard "behaviours" of computers are the product of male brains and end up imitating male brain function. The operating systems tell us something about those of males. For example, when a computer is not being used for a while, it will go into "sleep mode" — it will zone out. When it is not needed, the screensaver comes on because there isn't much processing required. The male brain tends to function similarly. When it is not actively being stimulated (or when it is bored), it too will go into "sleep mode."

We very often see this phenomenon in the classroom. If the task is not stimulating or there is too much language, some boys naturally zone out. They are not being oppositional, defiant, or lazy — they are behaving according to a natural rhythm. What does one do when the screensaver comes on? You touch any key and "tell" the computer that it is needed again. The same thing can be done with a boy; it is called "cueing." There are three main kinds of cueing: visual, verbal, and tactile. Visual cueing involves making eye contact, thereby calling the student back to the task. As we have found out, boys are very sensitive to eye contact. This is the subtlest form of cueing and is most effective with "mild" cases of zoning out.

Verbal cueing means talking directly to the student and calling them out of their reverie. The third method, tactile cueing, means touching the child in some way — a tap on the shoulder, a hand on the back. Tactile cueing can even include just walking up and standing close. Even simple proximity can pull a boy out of the zone.

William used to zone out in my grade twelve English class. Whenever I was teaching something that I knew was going to be on the exam, I made a point of checking to see if he was paying attention. If he was zoning out, I'd simply call his name, and when he looked at me, I would point to the board and say, "This is important." He would "come to" and start copying.

Bear Cubs: Connecting Through Rough Play

Michael Gurian called it "aggression nurturance." This would seem an oxymoron, but it is a good name for the way boys (and men) relate to each other. Let's watch Tyler on his first day of grade nine. He gets put in a period one math class where he doesn't know anyone. They are put into groups to do an activity. Everyone is nervous and there are lots of furtive attempts at "self display." Tyler gets a good vibe from another boy in the group, Chris. They make a few jokes and help each other with their work. Tyler likes this kid. Later in the day, Tyler is walking down a crowded hallway and sees Chris at his locker. It is time to cement the friendship. As Tyler walks past, he gives Chris a push into his locker. They make eye contact, smile, and the friendship is sealed.

This is aggression nurturance — connecting through rough physical play. It is a natural form of communication for boys, and should be understood and accepted. Boys push and shove and punch and pull as a way of making contact. They are less likely to hug, stroke, pat, as girls might do, to show affection and to nurture a relationship. Females often roll their eyes at this rough play, because it is not how they would choose to relate. Many schools have a zero-tolerance policy around bullying, allowing no rough touch at all, and, in some cases, no touching at all! In a zero-tolerance environment, this perfectly natural form of communication could send one or both boys to the principal's office. The cause of suspension will read, "conduct injurious to the moral tone of the school," when the real cause of the behaviour was a desire to connect and show friendship.

Most events at school take place while kids sit on chairs at desks. In the primary division in particular, boys are often happier standing at a table or working on the floor. The problem with the floor is that it's not a very structured environment. Sitting there becomes rolling around and then rolling with others. This is not always conducive to organized learning or quiet storytime! If you have a bodily-kinaesthetic boy at storytime, make sure he is at the edge of the group with room to roll. Expect it, allow it, manage it. If he is not disturbing others, it is not a problem, and though he appears not to be listening, he probably is. If he's not, it's simply because he doesn't find the story interesting, and that's okay, too. Of course, the old maxim still applies — freedom ends where the rights of others begin. You are free to roll around until you disrupt the listening of others. That is when the teacher's managerial function kicks in. If you can't control yourself, I will control you for you.

Some mothers are at a loss as to how to play with their boys in a way they enjoy. If a mother wants to connect with her son, all she needs to do is lie down on the floor. He will take it from there! When I came home to my four little ones (three boys and one girl), I would be too exhausted to "lead" any kind of play. I soon discovered that if I lay on the floor, things just seemed to happen from there. It did have much structure and involved a lot of rolling around and gentle-rough play.

Every morning in the hall, I pass two or three bear-cub fights. If I were to stop and "discipline" these boys, I would never make it to my classroom. If I sense the roughhousing is just a little too intense or could escalate, I simply stop and stand beside them. They know what I mean, and they pull back. This is the role of the adult in the midst of boys' rough play — watching to see whether they are able to keep it inside the boundaries or whether they need an external force to impose limits. Boys around fourteen to sixteen sometimes need this external policeman. The judgment centre is found in the frontal lobe, and researchers tell us that this judgment centre is slower to develop in boys. Having spent over thirty years with teenagers, this makes perfect sense to me. I have seen bear-cub pushing and shoving turn into full-blown fights because one boy could not judge when he had crossed the line, and the other could not restrain himself in response.

Problems arise for bear cubs when they become interested in girls. They will sometimes transfer these social skills to the boy–girl relationship. This usually doesn't go over very well. How many times have I had to stop in the halls and tell a fourteen-year-old boy to let that girl out of a headlock! This is not nascent male violence, it's typical boy behaviour being applied to girls. Boys need coaching in this area. I stand beside the boy, he immediately releases her, and I tell him confidentially, "Girls don't like that. They would rather talk," or "Find another way to show your love." The boy blushes, but he knows what I mean.

Aggressive play is a normal part of boy behaviour. It must be understood, tolerated, and managed, not punished, changed, or "pathologized."

One Thing at a Time

"I want you to go downstairs, take the laundry out of the washing machine, and put it in the dryer. On your way up, could you grab some hamburger buns out of the freezer? And, oh yeah, I think I left the phone downstairs last night. Can you bring it up?" All I have to do is say this in front of a group of women, and I get laughter. I don't even relay the topic or the context. They know they're at a talk about male-female learning differences and that I'm talking about males, and they laugh because they've seen the results of such instructions with the males in their own lives.

Boys prefer one task and one instruction at a time. They are not as good at multi-tasking. Some researchers say it's because the *corpus callosum*, the bundle of nerves connecting the left and right hemispheres of the brain, is much larger in women, allowing for greater "cross talk" between the hemispheres. Whatever the reason, it must be said that this is not a question of better or worse. It is merely a difference. The male brain tends to focus more intensely on one task.

Whose idea was it to put four burners on the top of a stove? I think of my wife cooking Christmas dinner. She has four pots with lids all rattling on the stovetop, a turkey in the oven, kids running around, and adult guests to talk to. Everything ends up on the table at the same time, even though it all took different lengths of time to cook! To me, this is an incredible feat. If I was cooking, I would cook the potatoes and set them to one side, then I would turn to the corn and cook that very well, and set it to one side. One thing at a time!

As I said earlier, one can understand the male mind by looking at computers. When you are online, you can only do one thing at a time. Even if you have many screens open, there is one mouse and the cursor is always in one place. The male brain is most comfortable in this environment, where nothing unpredictable can happen. If the female brain had invented the PC, there may have been several cursors moving around at once! In cyberspace, one only has to deal with one thing at a time. Drop-down menus are interesting as well. They are lists of choices from which you choose only one.

One of the strategies I suggest to teachers of boys is the use of lists, menus, or schedules. I put the schedule or agenda of each day's class up on the board and tell the kids that this is what we will be doing. I find the males, in particular, like this. They seem to take comfort in knowing what is coming.

Calendars are another helpful strategy. I always have a calendar on my side board, and it is the boys who check the date, wanting to "place" themselves in time. One woman came up to me after one of my talks full of anger about her husband's need for lists. "Whenever I go out or am away for an extended period of time, he wants me to leave him a list of things that need to be done! What is he — a child?" No, I told her, he's a typical male, and there's nothing wrong with leaving lists. In fact, a helpful strategy for kids with ADD or discipline problems around certain routines is to post a list itemizing what a particular job entails. Getting everyone out of the house in the morning can be a huge stressor in many busy families. A list on the bathroom mirror of the five things that need to happen before you go out the door to the school bus can be very helpful. This leads to the next issue — transitioning between tasks.

From This to That: Transitioning Between Tasks

Boys do not transition between tasks as well as girls, and the more focused a boy is, the harder it is for him to transition. Some will "hyperfocus," making transitioning even harder. We have all heard parents talk about the child who could continue doing something "even if a bomb went off." This is hyperfocusing, which is very common in males. It is a positive phenomenon and can lead to great accomplishments. The Olympic swimmer Michael Phelps, who has ADD, has used his ability to hyperfocus to great advantage.

The difficulty with hyperfocusing comes when the external world demands transitions to another task. We see it in school, where transitions are required regularly. Any aware teacher will tell you that many of the behavioural issues occur during times of transition. The boy is pulled out of something before he is ready. He can feel frustrated and confused, but he doesn't express these feelings in words — "I was really into that math problem. I wish I could just finish it." He does it through action — often disruptively. We see the same phenomenon at home, particularly around video games. A mother calls her son to supper, and he seems to totally disregard her, is rude to her, delays coming, or comes to the table frustrated — with an attitude to match.

Give Warnings

I have four pieces of advice for teachers and parents when it comes to transitioning. First, give warnings — in as few words as possible. (Less is more when talking to a hyperfocused male.) "We're going to be eating in thirty minutes. You need to start coming off the computer." Repeat this warning every ten minutes. He may not respond, and he may not appear to be listening, but it is probably registering on some level, and he is starting to pull out. In the classroom, the teacher can say, "We're going to spend fifteen more minutes on this math and then we're going to switch to spelling." Again, the warnings are repeated at five-minute intervals, so that when the big transition does come, it is not a surprise, and the male brain has, on some level, prepared for it.

Allow for Stragglers

The second strategy is simply to allow for stragglers in the classroom or for straggling at home. I used to begin every class of grade nine English with the students writing eight lines on a topic.

Daniel was a boy with a very slow rate of language processing, but he was able to focus very well. He focused intensely on thinking of something to write, and then on writing it. The problem was he took as long with the first step (thinking of what to say) as most other students took with steps one and two (thinking and writing). Every day we would listen to a couple of kids read their compositions. By the time we were done this third step, Daniel was just starting on the second step, putting pen to paper. The class would move on to grammar, and Daniel would happily keep writing. In the beginning, I made everyone close their journals, and move along with the crowd. I could see Daniel was very frustrated. Usually a nice kid, he would sometimes become rude or disruptive, and he had almost nothing in the journal section of his binder, making him feel "stupid." I decided to allow for his straggling (and his slower language processing). It was not essential that he transition along with us. He was quite happy when he was allowed to focus on each task and transition at his own rate. Eventually, he would even put his hand up during the grammar lesson and ask if he could read his entry!

Allow for this kind of straggling at home as well. If a child does not "jump to" at the first command, it need not be cause for World War III. Getting off the computer, especially leaving a video game, can be very difficult for the hyperfocused boy. Video games are very goal-oriented and structured in terms of levels, sessions, missions, etc. Completing one of these "units" is of utmost importance to the male brain. We talk about the importance of finishing what you start, so his reluctance to come off the computer could be seen in this positive light — he is goal-oriented and very good at following through on a task.

Set Time Frames

A third strategy is the negotiating of time frames. "I'm going to start dinner now. You tell me when you'll be able to come and set the table." "You said you have to write a paper tonight. You tell me when you're going to get off the computer to start it." When a child is involved in setting the timeframe, they are more likely to honour it.

A strategy I use a lot in the counselling or tutoring situation is the timer, and I recommend its use in school and at home as well. In my sessions, we usually alternate between play and talking. Ping-pong is very popular. Before we play, I set a timer at the child's age in minutes. They all happily agree to this. The key is that when the timer goes and we stop, it's not me taking their fun away. The timer provides an impersonal, objective boundary for the activity — one in which they had some input.

Timers can work for limiting pleasant activities like playing video games. "Let's set the timer for how long you're going to be on the computer." Timers can also be equally useful for limiting unpleasant tasks. "You have to do these math questions tonight for homework. Let's set the timer for ten minutes and we'll see how much we can get done, then we'll take a break." "Let's see if we can clean up this room before the timer goes in ten minutes." Knowing that there is a finite amount of time can make all the difference. Kids are often reluctant to start an unpleasant task, because they feel the unpleasantness is going to go on forever. If the time is limited by the use of a timer, it is easier to cope with. I often find that after the bell rings or the buzzer goes, the child keeps working. Again, this goes back to the transitioning issue. The child launched into the task knowing the time limitation, but unintentionally became quite focused on the task — leading to a longer time spent on it than planned.

Verbal Rehearsal

The fourth strategy for helping kids transition is verbally rehearsing what is about to happen. I counsel a boy who finds transitioning very difficult, not to mention that he really likes coming to see me and hates leaving. At the end of our sessions, he will always begin to act out his feelings, doing things to try to provoke a response from me — refusing to put something down, refusing to walk out the door. I have to be careful not to let his behaviour in the last five minutes of our session spoil what has been an excellent time together.

I have adopted two strategies. I give him time warnings: "We have fifteen minutes left … we have five minutes left," and at the end of the session I say something like, "You're going to get up from the chair and we're going to walk out the door together. We're going to meet your mom, and you're going to walk out to the car with her." As odd as this may sound, it works like a charm. It gives him a mental picture of what's about to happen, and he plays out the scenario just suggested.

The Biggest Transition of All: Falling Asleep

The biggest transition we all go through each day is from wakefulness to sleep. I am surprised how many boys tell me they go to bed at nine or ten but don't fall asleep until midnight. For many, coming down from the stimulation of the day takes a long time. Kids who have a hard time falling asleep may need to start the bedtime routine earlier. Barbara Coloroso talks about bedtime routines in her book *Kids Are Worth It*, the importance of cues that signal the arrival of bedtime and consciously or unconsciously help the child make the transition from stimulating daytime to quiet nighttime. Getting into pyjamas, bedtime stories, brushing teeth, and the bedtime snack are among the various components of the ritual that can be started earlier and perhaps extended over a longer period.

The Zen of Boyhood: Living in the Moment

There are Buddhist monks who spend their entire lives trying to achieve the goal of being totally present to the moment, living in the "eternal now." Many boys have already achieved this state of enlightenment! In fact, it comes naturally to them. "Why would I work on a project today that isn't due until next week?" "Why would I leave this to go and do that when this is so interesting?" These sentences make total sense to the Zen-minded boy. We adults spend so much time mulling over the past and fretting about the future. Instead of trying to change our boys to be more like us, maybe we should try to be more like them — enjoying the moment, totally absorbed in a task, staying with it until it's done. The problem is the real world, including places like school, does not allow for this kind of approach. Things happen according to a set schedule in the real world — a schedule that does not always make sense to the Zen-like boy.

How can a parent or teacher help a boy (or any student) who has a hard time meeting deadlines? One strategy is "chunking," or simply breaking down the task into manageable parts, only worrying about one part at a time. "You have to hand in a Bristol board display on a Canadian aboriginal tribe by Friday. Today is Monday. Tonight all we have to do is go on the computer and pick the tribe." You go on the computer, you find some good websites on the topic, and the child picks his tribe — the Mohawks. Homework done. The next night: "Let's find some websites that tell about the Mohawk and we'll make ten point-form notes and print off a couple of pictures." The child does this. Homework done. On it goes like this, each night having a manageable amount of work. In my experience with this technique, the child usually does more than the "chunk" planned. This is a good strategy for students of any age who suffer from procrastination or perfectionism. The two are often linked. I don't start it because I know it won't be perfect, and if it can't be, there's no sense starting it.

"Chunking" is like amortizing your stress over time. Instead of the awful stress that comes with doing a whole project the night before it's due, amortize that stress over a week or two weeks. As soon as you have the assignment, break it down into parts and plot those parts against time, a little bit each night.

The boy who lives in the moment can find calendars very helpful, as they provide a concrete representation of time in space. A calendar is like a map of time. Maps lead us through space; calendars can lead kids through time. Have a large calendar on the kitchen, bedroom, or classroom wall and talk about what's on it. This last point is crucial — talking and thinking through where we are in time, what has been accomplished or experienced in the past few days, what is on the agenda for today, and what is coming up in the future. Mel Levine distinguishes between two neurodevelopmental skills: spatial ordering (the ability to organize oneself in *space*), and temporal ordering (the ability to organize oneself in *time*). Some kids need coaching in both of these areas, but the Zen-like boy especially needs help with temporal ordering — hence the importance of standing in front of the calendar and talking things through.

The dark side of living in the moment is a disregard for consequences. Many boys will act in the present without any regard for what may happen, either in the present or several steps down the line. Sometimes boys need to be "watched over" or coached in this regard. Gabor Maté calls it "forgetting to remember the future."

Boys and Eye Contact

We all have five senses. For males, the most highly developed of these is sight. If that's true, then why don't men make eye contact? They don't precisely because it is so powerful. "What started the fight?" "He looked at me!" One male looks at another too long and the other feels threatened. "What are *you* looking at?" Males do not hold sustained eye contact because they find it invasive and threatening. This is important information for females, who enjoy eye contact and do not find it nearly as charged. They seek it. "Look into my eyes and tell me you love me." This is asking a lot of a man! "Look at me when I'm talking to you!" When being yelled at, the last thing a boy wants is to be forced to make eye contact with the person doing the yelling. He already feels invaded and humiliated by the raised voice; eye contact only strengthens those negative feelings. Women need to realize that eye contact is not essential when talking to a male. In fact, it can get in the way.

I worked with a boy, Sean, who kept his head down during class, which bothered his female teacher very much. He explained, "If I put my head down, I can listen better. When my head is up, I'm looking at all the other things in the room. When I do that, I don't listen as well. It's like my seeing is stronger than my listening, so I turn my eyes off and then I can hear better."

This is important anecdotal information. There are at least three main kinds of distractibility: visual (by what you see), auditory (by what you hear), and tactile (by the things you can touch). Sean was most susceptible to visual distractibility, and he had devised his own way of focusing! Again, eye contact is not a requirement for listening. Most of us are familiar with car-ride-therapy, even if we've never thought to call it that. This is the phenomenon experienced by many parents who cannot get their adolescent sons to speak to them face-to-face, but put them in the car and they open up. Why? Because the threat of eye contact is gone. Everyone is looking straight ahead, and the conversation from the males flows better than it would face-to-face.

Because males love looking, video games are here to stay! They will become more popular and more sophisticated. The whole world of cyberspace is a feast of looking and not being looked at. It is no coincidence that the central metaphor for Microsoft's operating system is "windows" — looking through a framed screen into limitless space. Every screen is, in essence, a window. Males are very comfortable and feel a strong sense of control when they can see clearly and are not being looked at themselves.

Tone of Voice: Stop Yelling at Me!

Just as for boys seeing is the most important of the five senses, hearing is the most important for girls. There is a direct correlation between the female brain's facility with words and her highly developed sense of hearing. The two work together: speaking and listening. Females hear words in a much more complex way. For males, words are sounds that denote specific objective meanings. For females, words have at least two important aspects: the specific objective denotations of the word, and, in addition, the tone used in speaking the word. For the female brain, tone of voice is extremely important. In fact, sometimes the tone carries more information than the words.

A woman can ask her friend how she is feeling. The friend responds, "Fine," and the woman responds, "What's wrong?" She could tell from the tone that her friend is not fine. She has learned more from that than from the actual words. It seems we can camouflage our thoughts, but it is hard to disguise our feelings.

Problems may occur when the female speaker assumes that the male listener has the same ability to decipher tone as she does. Her husband asks her how her day went. She responds, "Fine," and he continues doing what he was doing. She feels ignored or that he is unsympathetic. Through her tone, she was actually saying, "I had a terrible day, and I want some time and attention while I talk about it." Her husband simply did not "hear" this.

Very often, women communicate through tone and the male listener senses there is another level of meaning, but he cannot figure it out. "I know she's mad about something, but I don't know what it is." The secret when talking to a male is to say exactly what you mean!

Females often hear with their hearts, not their heads. The emotional tone can far outweigh the objective meaning of the words themselves. I might sternly ask my daughter to do a job, and her response is, "Stop yelling at me!" She feels my impatience and hears the negative feeling as a kind of volume. Kids will often talk about teachers or adults who were "yelling" at them when, in reality, the teacher was speaking with a frustrated or impatient tone. This is another reason why adults have to be aware of their own emotional state when speaking to a child. If we are tired or frustrated or angry about something else, this comes into our words, and the child concludes that he is the cause of the feelings.

ADD or NORMAL BOY BEHAVIOUR?

ADD in Historical Context

Thom Hartmann was the first to present the theory that people with ADD/ADHD are really just genetic survivors from our hunter-gatherer past, trying to cope in a farmer's world. The more I thought about this, and the more I applied it to my observations of particular boys, the more sense it made. Our own species, *Homo sapiens*, is estimated to have been around for about 200,000 years. For most of this time, we lived as hunters and gatherers. Hunting involved a lot of moving through space. Some archaeologists have estimated that the average male *Homo sapien* may have walked about fifteen kilometres each day. The male brain evolved to be proficient at moving through space. We also lived in close harmony with the natural world, where, Hartmann says, impulsivity, distractibility, and hyperactivity were "genetic positives."

About 10,000 B.C.E, most humans stopped moving from place to place. The agricultural revolution meant the domestication of crops and animals. Men became farmers. There was still much movement, and males continued their close connection with plants and animals, but focused attention and delayed gratification became more highly valued. In this society, the processing of printed text and sitting at desks for long periods was practiced by only a tiny minority of scribes.

Around 1450 C.E., Gutenberg perfected the printing press, which led to the mass production of books and to mass literacy. To be educated, to be an adult, to be ready to participate in society, increasingly came to mean being print-literate. If the hunter-gatherer found farming "boring," imagine how he would have found print literacy!

Then in the mid-eighteenth century came the Industrial Revolution. The economic foundation of the West changed from agriculture to manufacturing. More and more people left the rural environment to work in factories. People stopped moving around, and their connection with the natural world was drastically reduced. The hunter-gatherer went inside and was required to work at the same task for ten to twelve hours.

With the Baby Boom after the Second World War, an unprecedented number of children had to be educated. Factory schooling was born, and the factory provided the template for our modern educational system. Children were housed in large buildings for many hours a day, where they were required to become proficient at print literacy, there was very little movement, and the connection with nature was lost. Again, think of the hunter-gatherer sitting in this confining environment.

In the second half of the twentieth century, an electronic revolution transformed mass media from a print-based to a visual–spatial format. The word was replaced by the image and the new information environment, "cyberspace," was born.

Against this historical background, a behavioural phenomenon began to appear. Boys were finding it increasingly hard to sit still and pay attention. They did not have this problem in cyberspace. Only in the environment of the factory school did this problem show up. It was labelled a problem because the processes of the school required sustained attention to print as an "input" in the form of reading and as an "output" in the form of writing.

Have boys today lost the ability to focus on reading and writing, or have they simply recovered a more innate ability that was once given more value and opportunity for use — namely, movement through space? Are boys with ADD still hunter-gatherers? Are they still farmers? Are they suffering from a loss of connection with nature? Ironically, we may have returned to a "spatial" world in which movement, distractibility, impulsivity, and hyperactivity are useful once again.

Watch a boy moving in a first-person shooter game. Is he hearkening back to his primal hunter past? How many boys have I seen over the years who, by two o'clock in the afternoon, are ready to explode after sitting at desks for five hours. They would give anything to get out in a field and plough, get into a barn and throw bales of hay. They want to use their muscles and do something productive. They do not see the value of long stretches of reading and writing. Math they can tolerate, but it also requires long periods of sitting still!

Facts About ADD

In this book, I will use the term ADD to denote both ADD (Attention Deficit Disorder) and ADHD (Attention Deficit Hyperactive Disorder). ADD is the most common psychiatric disorder affecting children. It is usually assumed that a child with ADD has trouble paying attention, but it is actually a problem with the regulation of attention. Children with ADD are just as likely to hyperfocus on something as they are to move from thing to thing. This is one of the reasons video games can be so engrossing for kids with ADD. They allow for both hyperfocusing on the game as a whole, and rapid shifting of attention because of the constant novelty involved in the game. ADD is also characterized by inconsistency of focus — being able to focus one minute and not the next, working hard on a project in the morning and being totally unable to focus in the afternoon. One of the most interesting characteristics of children with ADD is their tendency to focus on what observers call "inappropriate objects of focus," but, of course, this raises the question, inappropriate to whom? One of the reasons these kids have so many problems in the school setting is they are unwilling to focus attention on things that don't matter to them. Is this a disability or a natural way of functioning?

The Diagnosis of ADD

The *Diagnostic and Statistical Manual of Mental Disorders (DSM-IV)* is a guideline published by the American Psychological Association used to help psychologists determine whether or not a mental disorder exists. Under the entry for Attention Deficit Hyperactive Disorder, the following criteria must be met in order for a diagnosis to be applied:

DSM-IV Criteria for ADHD

I. Either A or B:

Six or more of the following symptoms of inattention have been present for at least 6 months to a point that is inappropriate for developmental level:

Inattention

1. Often does not give close attention to details or makes careless mistakes in schoolwork, work, or other activities.

2. Often has trouble keeping attention on tasks or play activities.

3. Often does not seem to listen when spoken to directly.

4. Often does not follow through on instructions and fails to finish schoolwork, chores, or duties in the workplace (not due to oppositional behavior or failure to understand instructions).

5. Often has trouble organizing activities.

6. Often avoids, dislikes, or doesn't want to do things that take a lot of mental effort for a long period of time (such as schoolwork or homework).

7. Often loses things needed for tasks and activities (e.g. toys, school assignments, pencils, books, or tools).

8. Is often easily distracted.

9. Is often forgetful in daily activities.

Six or more of the following symptoms of hyper-activity-impulsivity have been present for at least 6 months to an extent that is disruptive and inappropriate for developmental level:

Hyperactivity

1. Often fidgets with hands or feet or squirms in seat when sitting still is expected.

2. Often gets up from seat when remaining in seat is expected.

3. Often excessively runs about or climbs when and where it is not appropriate (adolescents or adults may feel very restless).

4. Often has trouble playing or doing leisure activities quietly.

5. Is often "on the go" or often acts as if "driven by a motor".

6. Often talks excessively.

Impulsivity

7. Often blurts out answers before questions have been finished.

8. Often has trouble waiting one's turn.

9. Often interrupts or intrudes on others (e.g., butts into conversations or games).

II. Some symptoms that cause impairment were present before age 7 years.

III. Some impairment from the symptoms is present in two or more settings (e.g. at school/work and at home).

IV. There must be clear evidence of clinically significant impairment in social, school, or work functioning.

V. The symptoms do not happen only during the course of a Pervasive Developmental Disorder, Schizophrenia, or other Psychotic Disorder. The symptoms are not better accounted for by another mental disorder (e.g. Mood Disorder, Anxiety Disorder, Dissociative Disorder, or a Personality Disorder).

Based on these criteria, three types of ADHD are identified:

IA. ADHD, Combined Type: if both criteria IA and IB are met for the past 6 months

IB. ADHD, Predominantly Inattentive Type: if criterion IA is met but criterion IB is not met for the past six months

IC. ADHD, Predominantly Hyperactive-Impulsive Type: if Criterion IB is met but Criterion IA is not met for the past six months.

(Taken from *American Psychiatric Association: Diagnostic and Statistical Manual of Mental Disorders*, Fourth Edition, Text Revision. Washington, D.C.: American Psychiatric Association, 2000.)

Over the course of my career, I have certainly seen an increase in the number of students diagnosed with ADD. Do more kids have it than before or have we just become more aware of it? Is the increased incidence just a by-product of our increasing tendency to label and calibrate the spectrum of normal childhood behaviour?

The fact remains that there are some kids who have real difficulty with attention control.

There is no blood test or urine test to diagnose ADD. There are brain scans that can show deficits in brain functioning, but these are very seldom used for ADD diagnoses. ADD is most commonly diagnosed by means of a psycho-educational assessment. This process almost always involves parents and at least one teacher filling out an observation checklist. Sometimes these checklists tell us more about the person filling them out than they do about the child.

I have said earlier that the typical attention span of a child is his age in minutes. If a parent or teacher expects that a ten-year-old should be able to focus uninterrupted for twenty or thirty minutes, those are unrealistic expectations. When the adult gets to the part of the questionnaire that says, "Often has difficulty sustaining attention in tasks or play activities," she has to check off one of the following modifiers: always, often, sometimes, rarely, or never. Because of her expectation that a ten-year-old boy should be able to focus for twenty or thirty minutes, she is likely to check off always or often. Is this realistic? Will these kinds of answers lead to a diagnosis of ADD in a boy whose behaviour is perfectly normal?

Two other statements on the questionnaire are, "Often leaves seat in classroom or in other situations in which remaining seated is expected," and "Often has difficulty playing or engaging in leisure activities quietly." Let's imagine a December-born boy in grade one sitting with a January-born girl on each side of him. How will he appear? Does he have ADD?

I have heard it suggested, and I completely agree, that no child should be assessed for ADD before the age of seven, and even that is pretty young. The "clay" is still very soft. In our modern schools, where we are in the business of making kids "normal" and measuring normalcy, our yardsticks may be flawed. Our standards for normal have two aspects: the tools we use for measuring, and the attitudes and expectations we bring to interpreting the results. We should have great humility when it comes to diagnosing kids. Are our tools accurate and our expectations realistic?

To Medicate or Not to Medicate

Most ADD medications are stimulants. It sounds strange that we would be trying to stimulate a hyperactive child, but what these drugs stimulate, to use John Hallowell's metaphor, are the brakes in the brain. In Gabor Maté's analogy, they wake up the sleeping policeman in the frontal lobe, the judgment centre that says, "do this, don't do that."

Kids with ADD have trouble filtering incoming stimuli, so everything is equally interesting and important. Sitting in a visually stimulating classroom, their eyes wander over everything without discrimination. A problem arises when the teacher has a very different idea of where the kid's eyes should be. Kids with ADD also have trouble inhibiting outgoing stimuli — also known as behaviour. They appear impulsive or hyperactive because they have no internal pullback mechanism. They have poor self-regulation. The child with ADD is always at a green light, to use my classroom metaphor.

We are all aware of the increase in the incidence of the diagnosis of ADD as well as the accompanying increase in prescriptions of ADD medication. There are two ends of the spectrum when it comes to attitudes toward dealing with ADD. On one end is the idea that any use of medication is wrong. I have spoken to many parents and teens over the years who are completely opposed to using medication. On the other end are those who have no problem with it. My own attitude falls in the middle. I have seen some kids who benefited greatly from medication. They are better able to focus, their marks improve, and their overall sense of success and self-esteem are rescued. At this end of the spectrum we are assuming that school is a given and, for better or for worse, people are deciding to make the child fit there, even if through chemical means. Unless or until school is willing to change, the pharmaceutical option will continue to grow in popularity. As discussed earlier, boys coming out of cyberspace are finding school space harder and harder to negotiate. For some, medication may be the only answer. It can certainly be the quickest one.

Mario came into grade nine looking for a new start. He had a terrible reputation at his elementary school because he had difficulty focusing, and his behaviour was very impulsive. He had a hard time staying in his seat and was always on the lookout for negative forms of stimulation to keep things interesting. I taught him during first period, and as the day progressed his behaviour deteriorated. I would meet him in the halls as he took his tenth bathroom break. Teachers were letting him go just to get him out of class. When I spoke to his mom, she was at her wit's end. His behaviour at home was a daily issue, and he was starting to spend a lot of time "roaming the streets" (a typical ADD pastime — again, trying to keep things interesting through constant novelty and movement). She wanted him to try medication, but Mario was against it. He had tried it in grade six for a couple of weeks and didn't like the side effects. He said it made him feel "out of it."

When I spoke alone with Mario, he said he was very upset about the way grade nine was going. He had really been looking forward to a fresh start and wanted to establish a more positive reputation. He found himself back in the role of "class clown" and "bad kid." He especially wanted the girls to think well of him, and he knew they were slowly writing him off. In addition, I saw the familiar pattern of the grade nine or ten boy who is having trouble fitting into the mainstream and begins to seek out friends and activities on the fringes of school life. He found the smoking area and the company of other kids for whom school was not working. Many of the students we see in the smoking area or otherwise living on the fringes have issues with attention control and impulse control.

Mario was what we call a "student at risk." Because his "symptoms" were so severe, I encouraged him to try the medication again. He agreed, and the change was remarkable! With the medication and the support of particular teachers, he was able to completely turn things around. He could stay in his seat and focus on the task at hand. Sadly, because he had spent so many years in a negative role, his study habits, problem-solving skills, and general work ethic had all suffered. It was one thing to be able to sit down and focus; now he was faced with the intellectual task of actually doing it, but at least he went from failing to passing grades in all his courses.

Prescription Drugs, Marijuana, and Alcohol

Many kids are using mood-altering substances as a form of self-medication. We can't really condemn them for this. Our culture completely condones the use of substances to alter mood, the two main ones being caffeine and alcohol. We use these chemicals to help us cope, and that is what many teens are doing with cigarettes, marijuana, and alcohol. They are trying to cope with school, parents, peers, a part-time job, an over-stimulating culture — the list is a long one.

Zack was a student with ADD who refused to take medication. Ironically, he was not averse to using a more organic form — marijuana. Even tobacco helped calm his hyperactivity, and he was a regular user of both. Zack was still having trouble with school — paying attention, handing in assignments, and getting along with teachers. As he came into grade eleven, it slowly began to dawn on him that graduation was not far off, and he was behind in his credits, which would mean more time at school. He decided to try a prescription drug called Concerta (methylphenidate). The medication made a huge difference in his ability to cope, and amazingly, when he started taking it, he stopped using marijuana immediately. He told me he just didn't need it any more.

For some kids, ADD can lead to anti-social behaviour or even illegal activity. Poor impulse control and the need for constant stimulation can lead a young person into some sticky situations, especially when they are not being supervised or monitored. In some cases the decision about using medication ends up being one about how often a child is going to sit in the principal's office, or worse, the police station.

Medication and Classroom Control

Medication is often used as a method of controlling children in the same way that the strap once was. I am old enough to remember the strap. I never got it, but I remember how it looked, I remember others getting it, and I remember the power it had over all of us. It was one of the things that kept us in line, the most primitive form of external control. We behaved out of fear of physical pain.

The strap is gone, but the desire to keep kids under control is still there. Teachers and administrators have had to come up with other ways of achieving compliance. Ideally, they might use rational argument, but in the less than ideal world of the modern school, yelling and other low-level forms of verbal abuse have taken the place of the strap. In the last decade or two, a new "tool" has appeared in the form of drugs that alter moods and modify behaviour. It is not too cynical to suggest that medications of various kinds are increasingly being used as a means of social control.

Some of the main obstacles teachers face on a daily basis are negative attitudes toward school and sabotaging behaviour in the classroom. Faced with thirty students, a curriculum that needs to be covered, and a system that is not sufficiently self-critical to change its practices, the teacher is often left feeling powerless and confused. Political scientists use the German word *realpolitik*, which means doing what works in the moment despite one's ideological convictions. In classrooms today, we are seeing a lot of *realpolitik* — doing whatever works to get through the day. In this kind of environment, it is not hard to see why a teacher might suggest medication. Classroom control has become the primary and most problematic goal for many teachers and, with respect to medication, adults increasingly believe the end justifies the means.

DISTRACTIBILITY, IMPULSIVITY, AND HYPERACTIVITY: ALTERNATIVE DIAGNOSES

We have looked at three fundamental facts about boys: a year-and-a-half difference in cognitive and biological development compared to girls, the need for movement and space, and the preference for action over words. Let's apply this information to the three "symptoms" of ADD and see if we can find alternative explanations.

Distractibility

There are four types of distractibility: auditory (by extraneous sounds), visual (by extraneous sights), tactile (by the desire to touch things or people), and temporal (by thoughts about the past or the future).

Distraction is an interesting word. It implies that the child is distracted *from* something. Usually that something is what *we* want the child to be focused on. It could be argued that it is only from our point of view that the child is distracted. From his, he is focusing precisely on the most important thing — the thing *he* wants to focus on. It could be argued that ADD is just an unwillingness to focus on things one doesn't find interesting. In the definitions above, I used the words "extraneous sounds" and "extraneous sights." Perhaps these things are extraneous from our point of view but *central* to the child's.

Auditory and visual distractibility are closely related. Since the visual trumps the auditory in the male brain, looking will often override listening. This is especially true for the child with poor receptive language skills, common in boys. Earlier, I used the analogy of the waterfall and the thimble. Perhaps the boy ended up in a classroom (or a family) where there is a lot of talking and he feels overwhelmed by all the words flying around. The solution might be to use fewer words, to make instructions short, simple, and emphatic.

When he reaches his language saturation point, he will move on to other things. He will most likely revert to his preferred sense — looking. He will start scanning the room for visual stimulation. To the people talking to him, he may appear distracted. It is true that he is not listening, but that doesn't mean he is distractible. It means he has a limited capacity for the sustained processing of complex language, and his preferred mode — looking — has taken over.

If the classroom is very noisy or the boy is sitting near kids who love to talk, the solution may be to remove him from this over-stimulating language environment. It is a constant source of frustration to me that removing kids from particular environments, especially group situations, is seen as some sort of punishment. As someone who loves to be alone and finds group situations overwhelming and stressful, I see the opportunity for "quiet time" or "time-out" as very positive. In my English department, we have become quite good at using the "time-out" as a non-punitive strategy for acting-out behaviour. So many times I have seen a student who is not functioning at all in the classroom brought to our office, where he can work at a table. Once alone, the clearly over-stimulated child opens his books and starts to work. The office is quiet. There are other adults role-modelling focused attention, and the child's demeanour changes completely.

Impulsivity

When I talk about "acting-out behaviour," this leads to that other symptom of ADD that abounds in our classrooms: impulsivity. Recall that boys' brains develop at a slower rate. The pre-frontal cortex, the area of the brain that forms judgments and inhibits behaviour, is not as developed. We should *expect* boys to be more impulsive. Instead of seeing it as dysfunctional or disordered, we could just as easily view it as normal. Our job is not to change or shame it but to manage and accommodate it in the complex social setting of the classroom. This will always involve compromise on both the student's and teacher's parts. Again, going back to what we learned earlier, the need to move is fundamental in boys. Is this a disorder or is it natural behaviour? It can be disruptive to classroom decorum, but it doesn't mean the child has a problem or is bad. The challenge for a teacher is how to contain this energy among all the competing interests she faces in the classroom. It is not easy, but medication is not always the answer.

Hyperactivity

Boys are more likely to express themselves in actions than words. When they experience feelings, they move, and when the feelings are strong, they move even faster.

Dylan was a compliant boy who gave his teacher very little trouble until his parents separated and eventually divorced. One Monday morning, he came into the classroom and started run-ning around the perimeter, going faster and faster with each lap.

Eventually, he purposely crashed into the Christmas Nativity scene. When the teacher sat Dylan down to find out what was going on, it turned out that he was full of strong feelings. He had spent the weekend with his dad, who had a new girlfriend, and on top of everything, it was nearing the family's first Christmas apart. Many of the kids we see are literally acting out their feelings. Movement is their way of getting those feelings *out* — discharging affect. There is more of this going on in our schools than any of us realize!

Behaviour can be an expression of positive feelings just as often as of negative ones. Josh and his mom came in on a Thursday night. Mom looked haggard. "We've had a terrible week! Phone calls from the teacher. Josh was sent to the office. I don't know what's gotten into him." I talked to Josh, and it came out that tomorrow was "Medieval Fair Day," and all week had been spent preparing for this big event — constructing swords, shields, and castles out of cardboard, practicing plays, preparing food. Josh loved the Middle Ages, and he was just so happy and excited about everything to do with this event. His happiness and excitement found expression in action — often "hyper-action," disruptive to the adults trying to organize something fun in an orderly fashion.

Josh's behaviour was natural and predictable. What he needed was some coaching on limits and maybe a couple of time-out sessions when the whole thing became too overwhelming. His behaviour, though it appeared very negative to the adults, had a very positive source. He was totally motivated and engaged.

A teacher can sit with a child who seems to be acting out and ask him to translate his behaviour into words. "I get the impression from your actions that you're having a lot of feelings. I can't understand your actions. Can you translate them into words for me? I understand words better." Kids often need help differentiating between feelings, because they don't always have a very good emotional vocabulary. One thing we can do is explicitly teach them one.

I deal with so many adolescents, boys in particular, who are either out of touch with their feelings or cannot describe them. In my mentoring sessions, I use what I call "feeling stones." I have a little green bag full of small stones. I lay down a sheet of paper that has a list of about twenty feelings. The child's job is to put the stones beside the feelings he is experiencing. The stronger the feeling, the more stones go beside the word. I have found this technique invaluable in opening up conversations. The list helps us both focus in on particular issues in the child's life.

One of the most popular handouts at my workshops is this list of feelings. I tell teachers to post it in a central place and parents to post it on the fridge door. When it's time to identify feelings, the list can be used as a reference for kids to point to or check off the feelings they're having.

Here is the list:

Feelings

angry	happy
sad	excited
nervous	relaxed
trapped	smart
stupid	calm
confused	surprised
tired	quiet
frustrated	loving
bullied	friendly
depressed	comfortable
pressured	satisfied
bored	secure
lonely	safe
hungry	brave
tense	appreciated
powerless	powerful
weak	strong
excluded	loved
thirsty	hyper

PRACTICAL STRATEGIES that WORK with ALL BOYS

Kids with ADD can experience the same issues with certain areas of neurodevelopmental functioning as many boys. These issues are not necessarily disabilities or dysfunctions. They are differences and should be understood as such. Most commonly they include central auditory processing (the rate of receiving, processing, and responding to auditory inputs), graphomotor skills (the physical act of writing), written output (spelling, punctuation, grammar), executive functioning (putting it all together), spatial ordering (being organized — think of binders and backpacks!), and sequential ordering (time management). In addition to these more academic issues, the biggest challenge many boys deal with is impulse control, an issue that quickly translates into the label "behaviour problem." The practical strategies that follow are intended to address these particular areas. They will work with all boys, not just those with perceived "problems."

Exercise

We have talked about the male brain's need for movement. Exercise reduces physical and emotional stress, releases endorphins, and raises dopamine levels. Organized sports are good, but one of the things we see a lot of is standing around waiting your turn, particularly during practices. Bike riding, skateboarding, swimming, and road hockey are examples of activities that involve sustained movement. One of the reasons boys like video games so much is that you don't have to wait your turn. During classes and homework sessions, adults should always incorporate breaks that provide some kind of movement. A child will focus much better, especially after moderately strenuous activity that increases aerobic or cardio-vascular rates.

Homework

Boys work better with structure and routine. When things are done the same way every time or in the same order, it is one less thing to think about. Make homework time the same every night. Some kids are willing to do it as soon as they come home, while others need a break and will not work on it until after supper. I advise parents to let the child make this choice. It is best to position homework time near some other routine activity to provide a natural boundary. For example, if it's right after school, then you have to have it done before dinner and before any screens come on (this is a way of lumping TV and computer together). If it's after supper, then get the books out right after and, again, say "no screens" until homework is done. In this way, the homework routine leads predictably out of another and there is a reward or incentive for getting it done. In one family I worked with, the parents would get the kids started on their homework then sit down to watch TV themselves. This is not a good idea. Parents can be cleaning up, reading the paper, or just sitting quietly by, available should the kids need it.

I recommend letting kids take the lead in their own homework as much as possible. When parents are too closely involved, it can quickly become the parents' homework. Psychologists talk about "learned helplessness," a state in which one has learned they cannot solve a problem or perform a task alone. They "learn" that they are helpless and always need someone else. Lines like, "I can't do this," or "This is too hard" are repeated until they get the desired result — help for their helpless state (or "rescue" might be a better word). This phenomenon also goes by the name "stimulus response"; the child is training the parents to respond to a particular stimulus. The parent has to resist this training, putting the centre of gravity back with the child. One strategy is to call the child's bluff and say, "Okay. Just leave it then."

Sometimes completing homework becomes more important to the parent than the child, and the parent's thought is, "What will the teacher think of *me* if my child doesn't have his homework done?" The child senses that completing homework carries some special emotional importance for the parent, and he capitalizes on this. "If you think this is so important, then you better help me get it done."

This cycle has to be broken. The ownership should stay with the child. If he doesn't do it, he will face the consequences tomorrow. Let the teacher judge you. You are trying to raise an autonomous, self-regulating child, and always being there to "rescue" them will not teach self-direction.

Another tip I give parents and teachers is quality over quantity. Kids' frustration levels rise understandably when they are required to do ten questions that are really about one simple concept. One example would be writing out numbers as complete words: 4,361 = four thousand three hundred and sixty-one. Once you have the idea behind this, there is no need to do it ten times. I worked with one boy whose homework was to write out the steps of long division questions in words: 84 divided by 7. Here is his written answer: "First you ask yourself how many times seven goes into eight. It goes in once. You write a one above the eight. Then you say seven times one is seven. You write the seven underneath the eight. Then you subtract eight minus seven, which is one. Then you bring down the four and you have fourteen. Then you ask yourself how many times seven goes into fourteen, and it goes in twice. So you write a two above the four. You multiply seven times two, which is fourteen, and you write that under the fourteen, and you subtract and you get zero. So the answer is twelve." He had to do this for *ten* questions!

This was a boy who loved math and hated writing. The exercise reinforced his hatred of writing (and school generally) and weakened his love of math. He was full of resentment and frustration. I advised the parent to write a note to the teacher saying that Matthew understood the concept, and we did not see the need to repeat this ten times. Repetition does have value, but not when a fact, concept, or skill has been mastered. Then it becomes drudgery.

Repetition and Memory

When it comes to remembering facts, repetition does have value. I say it over and over again: repetition is the key to learning. We seldom learn something after hearing it once. Curriculum content is often only presented one time. The teacher can say that the material has been "covered" — but has it really been retained or learned? Recall is required up until the test, and after that, the information is never repeated or called on again. Learning happens when information is recalled over longer and longer intervals.

We live in a culture that values constant novelty. Fun is a word used to describe anything that is always changing. Boring is used to describe anything that stays the same. Facts stay the same; the multiplication tables can only be learned by rote repetition. Phonics rules can only be learned the same way. If handled right, I have found kids feel a sense of mastery and pride when they can store and recall facts. What they need is an adult who asks them their times table or how to spell a word *and then asks the same question again later!* I remember being in grade four, learning my multiplication tables. One day I must not have been able to answer the question 7 x 8. The teacher took it upon himself to ask me this particular question at random times throughout the day, not just during math class, which gave it a "fun" quality. He also kept asking over days and weeks to the point where it became comical. To this day, 7 x 8 = 56 is burned into my memory more than any other multiplication question.

Competition

Boys like competition. It is fed by testosterone and other chemicals in the brain. Boys like something to be difficult and the outcome of an action to be uncertain. These two things create a positive tension they find "fun." Competition can happen with a clock, with oneself, or with others. When I am working with kids and flash cards for multiplication or sight-word recognition, I set the timer for anywhere between one and three minutes. We record the date and how many cards we went through in the allotted time. The goal is to increase the number of cards read each time. Here the competition is with the clock and oneself. I will sometimes mention how other kids have done, and the goal becomes trying to beat "the record."

How many homework questions can you get done in fifteen minutes? Can you have the dishes done by the time a certain TV show comes on? Can you clean your room before Mom gets home from work? Creating this kind of time-based tension can be very motivating. However, it can become negative when there is strong sibling rivalry, especially between brothers close in age, and it might not be a good strategy for projects requiring care and attention to detail. Boys fall very quickly into the "just-get-it-done" mode — with quality going out the window.

Push the Reset Button

This may seem to contradict what I have said many times elsewhere, that eye contact is not essential for listening. A boy may be listening intently, even though he's not looking at you. We also learned that males find eye contact invasive and threatening. One of the ways we can bring a boy back to attention is by using this sensitivity.

I saw two little boys in the public library one day, about five or six, who were obviously very excited about storytime. They were over-stimulated by their feelings of excitement, each other's company, and all the things to look at in the library. They were talking very loudly and pushing each other up the stairs, drawing lots of attention (and looks of disapproval) from the adult patrons. Their mother followed behind with a constant stream of admonitions, threats, and shushes. Her words were no more significant to these boys than the sound of the air conditioning. As soon as it became apparent that the boys were over-stimulated, she would have done well to stop them, get down to their level, look them in the eye, hold their hands or arms, and give one very specific instruction. Something like, "Whisper in the library" or "No talking until we get to the kids' area."

Sometimes the adult has to wait until the child is focused and ready to hear the command; sometimes the adult will speak too soon. Allow time for the child to come back into himself and *be* there. This is a critical step and requires presence of mind, especially if you just want the behaviour to stop as soon as possible. The adult too feels rushed and over-stimulated. I like the metaphor of pushing pause or the reset button. I have found this strategy tremendously helpful with an over-stimulated child whose impulse control is almost totally gone.

Lists

I encourage parents to post lists around the house. The morning routine on the bathroom mirror: wash your hands, wash your face, brush your teeth, comb your hair. By the bedroom door: get dressed, make your bed, pick things up off the floor. These lists must be as short and concrete as possible. They also must be reinforced verbally, but just as importantly, physically. This means standing in front of the list and pointing to each thing. Your finger is like the cursor on a screen. You don't even need to read what's there. Let the child read it, and he will respond. This silent going down the list more accurately imitates what he will be doing when alone. It also takes away the "nagging" voice and reduces the activity to a mechanical one that you are trying to train.

Mirroring

One way we can teach self-regulation is through mirroring. Many kids cannot "see" themselves. They do not have this reflexive ability to leave their own point of view and see themselves as others do. One of the ways we can coach them is by simply describing what we see or hear. "I see you running around the room." "I hear you talking the most in your group." "I see the other kids getting irritated by your constant joking." These reports do not involve moral judgments; they are objective and factual descriptions. The child is then in a position to make his own judgment about his actions. This kind of coaching can happen in the situation or afterwards. It must always be done respectfully and in private.

Prepare for Unstructured Time

Kids with poor impulse control often have trouble with unstructured time. Riding in a car or waiting in line are two common examples. When my kids were small, we used to keep a big plastic globe-shaped container in the car. It had a small opening at the top. We put all kinds of little "doodads" into this container (things that could be held and fiddled with) and, in fact, we called it "the doodad jar." When one of the kids was bored, he or she would say, "Pass me the doodad jar," or if one was starting to get restless and act out, we would hand him the jar and say, "Pick something out of here." Every time I pass by a toy retailer, I always have a look for little doodads. It is best if the object has some moving parts, or you can do something with it. The checkout counters in a lot of stores will have this kind of thing as an impulse item — a small flashlight, an unusual key chain.

A mother's purse is another great place for keeping things to occupy kids during unstructured time. My wife always kept a deck of kid-sized playing cards. Go Fish, War, Old Maid — there are lots of simple games kids love to play.

Songs and games are another great strategy for filling unstructured time — especially in the car. When things really get out of control, I recommend one of my favourites, the Quiet Game. "Let's see who can be quiet the longest. The first person to talk loses." Google "games to play in the car" and you will get over sixty-five million results!

The same strategy can be used by teachers. Kids can have a doodling book to pull out of their desk, a novel, or some ongoing colouring project. Because kids take different amounts of time to complete assigned tasks, there should always be ongoing ones held in reserve for those in-between times when they have nothing to do.

Make this free choice an explicit instruction. "We have five minutes until the bell rings. You can put your head down, doodle, or talk quietly among yourselves."

The Prepared Environment

One of Maria Montessori's greatest contributions to education was her idea of the "prepared environment." She said that the school needs to fit the child. Children learn best in an environment that allows for independent learning and exploration. This means an environment rich to all the senses — especially sight and touch. A home can also be a kid-friendly, prepared environment. Educational stores have great wall charts like maps of the world, maps of the solar system, times tables, parts of speech, the cursive alphabet — the list goes on. And these graphic displays don't need to be store-bought. Parents can make them or kids themselves can. The point here is that learning requires a space to help facilitate children's natural curiosity.

Most learning is active. School emphasizes passive learning. Here, the teacher is the active person "delivering knowledge," and the child passively receives it. In active learning, the child decides what is important. Active learning is hard to track, monitor, and measure because it happens inside — often in mysterious ways and often unconsciously. All of a sudden, our child will talk about something, and neither you nor he has any idea where it came from. What we can do is prepare the environment in such a way that lots of "information" is available in the form of books, pictures, and objects.

The Internet has great potential as a place for independent, active learning, because any question can be answered instantly. All kinds of text, images, and graphics can be brought up instantly, and any train of thought is followed instantaneously.

The Kid-Friendly House

Montessori taught that the school must fit the child. I would suggest that the home must also fit — or at least a significant part of it. You would never know there were children living in many homes. Sometimes there will be a "play room" which is allowed to look like a tornado hit it, but the rest of the house is like a catalogue photo spread.

Parents live under the oppressive influence of a consumer culture that dictates exactly how one's property should look. In none of these commercial images do we see any indication of the presence of children. This becomes a kind of "norm" parents try to imitate — at a huge cost to their own sanity and the happiness of their children.

Children have no interest in how things "look." They are, by nature, "messy" because they are immersed in their environment. They do not see it as something separate from themselves that they would simply look at. Messy is a pejorative word used by adults to describe what is a natural and beautiful state. Neat and tidy are not values for children. These are adult constructs that can range from relaxed tidy to neurotic neat.

Parents should make an imaginative leap back into the perceptions they themselves once had as children. This is not easily done when all of our adult programming is about maintaining the appearance of order and control. One of the greatest gifts we can give our children is a kid-friendly house, a relaxed environment where their presence and activity are just as valid as those of the adults.

QUIET TIME

Montessori used to play "The Silence Game" with her students. She would ring a bell or hold up a card with "Silence" written on it, and all the children would go quiet. After about thirty seconds, she would whisper each child's name, and when they heard their name, they would come and stand by her. The students were taught not to make a sound while moving toward the teacher. The experience was intended to heighten their awareness of sound through creating silence. She described this game as a religious experience similar to meditation.

The closest thing I have experienced in my own classroom would be silent reading time. I try to incorporate this into all my classes, no matter the age level. Part of the value lies in the kids just getting some reading done, which they find very hard to fit into their busy (over-stimulated) lives. The other value lies in the rare experience of silence. I find that once we achieve it and are able to sustain it for, say ten minutes or more, nobody wants to disturb it. The kids will naturally avoid making any sounds or sudden movements that might disrupt the atmosphere.

Of course, the only way I could ever achieve this level of silence is by sitting very still and reading quietly myself. It is not possible with every class, but it is certainly something the kids appreciate. I won't say they "enjoy" it in the sense that it is "fun." They appreciate it in another way — one we don't really have a word for in our noise-loving culture. Perhaps one could apply Montessori's adjective that there is something "religious" about it. Every classroom and home could benefit from some "quiet time," as little as fifteen minutes, half an hour, or even an hour when all electronics are turned off and everyone stops talking. Silence has a calming and grounding effect. It brings one back to oneself. We are so much outside of ourselves.

Redirecting: Make Yourself a Distraction

One way to deal with a distracted child is to make yourself even more of a distraction. This can mean a touch or a hand on each shoulder steering a child in the direction you want him to go. You want him to put something down? Gently take it out of his hand. You want him to pick something up? Put it in his hand. It's called redirecting, and it can be physical or verbal.

Redirecting also works in the fight situation. I've broken up more than a few in my teaching career, and redirecting works in the early stages of the conflict, the verbal taunting stage, before the first physical contact. I am talking here about teenagers standing nose-to-nose, ready to go at it. First simply walk between the two combatants. This seems to break a kind of spell. In disrupting the space, the territorial aspect seems to disappear. As they stand nose to nose, it seems to be a question of who's going to cross the line first. You walk through and mess up the line, and you create static interference in the electrically charged connection they've established.

The second step is to crowd one of them so that he moves back or away. You point him in another direction and say, "Walk away." In my experience, most boys do not want to fight. They feel threatened and are usually scared, and they actually welcome some external force that gives them a way out and allows them to save face.

With younger kids, you can ask one of the fighters a question that does not relate to the fight. Start talking to both of them about something completely unrelated. Two boys are fighting over a pail and shovel at the beach. You pick up a toy bulldozer and start lifting sand. "Hey, this picks up a lot in one scoop. Does it pick up as much as the shovel does?"

Allowing Gross Motor Movement in the Classroom

I have mentioned boys' need for movement and how sitting for long periods of time can be frustrating, leading to acting out. What can be done to get boys up and moving? In the course of a typical day, there are countless little jobs that need to be done. Give those jobs to the bodily-kinaesthetic boy. Delivering messages to the front office, carrying things, cleaning the boards, handing out or collecting papers or books are all jobs that would provide some movement and therefore a discharge of energy.

Another strategy is to have the class stand up and do some simple exercises. The bodily-kinaesthetic boy will even be happy to do these on his own. Ask him if he wants to do fifteen sit-ups before he starts his silent reading. Have him try to beat his previous record. Hold a competition between the most bodily-kinaesthetic boys to see who can do the most sit-ups. The trick is to keep it serious and not let it turn into a circus.

Some classrooms have adopted a sitting-optional policy. Students are allowed to stand at their desks to work if they prefer. While standing, they will move their legs, bend over the page, twist and turn. This need not be seen as a distraction, since it usually involves no noise. If it is visually distracting to the class, then place the standing boy near the back.

Allowing Fine Motor Movement in the Classroom

As I have mentioned in other chapters, many boys think, concentrate, speak, and listen better when they are moving. This includes both gross and fine motor movement. Fine motor movement is much less disruptive to the classroom routine and can have huge benefits. Anything done with the fingers qualifies: doodling, drawing, colouring, fiddling with any little object. The best one I have seen is Silly Putty.

My notebooks in elementary school were covered in doodles. I can remember feeling more relaxed and focused when I doodled. My grade three teacher used to make everyone sit on their hands while she read stories to us. I don't remember anything about those stories. All I can remember is the burning feeling in my hands. My grade four teacher allowed us to doodle while we listened, and I can still remember particular parts of the stories. In one the characters were ants, and I can remember being down there in the grass in my imagination, watching these ants move around and interact. I listened better because my hands were busy.

Seating in the Classroom

A teacher's seating plan can have all of the logistical elements of a military general's battle plan or a coach's game plan. The expert teacher is always studying the seating plan to see which placements would maximize "efficiency." Some students can be put anywhere. Others require careful consideration — most commonly the easily distracted child, the impulsive child, and the bodily-kinaesthetic child. The bodily-kinaesthetic child should be seated near space, at the back, the front or near a window.

If a child is susceptible to auditory distractions, then the best placement may be at the front, where he can focus on the teacher's voice. Here the teacher can repeat, encourage, connect, and provide feedback without having to move very far. The child easily distracted by auditory stimuli should be seated away from heaters and loud air conditioners as well as talkative students. Boys are not as good at discriminating between foreground and background noise. The voices of talkative students nearby are equal in value to the teacher's at the front of the room.

The visually distracted child is usually best near the front, where all of the "distractions" are at least related to the curriculum. Sometimes the back is best for the visual child who wants to see everything and is therefore not always turning around to see behind him. Sitting at the back takes away his "audience" and allows him to stand up without distracting others.

The impulsive child should be seated away from high-traffic areas like the doorway, the pencil sharpener, and the garbage pail. Most importantly, he should be away from other easily distracted or impulsive students.

Having said all that, the playing field of a classroom is quite small, and there can be as many as twenty-five or thirty players on the field at once. The task of strategic placement is not an easy one.

BOYS, READING, and WRITING

READING

What Kinds of Books do Boys Like to Read?

Boys want to read books in which something is happening all the time. One of the reasons *Harry Potter and the Philosopher's Stone* grabbed the attention of so many new readers, including non-reading boys, was the fact that the action moved along so quickly.

There are four elements to any story: plot, setting, character, and theme. It is not hard to guess which one boys like best — plot, plot, plot! The other element that will draw a boy to a book is a male protagonist the same age as himself. The kinds of fiction boys like best are stories involving sports, action, and adventure. They are also drawn to non-fiction books that relay facts about things they are interested in. This kind of reading material is as valid as fiction.

Most school literature is chosen by women. They make up the majority of school librarians, elementary school teachers, and secondary school English teachers. I often recommend to school librarians that they let male teachers have a look through the catalogue before purchasing. What would a male reader be drawn to? Chances are the male adult will pick things a woman might have passed over. I remember reading a book with my grade nine remedial English class. The cover had a picture of a boy in a First World War uniform — great! We started reading the two-hundred-page book, and he didn't make it overseas until past page one hundred! Up until then he was having all kinds of relationships that involved all kinds of talking. When he did get to the battlefield, he never got to fire a shot. There was not enough action. The emphasis was on relationships and his feelings about various people.

The book had one of those gold medal medallions on the front that I neglected to look at closely. When I was finished reading, and the response had been pretty flat, I finally took a closer look at it. The award was from the Imperial Order of the Daughters of the Empire. The women who sat on the awards committee obviously loved the book. My grade nine class of reluctant-reader boys did not.

"How Do I Get a Boy to Enjoy Reading?"

We sometimes fall into the trap of treating reading like Buckley's Cough Mixture. "It tastes terrible, but it's good for you." Buckley's has even taken to implying that it works precisely because it tastes so bad. We talk about reading as though it was a chore or something difficult. We also tend to talk about it with kids as an end in itself. You just need to read for the sake of reading.

We must never forget that reading is a means to an end. Print is a "technology" with two main purposes: pleasure and information. The very act of reading may be so pleasurable to some that it doesn't even matter what they are reading, but I think this is a small minority. For most people, reading is pleasurable because of what comes from it. For some, fiction provides the greatest pleasure; for others, it is the information learned through non-fiction. Both goals are equally valid, and must be put first in any discussion of the value of reading.

When it comes to fiction, we must always put the love of the story itself ahead of any talk of the love of reading. We learn to love reading because of the great stories it can bring to us, and the special way it does — through imagination. Movies and television are great, too. They are another technology through which stories are communicated, but the medium is more literal and concrete than words on a page. These require the active participation of the reader. In movies and television, the viewer passively receives images created by someone else. This is one of the fundamental differences.

What the media share is the function of telling stories. No one would suggest that "watching" or "viewing" is pleasurable in itself. One watches in order to see *something*. It is the *something* that counts, not the act of watching. Similarly, we must always place the *something* that reading brings to the forefront. In the case of fiction, it is the story that one finds satisfying. In non-fiction, it is information that one finds interesting.

These last two criteria — that stories be satisfying and that facts interesting — points to the importance of personal choice. Kids are more likely to read what they chose themselves. Elementary school language arts programs are usually organized on this principal. When kids reach secondary school, curriculum reading becomes much more specifically prescribed. If you talk to teenagers who were avid readers as children and ask them when their interest began to wane, they will often report that it was in high school, when they were "forced" to read things they didn't like. Part of their dislike may have been the content of the work itself, but it could just as easily have been caused by the "forced" nature of the enterprise. We all show more commitment to what we choose ourselves versus what other people tell us to do — and this is doubly true for teenagers.

Reading Strategies for the Classroom (and the Home)

Read aloud to kids. This is a fundamental foundation for all future reading. I am not just talking about the little ones. Read to kids as long as they will accept it, and, in my experience, some kids will allow it right into their teen years. One night, I was reading to my ten-year-old son and decided it was time to stop. From two doors down the hall came the voice of my fourteen-year-old, who had been working at his desk. "Don't stop!" He had been listening the whole time.

Kids need to hear language read aloud. It is very different from conversational language. In fact, it is in a class unto itself. It sometimes has the quality of drama about it, especially when the reader reads dialogue with expression. When the narrator speaks between the characters' lines, it becomes entirely unlike any other kind of discourse. Kids will be better readers (silent and oral) if they have experienced role modelling of the very particular pacing, rhythm, and cadence of reading.

When I am reading one-on-one with kids, I will often have us take turns reading aloud, and I will go first. I find that the child's pacing and rhythm improves as he falls into the tempo set by me. There is a kind of silent metronome that moves the voice along. Imagine if we were able to plug a speaker into a child's head and hear his silent reading voice. It might be quite garbled, with a lot of gaps and faltering. Some kids may dislike reading because of this poor sub-vocalization. They become better readers when they hear it done aloud.

Reading Trauma

One of the most important and interesting lessons I absorbed as a teacher is just how fearful some students are about reading out loud. They have come up to my desk at the beginning of class on the first day of school, throwing all other nervousness and self-consciousness aside, to tell me, "Sir, there's one thing I want to tell you. I don't like reading in front of the class. Please, whatever you do, don't ask me to read out loud!"

I have worked one-on-one with a fourteen-year-old boy for the past four years. Every time we read, he has to make sure the door is closed so no one will hear him. Where does this fear come from? I can only guess from early experiences of humiliation while reading in front of peers. A giggle, a smirk, a laugh can have a devastating effect. Some kids are more sensitive and self-conscious than others. For this reason, I advise teachers to *let kids decide* whether they want to read and for how long. I ask, "Who wants to continue reading?" I usually get a volunteer, but if I don't, I just keep reading myself — no pressure. If a student volunteers, I tell him to stop when he feels like it. He can read five lines or five pages. Again, no pressure — it's not a contest.

Some of us may remember the way reading out loud was handled in class. The teacher calls on a student at random. No one, including the student, knows how long he will be required to read. At the end of each paragraph there is a hopeful pause. Eventually, the teacher will say, "Okay. Thank you." And then there is another pause while the teacher surveys the room looking for the next reader. I call this the lightning-bolt method. For most kids, it's not a big issue. For others, it is harrowing. Will I get picked? Will I humiliate myself? Teachers use this method because we want every student to read, but I find when I adopt the freedom-to-choose-for-yourself strategy, almost every student eventually volunteers. We should do whatever we can to make the experience of reading pleasurable, not stressful.

Movement and Reading

We have the idea that unless a child is sitting quietly looking at us, he is not listening. This is not the case. Allow fidgeting, doodling, and playing — as long as the child can still hear you. If I'm reading to a class, most like to follow along in the text. For those who don't, I encourage them to get out a piece of paper and doodle. When I'm reading one-on-one to a child, I always have Silly Putty available. In a previous chapter, I mentioned the grade three teacher who made us sit on our hands while she read and how my grade four teacher allowed doodling, which I found more beneficial. One boy I tutor brings little Lego men to class in his pocket and fiddles with them inside his desk while the teacher is talking or reading.

WRITING

Neil Postman used to say that every teacher should be required to spend a year teaching the subject he hates the most. Why? To find out first-hand what it feels like to be in the shoes of a child who finds the subject *you* love difficult — to learn empathy for the learner. I have always enjoyed writing. From an early age I was happy just to copy letters. I loved learning cursive writing and as I matured, I wrote almost every day. I find it hard to imagine how writing could be difficult, because it's not so for me. Now math is another story! My mind gets confused and I become tense around the simplest equation. I have to constantly remind myself that the way I feel about math is the way some kids feel about writing.

Writing and Executive Functioning

As I worked one-on-one with kids and read the work of Mel Levine, I began to see how writing was not one discrete task but really an amalgam of many tasks or skills occurring simultaneously. We can break writing down into at least ten component parts:

1. graphemes — knowing how to form letters (first printed letters, later cursive)

2. phonemes — knowing the sounds these letters make (phonics)

3. morphemes — knowing specific letter combinations (think of the word "eight")

4. semantics — knowing the meanings of words

5. homonyms — being able to distinguish between there, their, and they're

6. spelling — being able to combine the above five skills instantly

7. capitalization rules

8. punctuation rules

9. grammar rules

10. overall neatness (uniform letter size, keeping the writing down on the line, not trying to squeeze a big long word into the last quarter inch of a line, etc.)

When people write, all ten of these things are happening simultaneously. Most of us have mastered this very complex process. Psychoeducational experts refer to this ability as executive functioning, the ability to apply multiple skills and knowledge to perform a single task. When I'm talking to students about it, I use the analogy of juggling balls. Some kids can juggle all ten balls at once. Some can only handle two or three.

In addition to the list above, two other huge processes that go into writing, thinking and graphomotor skills, must be considered separately.

THINKING

Some people can think *as* they write. Others need to think first and then write. If we compare writing to speaking, it is easy to see that there are far fewer skills required for speaking — far less *technical* ability. This is why having a student dictate to an adult who writes it down or types it can be a better way of finding out what, in fact, a student thinks or knows. I will often get kids to say the sentence first and then, having formulated the thought in that easier way, write it down. Speech-to-text programs can also be helpful for students who find writing difficult, but I find the technology is still a bit cumbersome. The best scenario is the student talking out his thoughts to a fast typist.

Graphomotor Skills

The term "graphomotor skills" refers to the physical process of forming letters, but a large part of that process is invisible. Graphomotor activity happens at the interface between cognitive processing and moving the arm, wrist, hand, and fingers. It is the ability to move your thoughts from your brain, down your arm, into your hand, and onto the paper.

For some kids the physical act of writing is very difficult. They may know what they want to say and may even be proficient in the ten sub-skills listed above, but the act is such a chore that it takes them much longer, and there is general resistance because it is so difficult. I worked with one boy who had severe graphomotor dysfunction, and he avoided writing at all costs. One day he was wearing sandals and the pencil fell on the floor. He picked it up with his foot. I remarked on how well he did this, and he replied, "Oh yeah, I can write as well with my foot as I can with my hand." He proceeded to show me, and it was true. It was almost as though the graphomotor wiring in his leg and foot was the same as that in his arm and hand!

STRATEGIES FOR HELPING KIDS WITH WRITING

Students with poor executive function (who cannot juggle many balls at the same time) should be left to get their thoughts out in their own way, at their own pace, taking as much time as they need. Once the raw material of their ideas is on the page, then at least we have something to work with, and the student feels a sense of accomplishment for having produced something. The next stage is the tricky one: the proofreading stage.

Depending on the student's level of ability, proofreading can deal with just one issue, say spelling, or he can tackle two or three things at once, spelling, punctuation, and capitalization. Again, depending on the frustration threshold of the student, the adult can read the rough draft aloud, or the student can. Very often I find that if the student reads his writing out loud, he immediately sees the mistakes and will correct them. For boys, the biggest issue is speed. They just want to get it done! While the student reads what he has written, I use a pencil-shaped eraser to quickly erase the wrong word or the wrong part of the word. The child then re-writes it. This just speeds things up.

In a word processing program, this correction function can take place even faster. If the child simply doesn't see the error, then the adult should point to it and calmly ask, "What should this be?" If the child doesn't know, then the adult can simply supply the answer. Too much Socratic questioning can frustrate what the student already might feel is a tedious process. The trick is to keep the process moving and not get bogged down in mini-lessons or trying to get the child to remember something that has not been stored in long-term memory.

The three main strategies for helping students with severe writing problems are scribing (an adult writes from the child's dictation), the use of a speech-to-text program, and the use of a word processing program.

I think any student can benefit from the use of word processing. The neatness issue is solved, the spelling and grammar check functions alert the writer to possible errors, and the right-click function provides a list of corrections. This process ends up being a kind of drill in itself. Some researchers have even suggested that the use of two hands in word processing is superior to one hand in handwriting, that whenever both hands are engaged, both sides of the brain are stimulated, creating a more "whole brain" experience.

SPEAKING

There is a common misconception that males are not good at talking. As we learned earlier, the female brain is hardwired to prefer words, while the male is hardwired to prefer action. Conversational speaking involves at least three steps: receptive language, cognitive processing, and expressive language. Males generally have a slower rate of language processing. It's not that they can't talk; they just take longer to formulate their words. When talking to a male, one needs to be sensitive to their rate of:

1. reception (the time they need to process what you're saying)

2. cognitive processing (the time they need to think it over)

3. expression (the time they need to turn their own thoughts into words)

In practical terms, what this often amounts to is *waiting*. In my counselling sessions with boys where we are talking about feelings, even greater patience is required. I will ask a question, and the biggest challenge is to be quiet long enough to allow the boy to formulate his answer. William Pollack calls this "the timed silence syndrome." Many times, just as I have been on the verge of saying something to keep the conversation going, the boy will finally begin to articulate. With one boy, Todd, I have to be very careful to only ask one question at a time, and I can't rephrase it, because he will restart processing that revised version of the question. I have to pose the question in as short and simple a way as possible and wait for him to answer. Communication with a lot of males could be improved if this strategy was followed.

It sometimes helps to compare talking with a slow-processing male to playing catch. You throw the ball, he catches it, prepares to throw it back, and then throws it to you. There is only one ball (the topic of the conversation) and only one person can be controlling it at a time. When it's not your turn, all you need do is stand there and be quiet. It's beautifully simple. Complex conversations can sometimes look like two people juggling balls between them, which is very overwhelming to the slower language processor.

I tell teachers to wait longer for male hands to go up. Girls' hands will go up first because they have an answer to give. Very often, if boys' hands go up first, it's just so they can win the race and be picked first. It is very common for a teacher to call on a boy whose hand has gone up quickly only to have him start thinking of an answer after he's called upon.

Public Speaking

Many people hate public speaking, and one of the fears associated with it is being looked at, and, of course, judged. As we learned earlier, males find eye contact very invasive and threatening. One way of decreasing the intensity of the public speaking experience is to have something else besides oneself for the audience to look at. I find students speak much more easily if they have a visual aid of some kind — an object (as in show-and-tell), a Bristol board display, or a PowerPoint presentation.

LISTENING

Foreground Noise and Background Noise

Scientists tell us that boys in general do not hear as well as girls. We talked about this earlier in the section about tone of voice — that females were better at deciphering it. For males, sight is the most acute sense, whereas for females it is hearing. Researchers also tell us that boys are not as good at discriminating between foreground and background noise. A girl sitting in a classroom with extraneous noise can focus on the teacher's voice and keep the other sounds in a secondary position. For boys, this is not as easy, and all sound happens on the same level. Boys will often just focus on the closest or loudest sound. This takes us back to the military general's seating plan strategies! In some cases, the best place for a boy is right near the front of the class, where he can focus on the teacher's voice. It might be best to separate him from talkative students or not place him near a heat register or air conditioning unit.

Keep it Simple: Less is More

The female brain, loving words, has the idea that the more ways you say a thing, the better the message will get across. Repetition and elaboration make perfect sense. The male brain does not always work this way. Many boys are "flooded" by repetitive verbal stimulation (saying the same thing five different ways). They have a "surge protector" and will shut down when overloaded. They literally stop hearing! A teacher at one of the workshops I gave told us that, when giving instructions to boys, she tries to use the "ten-words-or-less" rule. She was applying exactly the correct strategy for reaching her male students.

Many schools have a no baseball cap rule. I have watched female teachers approach cap-wearing male students and say something like this: "You know you're not allowed to wear a hat in school. Why are you wearing it? I don't see any other kids around wearing hats. What makes you think you should be able to wear one? The principal talked about this just the other morning on the announcements. It's in the student handbook. What grade are you in? You've obviously been at this school long enough to know the rule about hats…." and on it goes. After the first sentence, the boy is no longer listening to the content; he is now operating on a much more visceral level. What is registering is the teacher's frustration and critical attitude. This is humiliating or threatening, and he reverts to a primitive defensive mode. The conversation now becomes about power and pride — a volatile area for males. The "fight or flight" response kicks in.

The fight response can take the form of physical or verbal acts of aggression. The flight response can take the form of running away or the emotional one of going silent. What was the original message? "Take your hat off." Five words instead of more than eight sentences. Once again, if you want a male to listen, keep it short and simple. Too many words will often muddy the waters. Remember the voices of the adults in the old Peanuts animated cartoons? "Wah-wah-wah-wah." We knew what they were saying by how the child characters responded. Charles Schulz has captured for us what adult speech can sometimes become in the ears of kids: background noise drained of all semantic content! I think sometimes the more adults talk, the less they are heard.

Other Strategies for Promoting Listening

One good way to get children to focus on what you're saying is to announce *what* you are going to say. Teacher: "Now, I'm going to tell you what your homework is." Parent: "Now, I'm going to tell you what's happening after supper."

In the flood of words from adults, the child is not always able to determine what is important. Sometimes it can help to have the context in which to put the idea — tonight's homework, the plan for getting to baseball practice after supper. It provides a box into which the child can put the information. When you *frame* the key information in this way, the child is better able to distinguish between essential information and filler. The objective should always be to cut down on the extraneous. Sometimes the child is left bewildered: where was the actual instruction in all those words?

Another good strategy I use and recommend to teachers is the use of some kind of bell, gavel, or noisemaker. I have gone through three gavels in the last ten years, and the last two were given to me by boys who said they really liked the idea. The use of the whistle in gym class or on the sports field performs the same function. It focuses the attention of the group on something important that is about to happen or needs to be said.

In *Kids Are Worth It!* Barbara Coloroso describes the very effective strategy she calls "the broken record" — giving the same instruction over and over again with the exact same words until the child complies. "You need to turn off the TV. You need to turn off the TV. You need to turn off the TV." The simple repetition "jams" the airwaves, making counter-statements irrelevant and making it easier for the child to focus and process the information. The effect is so irritating that the child will comply just to get the adult to stop!

The EMOTIONAL LIVES of BOYS

Boys and Initiation

The life path of a girl is very different from that of a boy — particularly in relation to the mother. When a girl is born, her first experience of love and nurturance comes from her mother. It is an intense and beautiful relationship. At puberty the girl becomes even more like her mother and their lives continue on a parallel developmental path.

For the boy the story is different, though it starts out the same way. His first experience is similar. It is an intense and beautiful relationship. At puberty, however, his life path takes a very different direction. He has to answer an internal imperative to become something different from Mother. He will not "turn into" a woman like his sister; he must become a man. The person in a boy's life who can help him do this most effectively is his father.

Other male role models may perform the same function, but there is no exact substitute for the father in a boy's life. For millennia, societies have had initiation rituals in which the men of the tribe took the boy and initiated the process of becoming a man. The common elements of these rituals were separation from the mother, the endurance of some kind of physical pain or hardship, and the affirmation of a new identity. These rituals are all but gone today. They persist in some religious rituals, the Jewish bar mitzvah and the Christian confirmation, but these are pale imitations of the dramatic rituals that once existed and still do among some pre-industrial and indigenous cultures. We also see vestiges of these in the world of sports, the military with its hazing rituals, and even in some high schools you will still find official and unofficial grade nine initiation rituals. None of these, however, should be considered legitimate models to be encouraged.

What is mainly missing in initiation rituals of today is the positive adult male initiator or "elder." In the absence of male mentors, boys will initiate each other or themselves. Peer initiation takes the form of teasing and bullying. When boys do this, there is often an element of trying to toughen each other up. Bullying includes many of the ingredients of the initiation ritual. Male bullying always occurs away from Mother and all things feminine. It is always a rejection of the feminine, and an embracing of hyper-masculine traits. In the "ideal" bullying situation, there is a feeling of risk, some experience of pain (emotional or physical), and the demonstration of endurance (being able to "take it").

In the absence of positive male mentors, boys will not only initiate each other but also themselves. Self-initiation can take many forms, the most common being self-mutilation (piercing and tattooing) and high-risk behaviour. Part of the allure of piercing is the pain. The aura of danger and risk around piercing is part of its attraction. Body piercing is one of the oldest rites we know of. Not only does it involve the endurance of pain, but it also signals in a very public and visual way the assumption of a new identity. It says, "I am not my mother's little boy any more. I have become something new and unique." In this sense, we can see piercing as a positive thing, a way of asserting one's individual identity — something essential to healthy psychic development.

High-risk behaviour is a little different. Driving fast and dangerously, performing daring skateboarding tricks, drinking or drug-taking to excess — these are all examples of high-risk behaviour. The negative common denominator is that they can seriously harm or even kill the person doing them, and in some cases seriously endanger others.

So much high-risk and anti-social behaviour in boys is the direct result of the absence of positive male mentors. We see negative male mentoring in gangs when older boys and men take males into their sphere of influence for less than noble purposes. It cannot be denied, however, that on some level the initiation function is being fulfilled. These boys are seeking older males to help them establish a distinct masculine identity.

When are men going to come back into our culture as a positive social force for children? They perform an essential role in the psychic development of both boys and girls. Men seem to have retreated into sports, computers, and jobs. Perhaps it's been this way since the Industrial Revolution, when generations were separated from each other. The agricultural image of the boy working alongside his father is gone. Even the apprentice-master relationship of the sixteenth and seventeenth centuries is largely gone. There are very few opportunities in our culture for teenaged boys to associate with older men. Boys often find themselves living in feminine environments against which they begin to rebel in adolescence. The two main examples of this are schools and the single-mother home.

School has been shown to be a feminine environment. Not only are the majority of teachers female, but school is an environment that rewards behaviours and fundamental skills traditionally associated with women and which brain research shows come more easily to them.

The other feminine environment in our culture that can produce so much conflict and confusion is the single-mother home. If we go back to the all-important male project of adolescence — becoming a man — one of the ways boys achieve this is by rejecting the feminine in themselves and very often rejecting the mother as the prime feminine force in their lives. When a boy living with a single mother "turns on her," it is important to understand the underlying developmental need for independence and the psychological need to assert his masculinity. It must be emphasized, however, that this need does not give the adolescent any right to verbally or physically abuse his mother. For most boys, this stage will express itself not in physical violence but in an attitude of non-compliance and an unwillingness to speak. To do what Mom says or to answer her questions can feel castrating for the emerging male ego. In his attempts to feel his power and autonomy, any simple comment or question can be felt as a massive intrusion or attempt at control.

If the boy does not play out this psychodrama with his mother, he may do so with his female teachers. As head of the English department, a subject traditionally taught by women, I have often had to intervene in cases where adolescent males were making a project of harassing their female teacher. Often, the dynamic was fuelled by this male need for power and autonomy, and the need in adolescence, felt more strongly by some than others, to reject the feminine. In these cases, the female teacher becomes a lightning rod.

One of the most effective responses to this kind of situation is the intervention of a male authority figure. Some women find this advice troubling; it seems to imply that women are weaker, that they can't handle their own problems, or that they need to be rescued by men. It need not be seen in this negative light. There is a very positive opportunity here for the growing boy to see an older male step into a situation of injustice and present a positive masculine model — standing up for others, showing a creative assertiveness, and setting boundaries. Boys spend most of their childhoods having boundaries set by the mother (and other women). In adolescence, they seek to challenge or subvert these boundaries, and sometimes the new voice of a male imposing boundaries is a welcome and perhaps new experience. To "give in" to a woman is a very different experience in the adolescent's mind from "giving in" to an older male.

Male teachers must realize and embrace the profound role they can play in a young boy's life, whether that boy has a father or not. When I was in grade seven, I had the good fortune to have Tom Dalicandro as a teacher. He taught me several subjects, including literature and physical education. I can still remember his lesson on "The Secret Heart," a poem by Robert Tristin Coffin about a father's love. The imagery made a huge impression on my twelve-year-old soul. Mr. Dalicandro put the poem up on an overhead projector and uncovered one line at a time. We discussed the possible meanings of each line and built on the meaning of previous ones. It was my first experience of close textual analysis.

The fact that this poetry lesson was delivered by a man was a big part of the "lesson." I learned that men can do poetry, and words and feelings are not just feminine domains. Mr. Dalicandro was also my gym teacher. There I felt totally inadequate. In that all-boy environment, one's reputation seemed constantly on the line and public humiliation was imminent. When we were doing track and field, he divided us into groups by type of event. He pointed at me (I was one of the taller kids) and said without any hesitation, "You're a high jumper." I have remembered that moment all my life. I did do fairly well at high jumping and it was fun, but it was the way he looked at me, assessed me, and defined me in a positive way that felt so reassuring.

Over the course of my teaching career I have worked with so many boys (and girls) for whom the absent father was the central hole in their lives. Psychologists talk about "father hunger," and I have certainly witnessed this phenomenon in the classroom. The father undoubtedly plays a role in our psychic life that no other person can. This is not to say that father substitutes or other male role models cannot have a profound influence. They can and should. Male teachers are incredibly well-placed to play this role and should accept it when it arises. It can be very humbling to have a young person look up to you. It raises the question, "Am I at least in some way living up to that young person's idealized image of me?" Sometimes the projection is too much; the child puts you on too high a pedestal. And sometimes the emotional need is too great, and there is a danger of violating emotional boundaries.

The teacher has to hold these tensions in balance by being who you really are, not pretending to be more, by giving the child emotional support, even forming an emotional bond, without confusing your role as teacher with that of parent or friend. The teacher is described in legal terms as acting *in loco parentis* (in place of the parent), but this role is always a temporary and tacit one — a sacred trust.

The Highly Sensitive Child

Some kids are born with their "windows and doors" all open. Everything comes in and they react to it all. These children are called "highly sensitive" or "highly reactive." Elaine Aron, in her book *The Highly Sensitive Person*, did much to raise awareness about this group she estimates makes up 20 to 30 percent of the population. I'm not sure if there are more of these children around today or whether we've just learned to better recognize them. Or, perhaps because the world has become so overwhelming, their unique nature shows up more than it did in a quieter, slower, more nurturing one. Babies who have trouble settling or who wake easily, children with allergies and asthma, often turn out to be highly sensitive. This sensitivity doesn't really show up until their environment becomes over-stimulating. When children go into daycare or school, they can be overwhelmed by all the new information pouring into their central nervous systems. A lot of highly sensitive children learn to cope by becoming what we call "shy." They turn down the volume, avert their eyes, and they socialize with only a select few or sometimes no one at all. They often appear anxious.

When these children come into our lives, we should take special care of them. They are not disordered or deficient in any way. In fact, their sensitivity is a great gift, but one they will in a sense have to "pay for" in a world that lives by mottos such as "suck it up" and "just do it" — a world that explicitly rewards insensitivity. These children must be understood and honoured for who they are. Parents, teachers, and other adults need to help them manage their nature, by knowing when it's appropriate to protect them and when to challenge them to test their limits.

Carl Jung told us that there are basically two types of people: introverts and extroverts. While it is possible for an extrovert to be highly sensitive, most sensitive people are introverts. It helps to know which you are. Introverts' lives are focused more on what is happening inside. They usually have great emotional and interpersonal intelligence. They also often have rich fantasy lives, which they find easier to control than the unpredictable real world. They can also be very sensitive to the external world, seeing and hearing things that others don't, or they simply are more affected by them.

Introverts find social situations draining. Such a person comes home from a party and crawls quickly into bed. He has guests over for dinner and by ten o'clock is looking at his watch. The introverted child can be identified at social functions as the one with his nose in a book. Over the years, I have taught many introverted children. They do not put up their hands, but they tend to do quite well in school because they are very attentive in their own subtle ways. I will often credit an introverted child with excellent "participation" skills because of his keen attention and awareness of what is going on in class, although he may never have raised his hand.

Extroverts, on the other hand, are focused more on what is happening outside. They often have greater bodily-kinaesthetic, spatial, and social intelligence. They love to be with other people because they feed off the energy of others. Where the introvert finds social situations draining, the extrovert finds them invigorating. They drain the battery of an introvert but charge that of an extrovert, who comes home from a social situation and gets on the phone.

One way of being is not better than another, but it must be admitted that our society does more highly value the characteristics of the extrovert. The ability to function socially for long periods of time can give one a great advantage in school and business. The quiet, solitary figure is not a "poster child" for our competitive, fast-paced world. Introverts often feel inadequate. From an early age, they see the verbal, active kids getting more attention, be it positive or negative. They have thoughts and feelings that go unexpressed and are therefore unacknowledged by others. They often have fewer friends and sometimes no close ones at all. They can end up feeling lonely and isolated, especially in adolescence when social functioning becomes so prized.

Highly sensitive kids will often take refuge in a fantasy world of their own making, in the imaginative world of books or the virtual one of video games. These worlds do not require "going out" of oneself and are therefore much more comfortable.

I said that one way of being is not better than another. We may say we believe this, but we often act otherwise. Adults who are highly sensitive must "own" their nature, and such children must also be taught to accept and manage it. When they are required to be social, they must learn to apply those skills and remember that there will be time to re-charge the battery later. Knowing that it's okay to limit social situations or to take breaks from them can be very helpful. Remembering to schedule battery recharging time and finding a career that suits one's need for a low-stimulation environment are both important for the introvert.

I once presented these ideas on introversion and extroversion at a teacher's conference. Later that day, in the cafeteria line-up, a teacher turned to me and began to cry. She told me she had never understood why she felt so drained at the end of each day. She loved teaching, kids, and learning, but she found it all so exhausting. "How am I ever going to survive in this profession?" she asked through her tears.

"The first step," I told her, "is being aware of your nature and then arranging your life in a way that suits it. You need to pace yourself through the course of the day, take 'solitude breaks,' and you need to make sure you have significant time at the end of each day to re-charge your battery."

Teachers talk about kids who "eat them alive," who seem to have an insatiable appetite for attention. An introverted person can literally feel they are being "eaten alive" by other people. Introverts often have to put up physical or emotional boundaries so they are not totally depleted by the demands of others. Sometimes we have to "draw the line" for our own preservation. These skills are relevant not just for teachers but for any introverted person who lives or works in an over-stimulating environment.

This topic has particular relevance in a new kind of world so full of stimulation. Going back to the previous chapter on the trauma of media, we have to be especially vigilant when it comes to the television, movies, and websites that our children are exposed to. With all our advances in special effects technology, children can see the most overwhelming things in "high definition." The American Pediatric Association has counselled for many years that children under the age of two should not watch television at all. Today we have *Baby TV* and *Baby TV Online*. Parents are given no advice or guidelines regarding older children and media. All we have are movie ratings and video game ratings that use very broad categories. While most of these ratings might suffice for the average child, special care must be taken with the highly sensitive child who may be more affected by scenes of violence, horror, or sex.

Typical Boy, Typical Girl: Sex-Role Stereotyping

In the following sections, we will look at the unique natures of boys and girls. What might sound like over-simplification or generalization is only done for the sake of efficiency. We cannot ignore the vast amount of brain research in the past twenty years that has revealed fascinating differences between the male and female brains. At the same time, it must always be remembered that gender is not an either-or, black-and-white reality. We all operate along a continuum of gender, and we may even be at one place on the continuum in one area of functioning and at another in a different area. Gender is a complex blend of many factors and influences. In the pages that follow, we will talk about the typical male and female. Do such people exist? Perhaps. Some are closer to the "type" than others, but most people cannot be pinned down in this way, nor should they be.

We should honour, nurture, and protect the child who is not typical of their gender, particularly in adolescence when the pressure to conform to gender stereotypes reaches its highest pitch. The little girl who loves rough-and-tumble play, the "Tomboy," and the sensitive "Mama's Boy," soon receive the signal from their peers that it's time to get with the program, and, sadly, this program of gender can become quite narrow and rigid.

The lesson for feminine gender traits in adolescence goes something like this: "Girls, your role is to be pretty and submissive and slightly dumb. Any assertion of strong opinions will get you quickly labelled 'bitch' or worse, 'feminist.'" As Naomi Wolf documented in *The Beauty Myth*, Barbie is back with a vengeance. There has been what Susan Faludi called a "backlash" against feminism and female power in general. Women are reverting back or being pushed back into the submissive role of sex-object — valued for their appearance, for what Wolf calls their "beauty quotient."

In her book *Female Chauvinist Pigs*, Ariel Levy demonstrates how women have become complicit in their own degradation by embracing what she calls the "raunch culture" and calling this a form of empowerment. Ten-year-old girls wearing T-shirts that say "Porn Star," grade nine girls carrying handbags with the Playboy bunny logo — sleaze has become the new cool.

The lesson for masculine gender traits in adolescence goes something like this: "Boys, your job is to be rude, crude, insensitive, and also slightly dumb. You are ruled by your appetites — food and sex — and you don't need to exercise any self-control. Those jobs are for your mother and your girlfriend."

The common lesson for both genders is that it's cool to be dumb. In recent years I feel this rule has become even stronger among males. Media is now filled with the image of the stupid, irresponsible male. In sit-coms, the mother is the responsible one. She takes care of the kids and the husband as though he was one of the children. We see this paradigm best in *The Simpsons*. If we look at Bart and Lisa, we see a dichotomy. Lisa is allowed to be intelligent, socially responsible, and articulate. She is labelled a geek or nerd, but she has many options open to her in the future.

For Bart, everything is stupid, nothing is important, everything can be mocked. Bart is labelled a "cool dude." Someday he is going to hit a wall, and his coolness will count for nothing. A terrible kind of trick is being played on Bart of which he is completely unaware. I call it "The Bart Simpson Syndrome."

I have taught many cool dudes over the years who wake up one day to realize they are in grade twelve and it is now time to graduate. They have trouble reading and writing and applying themselves to tasks they do not find interesting, because they have not practiced these skills. They have had so few role models of intelligent, literate, committed male energy, and so few for deferred gratification. The two most common images of masculinity in media today are the stupid man and the violent one. The intelligent, articulate man is absent. I found it fascinating yet deeply disturbing that in the 2008 U.S. presidential race, Barack Obama had to downplay the fact that he had a Harvard law degree. What kind of society have we created where the person vying for the most important job must be careful not to appear too smart!

In our schools we see this growing anti-intellectualism, particularly among boys. The unspoken idea that academic success is reserved for girls is a scary one. Universities are now predominantly female. The affirmative action programs of the past twenty years have worked. "Girl Power!" "Go Girl!" These attitudes have pushed girls forward into non-traditional areas, and they are achieving at a much higher rate than males. It seems that what we learned in physics class might apply to societies as well: for every action there is an equal and opposite reaction. As girls have surged ahead, boys have fallen behind. The underachievement of males is becoming well-documented. Among the many causes of this is a general lack of understanding of male nature and the increasing difficulty males have functioning in the standard cinder-block classroom of the traditional factory school. These difficulties have become more apparent as boys are now coming to school not from the farm or the suburban home, but from cyberspace.

Male Liberation

For the past thirty or forty years, Western society has been dismantling and re-constructing traditional definitions of the roles of women. Women have been the victims of sex-role stereotyping, and one of the important projects of feminism has been to critique these stereotypes and liberate women from them.

I have always been a great supporter of feminism and the feminist project. For many years, I encouraged my senior students to read the great feminist writers. Many girls went on to women's studies programs at various universities. As I read these books and discussed the ideas with my students, it slowly dawned on me that males too are victims of sex-role stereotyping.

Growing up as a somewhat sensitive, verbal, literate male, I never felt I lived up to the cultural image of the strong, silent, sports-playing male. I was shocked and relieved when I found the following line in a book titled *Under Saturn's Shadow: The Wounding and Healing of Men*, by the American analyst, James Hollis. He said, "Men's lives are as much governed by restrictive role expectations as are the lives of women." The truth of this struck me like a thunderbolt. I had spent a lot of time analyzing the ways women were oppressed by social structures and attitudes, and I began to consider how men also suffer under these forces. Patriarchy had disempowered women. Could it also be said that males too were *victims* of patriarchy? Wasn't it supposed to *favour* men?

How many men's lives have been sacrificed to competitive corporate capitalism? For every Bill Gates and Donald Trump, how many Willy Lomans are out there — walking shells of men whose true lives have been stolen from them by the illusory hope of the American Dream? I began to read books by thinkers who later came to be lumped together under the heading "Men's Movement," Robert Bly being one of the most famous. These writers called for a men's liberation movement that never came. As media sought to reduce feminists to fanatical bra-burners, so was the men's movement belittled in popular culture as a group of drummers looking to reconnect with their "wild man." It's a shame this project never gathered much social momentum. As the feminist movement has gone underground, so too has the men's. Our society, it seems, is still not ready to re-think gender roles beyond a certain point.

The Emotional Entrapment of Boys

One positive vein of the men's movement, however, has continued in the recent attention being paid to boys and the way they are raised. William Pollack's book *Real Boys* and Michael Gurian's *A Fine Young Man* are just two of the hundreds of books and articles published in recent years dealing with the issues facing boys in school and in our culture. All of these books point to restrictive male gender roles as one of the problems plaguing boys today. William Pollock talks about the "cool suit of armour" and "the Boy Code" that keep boys in a "gender straightjacket."

Any discussion of the emotional lives of boys must begin with an understanding of this phenomenon. In infancy and childhood, boys are stereotyped, but it is really in adolescence that this process becomes debilitating. The range of behaviour permitted to them and which they permit among themselves becomes narrower as they move into the teenage years. About four or five years ago, I asked one of my grade nine classes, made up mostly of boys, to articulate their ideas about masculine and feminine traits. I asked them to make two columns. One was headed "Boys are…" and the other "Girls are…" Here is a compilation of the most commonly repeated words:

Boys	Girls
Cool	Sensitive
Tough	Kind
Cruel	Nice
Funny	Caring
Rough	Like to talk
Insensitive	Gentle
Stupid	Understanding
Jerks	Smart
Disrespectful	Like to flirt
Like to fight	Weak
Bullies	Dress nice
Loud	Spend a lot of money

Obnoxious	Wear a lot of make-up
Lazy	
Like sports	

This is a disturbing list, but I think it reveals in a very crude way some of the toxic thinking that goes on among boys, particularly in adolescence.

To understand this list, we must go back to the lack of male initiation in our culture. As boys try to define their masculinity, one of the ways they do it is by rejecting those qualities they perceive as feminine. These are qualities they probably felt very comfortable with as younger children and that they enjoyed very much in their mothers. They have therefore come to associate them with the feminine. In adolescence, the project of becoming male becomes that of rejecting all feminine traits and resorting to what has been described as *hyper-masculinity* — a very one-sided and restrictive range of behaviour.

How Boys Release Emotion

On the surface, this might seem pretty harmless, but many boys are left feeling empty and depressed by this denial of such important attributes, feelings, and behaviours. Look at the first eight words on the girls' side. What does the boy for whom these are essential attributes do? How does he live them out? Some boys just "turn down the volume" until the pressure cooker of adolescence is over. They put these thoughts and feelings "away." They become emotionally numb, and their numbers are growing each year. If there is one phenomenon I see growing among males, it is emotional numbing. Since no one can live like this all the time, teens have found ways to release emotion, some healthy, some not. Four of the most common forms of release are music, sex, self-harming or cutting, and drugs and alcohol.

Music

Music has become one of the most important release valves for males. It provides an outlet for their unexpressed and inexpressible thoughts and feelings. The ubiquitous image of the expressionless teen with his earphones and iPod is that of the sensitive child coping as best he can in a world that does not permit him full expression. In the music he chooses, his thoughts and feelings find expression, his soul is fed, and the tension is released.

As I say to my students, poetry is not dead; it's more alive than it's ever been. We have just returned to the ballad tradition, and every kid is walking around with his own personal troubadour (his iPod) onto which he has loaded hundreds of poems! It is true that some contemporary lyrics are raw and even controversial, but this represents a relatively small fringe, and the swearing and coarse sexual references could be viewed as the honest expression of teen libido. If we really want to understand our teenagers, we would do well to pay attention to some of these lyrics they are listening to (and writing!). While the sexual relationship theme will always be ubiquitous, many songs contain profound themes and messages about modern life, politics, parents, school — the list is endless.

Sex

Sex has become a shortcut to intimacy. Many teens, looking for friendship and connection, jump immediately over any kind of getting-to-know-you stage and use sex as a way of feeling "love" — or feeling anything at all. Before AIDS, teen sex began with petting and progressed through the various "bases" to intercourse. Since AIDS, and with the help of the Internet, it has fragmented into a whole array of behaviours that range from innocent and harmless to bizarre and dangerous. Expressions like "friends with benefits" or "friends with privileges" and "hooking up" all involve sex without commitment. The goal is not to form a sustained and sustaining relationship, it's to find release for pent-up emotion. This kind of casual sex or sex-as-entertainment is very alienating. Many teens feel a great sense of emptiness about these experiences, even if they are not aware of it or able to talk about it. To the extent that these kinds of practices have become normative in a particular peer group, they are just accepted and not questioned, yet many teens, especially girls and sensitive boys, find them profoundly dissatisfying — sometimes even depressing.

The proliferation of Internet pornography is another disturbing trend. Surveys of young males are finding that many prefer it to dating. Online, they are in complete control of the situation and there is no communication from the other person. In a real life relationship, there are complex social interactions involved with which many young males are choosing not to bother. Boys must be encouraged all through the developmental stages, but perhaps more so in adolescence, to get out there and take the risks involved in forming relationships with girls.

Self-Harming or Cutting

A line from the song "Pain" by Three Days Grace explains the psychology behind cutting and other forms of self-harm: "I'd rather feel pain than nothing at all." One condition shared by kids who self-harm is being emotionally blocked. As the range of acceptable emotional expression has narrowed, many teens have lost touch altogether with their emotional lives. If you ask them how they feel, they have no idea. Psychologists have coined a name for this phenomenon. It's called "alexithymia," the inability to name feelings. The thing is, feelings will come out whether or not one has the words for them. The physical pain caused by cutting and other forms of self-harm is a conduit and a metaphor for emotional pain.

I have worked with many kids who were cutting themselves to various degrees, and in every single case, the child felt socially isolated and emotionally blocked. What they need more than anything is a positive, nurturing relationship with someone who will take the time to listen. One key element must be consistency over time. One of the things I find so frustrating about public mental health services is their intermittent or even one-time format. Some of these kids need a strong connection once or twice a week, sometimes occurring over years. The African aphorism, "It takes a village to raise a child," means having villagers around with time. When children are small and cute and compliant, they are easier to spend time with. It takes a special kind of villager to form a connection with a silent, brooding teenager and commit to that relationship over time.

Drugs and Alcohol

Drugs and alcohol numb feelings of pain. Substance abuse is often referred to as "self-medication." The question becomes, then, what is the source of the pain? Substance abuse is the symptom, not the illness. Teens who are abusing substances have an underlying "condition."

The most common underlying conditions medicated by drugs and alcohol are feelings of stress, powerlessness, disconnection, frustration, and, most of all, anger. We are very uncomfortable with anger, and teens feel this conflict strongly, so it gets swallowed — but it can only be swallowed for so long. If there is one truth about our emotions, it is that they must find expression. If they do not find expression in healthy ways, they will come out in unhealthy ways.

Another of these underlying conditions might be a learning style or brain profile that does not fit in school. Many kids end up feeling hopeless and frustrated, as though they are a constant disappointment to their parents, their teachers, and themselves. Imagine going all through school and never getting any marks above a C. For some kids this is a reality. Every September, they hope for a change, especially when they enter high school. By grade ten, they give up. This is one of the common ages I see kids starting to experiment with mood-altering substances like alcohol and marijuana. While this may not be a healthy choice, it has its own inner logic.

The second emotional purpose served by drugs and alcohol is the breaking down of inhibitions long enough for the adolescent to say or do or feel what they truly want to. This function is particularly powerful for men and boys, who are not permitted to express emotion. The gender role dictated by our culture is one in which the male is silent, brooding, strong, and unemotional. Expression of feelings is equated with weakness. Emotions are feminine, and the only strong one permitted is anger. Happiness, even joy, is allowed, but only if it is associated with victory.

We see this most clearly on the sports field or hockey rink, where males can be seen hugging and laughing and screaming with delight. What is a male to do with the hundreds of other thoughts, feelings, and impulses that make up daily life? Most of these are repressed. The emotional tension builds and builds, and again, alcohol and drugs become a "logical" way of lowering the defences for at least a couple of hours. Most teens are not daily users, but rather "binge" users, especially on weekends. This is a clear sign that the substance is being used as a release for pent-up emotions.

William Pollack talks about the "shame-based hardening process." Boys shame the positive "feminine" traits listed earlier out of each other. They become "hard," by which we mean "emotionally numb." In extreme cases, some boys eradicate these positive attributes completely. They become so hardened that they may never make it back to full emotional functioning. If we are going to help them stay in touch with and communicate their emotional reality, we are first going to have to understand the unique ways in which they communicate.

Boys' Communication Styles

The first and most powerful way males communicate is through their actions. Male behaviour is always expressing something. The question for parents and teachers is: What is he "saying?" Self-destructive behaviour implies depression or anger. Manic behaviour can be fed by happiness, excitement, or anxiety. Altruistic behaviour communicates love. Casual sexual activity might be about a deeper need for intimacy. The list could go on, and the meanings could vary from boy to boy. Sometimes we need to get boys to "translate" their behaviour into words. We can say, "It appears to me from your behaviour that you're having some strong feelings. Can you translate those actions into words for me?" Then comes the hardest part of all, especially for those who like to talk: be quiet. Wait for him to respond.

As we discussed in a previous chapter, boys are indeed capable of talking, but males do take longer to formulate their thoughts and feelings into words. We must allow the necessary time for this processing. Sometimes we may have to wait a long time! Your son comes home from school obviously upset about something but won't talk about it. "I can see you're really mad about something. I want you to tell me what it is sometime before bed tonight."

When communicating with a male, remember that boys find eye contact invasive and threatening, and the communication does not require it. If we want to connect with our sons, we can *do something* with them. Boys are much more likely to open up and talk when the focus is not on them but on some task. Even if no talking happens, doing something together is still a positive bonding experience.

Many parents become frustrated with the repeated response, "Fine." No matter what the question, the answer is "fine." How was your day? How are you doing? How was the movie? Boys have told me that "fine" can mean one of two things: "I don't feel like talking right now," or, "My day actually was fine and I have nothing more to say about it." When I ask them about this, they express great frustration, even anger at the parent who tries to "tease out" more information or continue with what the boy feels becomes an interrogation. Sometimes we just need to let it go at "fine."

Another way to prevent the boy from crawling into his protective shell is to talk about something else besides him and his thoughts, feelings, or experiences. We can sometimes fall into what I have called the "Oprah Syndrome" where we become like a talk-show host interviewing our child. Talk about something in the news or something that happened to you that day and take the focus off the child. When an adolescent boy is asked even the simplest question, it may trigger that feeling of being under a microscope.

Teaching Boys to Care: Nurturing and Empathy

Nurturing and empathy go hand in hand. You cannot have one without the other. It is not that males cannot be nurturing and empathetic. It is more that they are not given many chances to practice being that way. There are two simple but important ways boys can practice their nurturing skills. The first is with pets.

Exposure to animals is therapeutic for anyone, and it is especially meaningful to boys. It doesn't matter what kind of animal: if it is a living thing, and it is dependent upon the boy for its survival, this is a powerful relationship. It is important to choose a pet appropriate for the age and personality of the child. If too much care is required, the child may not be up to the task and will become frustrated and disillusioned. It's okay for a parent to help out now and then if the task becomes too onerous, but the responsibility must always rest with the child. I work with a boy named Jeff who owns a hermit crab he calls "Sheldon." That crab means a lot to him! Every time we meet, I get an update on Sheldon's life. I think Jeff, who is a pretty sensitive kid, identifies with Sheldon and the way it crawls inside its shell for protection.

The other way to help boys develop their nurturing side is to create opportunities for them to be around younger children, even babies and infants. When a boy is dealing with a younger child, he is forced to leave his own subjective experience and make an imaginative leap into the experience of another. This is a vital life skill. At school, we have a peer-mentoring program in which senior students are matched up with grade nine students. This is an excellent opportunity for older males to practice nurturing and empathy. Other programs, like "Reading Buddies," accomplish the same goal. Senior elementary school students are matched up with junior-and senior kindergarten students for sessions in which one or both of the students read aloud. These programs can be very powerful. I have talked to grade twelve boys who can still remember with fondness their reading buddies from kindergarten as well as the kids they read to when they were in grade eight.

Our culture has become very narcissistic; we are encouraged to focus intensely on ourselves. Teenagers are naturally narcissistic anyway, and when you add this cultural influence, it can become quite toxic. The feelings of depression and ennui could be ameliorated by opportunities to focus on others. Craig Kielburger's book *From Me to We* gets at this issue, the moral as well as the therapeutic value of helping others.

BOYS and SPORTS

Many boys depend on sports for self-esteem. This is not a bad thing. It would be nice if we could all excel in at least one thing; for some kids, this thing is sports. Athletic ability should be celebrated and encouraged at every turn.

Connor's marks were going down at school. His mother asked me if she should take him out of soccer, so he could focus more on his schoolwork. Connor was a bodily-kinaesthetic kid, and his problems at school were not the result of his time spent on soccer, which was the most positive thing in his life, so I strongly advised her against taking him out of it.

The Positive Aspects of Sports

Sports satisfy a boy's need to move. School provides few opportunities for movement. Sports can also provide the opportunity for expression of emotions. In the world of boys, the sports field is one of the few places where such spontaneous and powerful expressions are allowed. Sports are a great form of stress relief as well; teams allow boys to connect through friendships and feelings of camaraderie. They are places where affection and touching are permitted.

Boys can gain a sense of mastery that they may not experience in school. The "goal" is very concrete and specific, the rules are clear, and competition is encouraged. In school, boys often find the goals vague, the rules arbitrary, and co-operation is valued above competition. The sports field makes more sense. School and sports share the common element of failure; the difference is the individual form of failure experienced in school versus the communal failure of the team. When one fails in school, one fails alone. You are the sole cause. Failure on the field is collective; if one makes a mistake as an individual, a good team will support that player regardless. There is more of a tribal feeling that can be missing in the classroom, and boys are drawn to this brothers-in-arms atmosphere.

One of the most important benefits of sports can be the role-modelling provided by the coach. He and other males assisting a team can be powerful influences. As a boy grows into manhood, he studies the behaviour of men and will copy that of men he admires. This implies a huge responsibility for coaches in providing a positive male role model. This is especially true for boys with no father at home, but even boys who do have one are studying the men in their lives for traits that resonate with their own character and interests. I'm sure my three sons have had many traits modelled by me, but I also know that we are very different people, and they have found models in other men that they would not find in me. This is as it should be. Boys require initiation by men — not just one, but all the men of the tribe.

Negative Aspects of Sports

While many boys have been helped by sports, there are those who have been harmed as well. First of all, the coach as role model can be a negative influence just as easily as a positive one. Coaches who bring a critical, negative, overly competitive attitude to the game can cause great damage to a boy's self-esteem. Giving constructive criticism is part of a coach's job, but there are those who use negative criticism and public shaming to try to improve player performance. These may achieve their goal, but only through fear. The player works harder not to please the coach or to win the game but rather to avoid the fear of public shaming. There is a lot of stress on such teams, and boys will eventually avoid it by quitting.

Many teenage boys have told me about their disillusionment with hockey when the emphasis on winning became too great. This pressure increased not just at the more elite levels, but at all levels of play as the kids got older. By thirteen or fourteen, many boys have had enough of the negative stress and pressure. By seventeen, after so many years have been invested in the sport, it is hard to leave, and I see a lot of substance abuse by players trying to deal with the pressure. Personal performance and team standings become closely connected to the teenager's sense of self-worth, and unless they are "NHL material," this pressure can be too much to handle.

Body image issues also arise in sports. Boys can feel a lot of pressure to "bulk up" to imitate media images of the perfect athletic male body. Some teenagers quit sports but keep working on their bodies. All the benefits are gone, and all that remains is the "look" of an athlete. I have known boys who had lots of muscle mass but were not particularly fit in terms of cardiovascular or aerobic capacity.

BULLYING

I became interested in the topic of gender differences in learning as a result of my studies of bullying. I quickly came to see that while bullying definitely happens among girls, it is more of a male phenomenon — fed by particular brain and hormonal factors and reinforced by developmental and social forces.

Bullying is the use of fear and intimidation to gain power and control. The things that are feared are physical and emotional harm, social exclusion, public humiliation, and shame. Power and control are gained through the perception of raised status in the group (real or imagined) and a feeling of heightened self-esteem.

The Spectrum of Bullying

Any discussion of the topic must deal broadly with the whole spectrum of bullying in our culture. To isolate it as a kid problem is to leave out significant factors that influence bullying. As we will see, bullying has nature-based causes, but it is also caused by external social factors. It can be learned or reinforced by adults and by the environment in which they are raised. Bullies can be other kids, brothers and sisters, parents, teachers, administrators, co-workers, husbands, wives, governments, and media images.

Jake was a fourteen-year-old from a hockey family. His two older brothers were rugged, athletic types. Jake had no interest in organized sports — he loved drama. Every day he went home to a beating from one or the other of his brothers, his own personal bullies.

Sometimes, when I call a parent about a child's academic or behavioural issues, I know right away that I am talking to a bully, and the child will be bullied after my call. I have listened to colleagues being bullied by parents on the phone, and colleagues have asked me to sit with them at parent-teacher interviews because they were afraid of being bullied by a particular parent.

I used to speak quite often to grade seven and eight classes on the topic of bullying. I would be ushered into the library or a classroom, and there were some occasions when the teacher would proceed to bully the students into silence and "appropriate" behaviour before my talk began by threatening them in a cruel tone about dire consequences. Some of the biggest bullies I have seen over the years have been teachers who use bullying as a classroom management technique.

I have worked with many administrators, and some of them have been bullies. Many rise through the ranks with no real vision of education and no strategies for dealing with non-compliance. Some administrators got out of the classroom because they were tired of the misbehaviour. Their strategy for dealing with it may have been bullying, and they simply bring that strategy to their new role. Not just school administrators but bosses in all sectors can be bullies.

I have spoken on this topic at a number of teacher conferences. After my talk, a few teachers always stay behind to tell me their horror stories about being bullied by colleagues. Some teachers are hounded by their principals, called up on every little detail of their work. One teacher told me she had to take a stress leave because of the bullying she endured from the head secretary, who was constantly challenging her and making her life hell. Another young teacher said she transferred schools because she could no longer deal with the bullying she endured from the custodian in her wing.

We all know about the scourge of domestic violence, but this is simply the most dramatic manifestation of the bullying that goes on in so many marriages. Low-level verbal and physical abuse in the home is more common than we think: wives who call their husbands "worthless" in front of the kids, husbands who give their wives a push or a shove.

Another area where bullying has become common is in international relations. The current "War on Terror" has a strong bullying element. The very word "terrorism" connotes the use of fear and intimidation to gain power and control.

Perhaps the biggest bully on the block today is advertising. In advertising, "control" means control over the spending habits of individuals. "Power" means economic power or market share. These things are achieved through fear of social exclusion, public humiliation, and shame. It is risky to give examples because they become outdated so quickly, but one will stick in many people's minds. It was the series of Apple commercials that featured a cool young "dude" as a Mac comparing his operating system to that of a PC, represented by a geeky, middle-aged man the viewer could see was at a distinct social disadvantage. The moral of the commercial: "If you buy the Mac you will be like the cool guy; if you don't, you will be like this nerdy guy and suffer the same kind of negative social judgments by your peers that you are passing on him right now."

Boys are bullied by other boys, but it is important to remember that they are growing up in a culture where bullying has become pervasive and subtle. It is part of the way we interact. Any discussion of bullying has to become one about how we relate to each other generally and how this cultural tendency can be eradicated.

Myths About Bullying

We all have certain "files" that have been "downloaded" into our heads by our culture and upbringing. Among these files we might find a list of myths about bullying. The first is the idea that the bullied kid deserves what he gets or that he's asking for it. "He's being irritating. He's being a geek. He needs to get with the program. He needs to learn that there are certain things you cannot say or do." This opens up into the whole area of socialization and the myth that bullying is just part of growing up. You have to "suck it up" and "tough it out."

Bullying becomes a way of teaching social norms. The bullied child learns that not only are certain behaviours and ideas socially sanctioned as normal, but bullying itself, as a form of instruction, is acceptable. I have counselled parents with wonderful, eccentric children who were trying hard to curb certain tendencies in the child's behaviour, with no success. Usually I advise them to let it go, to enjoy it, and let him enjoy it as long as possible, because the peer group, through its pedagogy of bullying, will soon lop off those tendencies or send them underground.

Where Does Bullying Happen?

In elementary schools, the high-risk times and places are recess, lunch-time, the schoolyard, and washrooms. In secondary schools, they are hallways between classes, changerooms, the cafeteria, and washrooms. At both levels, school buses are prime sites for bullying. What do all of these places have in common? The absence of a strong adult. Sure, there are teachers "on duty" in the schoolyard, but the ratio of teacher to students is huge. No teacher can keep effective watch over hundreds of kids. In addition, bullies are expert at not being detected. Their radar is constantly up, and they know exactly when to strike.

Beyond school, bullying takes place in the newly-invented largest playground ever imagined by humans: the Internet. "Cyberbullying" is a new phenomenon. Before 1993, the equivalent would have been the prank phone call. In its simplest form, cyberbullying can be cruel words or images passed around through email, Facebook, or MSN. Its most extreme form is the creation of sites devoted to attacking a particular person.

It is important for both bullied kids and bullies to realize that online content can be saved and used as evidence. The Media Awareness Network, a Canadian media education agency, makes it clear on its website.

Under the Criminal Code of Canada, it is a crime to communicate repeatedly with someone if your communication causes them to fear for their own safety or the safety of others. It is also a crime to publish "defamatory libel" — writing something that is designed to insult a person or likely to injure a person's reputation by exposing him or her to hatred, contempt or ridicule." Online bullying can be reported to your Internet or cell phone service provider. "Most companies have Acceptable Use Policies (AUPs) that clearly define privileges and guidelines for those using their services, and the actions that can be taken if those guidelines are violated. They should be able to respond to reports of cyberbullying over their networks, or help you track down the appropriate service provider to respond to. (*www.bewebaware.com*)

What Can be Done to Stop Bullying?

I am often asked what we can do to stop bullying. Unfortunately, there is no single answer. There are many things that can be done to reduce or try to prevent it, but it will always be with us. The closest I have been able to come to a sure method is the presence of an authoritative adult. By this I mean one who is willing to assume authority and who kids see as a legitimate authority figure. I do not mean an authoritarian adult, which is just another word for a bully. Kids are unlikely to stop bullying on their own. An external "force" has to be imposed that will disrupt the psychological dynamic.

What is the Psychology Behind Bullying?

Humans are social animals. To put it another way, we are pack animals. We prefer to live and move in groups. The essential feature of any pack that must be understood before bullying can be is the "pecking order." Every group has one, a social hierarchy perceived consciously or unconsciously. Whatever group we belong to — the classroom, the family, or the workplace — we sit somewhere in a pecking order. Whenever we enter a group, the first thing that has to be established is our place in that order.

None of us wants to be at the bottom. One of the unseen dynamics in any group is the constant jostling for position in the hierarchy. This dynamic is especially charged in school, where you have a group of twenty-five ten-year-olds in a classroom or between fifty and a hundred out on the playground. Within any group of ten-year-olds, there is a pecking order.

In the schoolyard, there is another pecking order, based largely on age or size. The grade eights rule, but the grade sixes have their place on the pavement. The grade sevens hover around the grade eights, waiting to take their place next year and learning social cues of dominance. When those grade eights go to high school, they find themselves flung back to the bottom of the social totem pole and the whole process starts over again.

Grade nine is one of the most charged social atmospheres because of this need to re-establish a social hierarchy. If the students come from a number of elementary schools, then previous hierarchies no longer apply. This can be a recipe for cruel and unusual behaviour. I see two kinds of kids in grade nine: those who are actively trying to establish a place in the pecking order and those who adopt the strategy of drawing as little attention to themselves as possible. The latter choose to wait until the top rungs have been filled and then will try to place themselves somewhere in the middle. They are also trying to stay out of the way of those who will make it to the top at their expense. They do not want to become collateral damage in someone else's ascent.

This leads to the foundation of bullying: put others down to make yourself feel good. In adolescence in particular, a lot of kids don't feel very good about themselves. They feel awkward, unattractive, insecure, self-conscious — the list of negatives goes on.

For some, the list is not only long but deeply felt. Every child deals with these feelings differently; some by bullying other kids. They are trying to fill an emotional hole. The loud, aggressive, intimidating bully is probably the weakest person in the group. He lacks self-esteem and will use any means to gain it, even though the esteem he gains from bullying is very hollow.

This is why bullies don't stop: they will never find what they are really looking for with this method. What they really want is love and acceptance, and it's what a lot of people who are scrambling to the tops of all sorts of different social ladders want. They also crave a feeling of dominance, but there are two kinds, negative and positive. The first is achieved by force and must be held by force. This is a very precarious kind of dominance. The second is gladly acceded to by others and comes from self-confidence and self-esteem. The false leader is working out of fear; the true leader is working from an inner core, an inner vision. The false leader is feared and obeyed, the true leader is loved and respected. This might sound lofty when talking about kids, but they know who the real and the false leaders are. In a healthy environment, these legitimate leaders do rise to the top of the pecking order. In a toxic environment, the domineering bullies, the false leaders rise to the top.

Bullying in the Workplace

Some of our civic and business leaders are true leaders. Others are shallow people motivated by a desire to prop themselves up. It can be very difficult to work for such a leader.

The American version of the television show *The Office* illustrates this phenomenon. While the boss, Michael, is not really a bully, he is incompetent and has achieved social dominance on false grounds. Everyone sees his shallowness except him. There are currently versions of *The Office* going into production in five other counties. They are not simply re-selling the American version; they are producing versions with their own actors and their own cultural nuances. This shows how universal the phenomenon is of the false leader achieving social dominance and the frustration felt by those more capable people who surround him. While Michael is a harmless fool, sometimes the false leader is a bully who has achieved his dominance through fear and intimidation. This is his *modus operandi*, and he continues to use it even when he has achieved his external goal. The inner goal of feeling better about himself is never met. He is haunted by self-doubt and feelings of insecurity, which he must mask with bravado.

The topic of workplace bullying is relevant to our kids for two reasons. First, school is a workplace for the adults there, and if the dynamic of adults bullying adults exists among the staff, it will have a direct effect on our kids who spend their days in this environment. The kids will feel this tension and may themselves become the victims of adult bullying. In the pecking order of the school, the students are at the bottom, and adults looking to fill their vacuum of self-esteem may turn on the students, putting them down to make themselves feel better. In the toxic environment of a bullying school, the kids become the final victims.

The other connection between workplace bullying and raising children is the possibility that one of the parents may spend their day in a bullying environment. This has a corrosive effect on the self-esteem of the parent, who brings those feelings home. In the pecking order of the family (if there is no dog), the child is at the bottom, and parents can end up "taking out" their frustrations on their children. Again, children become the indirect victims of workplace bullying.

The Rule of Cool

We might imagine that there was less bullying in the one-room schoolhouse. This is not because those were the "good old days" when nothing bad ever happened, but because there was a natural order dictated by age. With all ages in one room, the older you were, the more authority you had, the higher your status in the group.

In the modern factory school, age mixing is rare (except on the playground). Because everyone in the grade five classroom is approximately the same age, they have to find another way of creating a hierarchy. Here they turn to "the rule of cool," a quasi-religious cult which dominates our contemporary society. This rule means conformity to the norms of popular culture dictated by consumer capitalism. It seems there is a cool way to do everything, a cool form of every product, and a cool way to just be. One's status in the group rises or falls depending on their "cool quotient." Cool value can rise and fall daily like stocks, depending on what kids say, wear, do, or who they hang out with. It is an oppressive atmosphere dominated by fear of social exclusion, which might be precipitated by any misstep.

There are some kids who are "cool" in a different way. They are so cool that it doesn't matter what they say, wear, or do. They hang out with all different kinds of kids. They seem impervious to bullying — Teflon kids. In my experience as an observing teacher, I believe these kids possess confidence and strong core self-esteem. Bullies can "smell" fear and insecurity, and these kids just don't have that smell. They often have a sense of humour and irony, and they see the silliness of the social manoeuvring game. They are able to laugh at it and themselves. They do not take the arbitrary rules of kid world or themselves too seriously.

For some of these kids, it's just their innate nature. I think others learned this attitude at home. Their parents are grounded and real and do not wring their hands about their own or their child's social acceptance. They are not living under the rule of cool, and they have not taught their children to twist and contort themselves for social acceptance. These kids have been given a great gift.

Who is the Target of Bullying?

There are three attributes that can make a child more susceptible to bullying. The first is being different in some way. The second is having a self-confidence profile similar to that of the bully. The third is being a nice, well-behaved kid.

Packs or peer groups do no deal well with those who are different. Peer pressure has always been a problem, but in our culture of conformity, it has gotten even greater. When my son Thomas was in grade nine, another student asked him for some loose leaf paper. When Thomas handed it over, the other kid looked it over and said, "This paper is gay." The word "gay" is the antonym for cool. Apart from gender-related topics, it is a code word for anything that doesn't fit the norm. Bullies know these norms, and some are like the self-appointed "cool police." They scan the room or the hallway looking for violations of the cool code. When they find one, they swoop down like a SWAT team to punish the perpetrator, and the justice is swift. Kids can be bullied for a new haircut, a new backpack, using a big word, having a last name with a bad rhyme — the list could go on and on, but the common denominator is that the object or behaviour violated some code.

Targeted kids sometimes have a psychological profile similar to that of the bully: low self-esteem, lack of confidence, weak academic skills, or poor social skills. The bully goes after this kid because he understands him. He knows how to manipulate him because he knows where his vulnerabilities lie. I have often seen kids with poor academic records going after other low-performing kids. A child with low self-esteem can sniff out another — someone who is unlikely to fight back.

This leads to the next characteristic sometimes found in bullied kids. They are too passive. They are nice, polite children who have always done what they were told and have never talked back. When the bully comes along, they find it hard to push back, and the bully moves in for the kill.

The parent is the child's first bully. This sounds like a shocking statement, but go back to the definition of bullying: the use of fear and intimidation to gain power and control. The will to power is one of the strongest forces in all our lives, and the child will naturally desire more and more of it as he moves through the developmental stages. Often, these gains for the child are felt as a loss of power for the adult. In our attempts to keep power and control, we sometimes turn to fear and intimidation. One of the most subtle forms this takes is the threat to withdraw love. We end up with compliant children who fear making Mom or Dad angry.

We must ask ourselves how we deal with opposition from our own children. In some homes there is really no room for non-compliance. One unspoken rule is Mom and Dad are always right, and they do not deal well with being questioned or contradicted. Another such rule is that if you make them angry, it is your fault. You are responsible for their feelings, and if you anger them, they may reject you. If you want to keep their love, you must not con-tradict them.

This very compliant child, who seems so well-behaved, may just have become very passive, never having had the practice of talking back or expressing legitimate anger at perceived injustice. He learns early that it is better just to go along with whatever is happening. He has no right to "make waves." What makes it hard to watch these kids getting bullied is that they are just so nice and well-behaved. They don't deserve to be chosen as targets. They have become, or have been turned into, their own worst enemies. They do not know how to stand up for themselves!

The home can be the first place where we learn the power of our own voice and where we are permitted to speak up when we feel some important issue is at stake. The issue may seem trivial to the adult, but it is the underlying lesson of "taking a stand" or "standing up for yourself" that is so important. "Don't talk back to me!" is a strange thing for a parent to say. The tone the child used may be the problem, and the sentence is about disrespect, but on a deeper level I think the line sometimes means, "You are not allowed to disagree with me." Parental rules often *are* questionable. We are not omniscient gods, and we teach our kids a huge lesson when we open up decisions for discussion rather than ruling by decree.

Children who have their wills thwarted like this can have two reactions. They can become bullies and attempt to silence others — putting them in their place, or they become victims, unable to talk back when their rights are violated. Talking back and "breaking the rules" have their purpose, which is to teach personal power. You have the power to assess and react to other people's arbitrary actions. You have a voice and will of your own, and the power to choose your own behaviour. You have certain rights as a human being. These are all lessons that will come in handy on the elementary school playground and in the high school changeroom, and they can be taught at home from an early age.

Why Don't Kids Report Bullying?

The main reason kids don't report bullying is that they are afraid of drawing even more negative attention. This is not surprising. A victimized person feels very vulnerable and exposed. Our first response might be to fight back, but for many kids it is to try to disappear, to just ignore it or put up with it. The status quo, as bad as it might be, is better than the mess created by reporting. That is why it's so important to talk to the child about how the situation is going to be handled after he reports. If the aftermath turns into a disaster, then the child is re-traumatized.

THE TOP THREE STRATEGIES FOR DEALING WITH BULLIES

One: Avoidance

This might be seen as running away from your problems, but sometimes getting out of the way is the most reasonable response when faced with a threat. If you were being chased by an animal or found yourself in the path of an oncoming car, you would run or try to avoid a confrontation. The same is true when faced with a bully. Some can do a lot of damage. In addition, the bully is the one with the issue, and it's perfectly reasonable to try to avoid being entangled in someone else's psychological problem.

My first advice to kids who are being bullied is try to stay out of the bully's physical presence. This is where adults can play a constructive role. I taught a grade nine class where a particular boy was harassing another girl almost daily. I took the girl aside to ask her about it. She told me that this boy had been bullying her for two years, both at school and in her neighbourhood. It had reached a climax the previous summer with police involvement. My question is why were these two kids scheduled in the same English class? What would it have taken for a responsible adult to make sure this situation was flagged and these two kids were not put together? I have seen the same phenomenon in organized sports, where a bullied kid quit playing hockey when he found out the bully was on his team that year. This is a time for parents to step in and request a change of team and for coaches to respect the rationale behind the request, not falling back on the "macho" attitude that you can't run away from your problems.

If you can't stay out of his presence, then avoid eye contact. It has so much power to create a positive or negative connection in males. Psychologists talk about the phenomenon of "projection," where a person projects something in himself onto someone else. What the bully will sometimes project are his feelings of self-hatred. These get transferred and, all of a sudden, he "hates" that person for no apparent reason. The reason is psycho-logical, logical to the psyche. He seeks relief from his own self-loathing, so he gets rid of it by placing it on someone else. There is a reason why we put others down: to make ourselves feel better. Bullied kids should be taught explicitly about the psychology of bullying, so that they do not see the situation as originating in them or something they have done. So often the victim feels embarrassed or like a failure in some way, even though they are passive victims.

Bullied kids can end up dwelling on the bully. I tell them to try to put the oppressor out of their minds. It can almost become a kind of "fatal attraction." The bullied child with low self-esteem may unconsciously feel that he somehow deserves it, that the bully has found him out. This relates to what I was saying earlier about the common psychological profile between the bully and the bullied. The bully chooses that particular child as his target because he feels a sympathetic connection. By sympathetic, I simply mean a similar feeling about himself. Thinking about the bully too much can turn into the more generalized thought, "I am a victim," which can become a self-fulfilling prophecy. Kids should be coached with what cognitive behaviour therapists call "thought-stopping."

Another aspect of avoidance is not listening to what the bully says. This is much easier said than done, because we all know how hurtful words can be. A bullied kid I worked with wrote a poem with the line, "Sticks and stones may break my bones, but names will kill my soul." Bullied kids have to be coached not to listen and to realize that the words have no objective meaning. Sometimes it's easier to let something go if we stop and take a good look at it. I get kids to repeat the abusive lines to me. "What are you ... stupid?" "You can't play worth crap." "Fag!" The list goes on. We talk about the factual inaccuracy of these statements. They are not statements of truth. They say more about the bully than they do about you.

Two: Talking Back

When avoidance doesn't work, the child might just have to stand his ground and talk back to the bully. This is where some kids can really benefit from coaching in assertiveness. The training is a helpful life skill generally, apart from its usefulness with the bully. I have the child stand up, and we talk about body language. I show him how to stand up tall, hold his chin up, put his shoulders back, and look me in the eye. (In stage one: avoidance, eye contact is to be avoided. In stage two: talking back, eye contact is essential.) The results are amazing. The bullied child may have a posture that conveys passivity, insecurity, and feelings of helplessness. Just working on posture not only changes the impression he gives, but can also have a huge effect on the way the he feels.

The next step involves talking, and here again, some kids need coaching in using their voice more forcefully. I talk to kids about the difference between speaking from your mouth and from your stomach. This might require some role-playing. I play the part of the bully, and they have to talk back to me. I tell them to say what they are really thinking and feeling — a challenge for kids who are not used to that. Doing this is more likely to engage the stomach, because this is where a lot of kids store their strong feelings. I coach the child to keep it short and strong and tell the bully exactly what he wants to stop. Depending on the child's own moral code, repertoire, and comfort level with vocabulary, he will shout out, "Stop it!" "Shut up!" (or worse…) In order to be able to do this effectively, a child needs to feel in his core that he does, in fact, have rights and boundaries that he is entitled to defend.

Three: Reporting

If the first two strategies don't work, there is no alternative but to tell someone. Hopefully there is an adult the child trusts, one who will handle the situation respectfully and with some degree of wisdom. As I mentioned earlier, it is important for the victim to have a say in how the situation will be dealt with. He may want to remain anonymous. That is fine. I have seen it work both ways. Sometimes the kid wants the bully to know who has reported him. It is important that the intervening adult never interview the bully and the bullied kid together, unless the bullied kid specifically asks for that. Few will. The bully will go into survival mode and will say whatever is needed to get out of the situation with as little damage as possible. The victim also needs to hear it reinforced that he is not responsible for what might happen after he has reported. If the bully is punished in some way, this is not the victim's fault. The fault always lies with the perpetrator. It is very important to tell the bully that no retaliation will be tolerated and this must be followed up periodically.

I did not teach James in gym, but he was in my English class, and he confided that Dylan, who was also in my English class, was harassing him in the changeroom with verbal taunts and the occasion towel snap.

I approached Dylan one-on-one, away from any listeners. I kept my words as brief and direct as possible. "James told me that there is some bad stuff going on in the changeroom after gym class. [pause to let Dylan realize what I'm talking about. No more is necessary.] It's going to stop right away. [pause again] I'm going to talk to James tomorrow, and I'm going to ask him if anything bad happened in the changeroom, and I expect he'll say 'no.' I'm also going to ask him if you said anything to him about this talk we're having right now, and I expect he'll say 'no.' Do you understand?" Dylan nods.

Notice that I don't get into the particulars of who did what. I don't ask him to submit a plea. This would simply open up a whole court case of minor details, accusations, and counter-accusations that just distract from the basic issue. Whatever the details, the bottom line is that one kid feels threatened by the words and actions of another. This has to stop. The goal is not to decide who's guilty, it's to stop a particular behaviour.

Another important thing is to keep it short! I often find in discipline situations that there is just too much talking, usually on the part of the adult. Very little is actually registered. The long sermon about why this was wrong leads nowhere and is not taken in on a logical level. "Oh, yes, this makes sense. I can see now why I shouldn't behave this way." It is usually experienced emotionally: "They think I'm bad. I *am* bad. I need to say whatever will get me out of here as soon as possible."

One of the silliest "consequences" I have seen is the letter of apology from the bully to the bullied kid. When I discuss bullying with senior high school students and their memories of how it was dealt with in elementary school, this strategy is brought up as the most laughable. This letter is not written out of any genuine feeling;

it's the result of coercion and has very little authenticity. If anything, it teaches children to be insincere. They know what the adults want the letter to say, and they write that.

The most important part of any adult intervention is follow up. Both the bully and the target should know that the adult is serious, and in this situation especially, actions speak louder than words. The next day I spoke to James and asked if anything bad happened in the changeroom. Nothing had. I made sure to speak to Dylan, again, keeping it short and simple. "I spoke to James, and he told me nothing bad happened in the changeroom. I'm glad to hear it. I'm going to be asking him again in the future, and I assume he'll say no." I have commended him for his positive behaviour and tell him now that I will be keeping an eye on this.

If James had reported more bullying or threats of retaliation for reporting to an adult, I would speak to Dylan emphatically about it and about the next level of escalation. "You can stop this now, or we will have to move to a higher level. It will go to the front office, then it will go to suspension. If you were smart, you would stop it here, because I'm not going to let this go. You will not speak to James tomorrow in the changeroom at all. I will be checking up." The adult must always try to keep this from escalating into a public drama, which is what bullied kids fear most. They become re-victimized by the public exposure.

The Politically Incorrect Approach

After one of my presentations to a parent group on the topic of bullying, a tall, thin, reserved young man of about thirty-five came up to speak to me. This was his story:

"When I was in grade six, I was tormented every day in the schoolyard by a particular kid. It was terrible. He had it in for me. I don't know why. My parents reported it to the teachers and the principal, but nothing changed. I put up with it for two years. Then one day in grade seven, I snapped. I'd had enough, and nobody seemed able to help me. The kid made one of his comments and pushed me to the ground. I got up and jumped on him. He fell to the ground, and I just started punching him. Of course, the teachers all came running, and I got suspended for fighting. To this day, I say it was the best thing I ever did. My life totally changed after that. The other kids stopped bugging me, and I felt totally different about myself. I felt like I had proven to myself that I could deal with things. I feel confident today as an adult, and I know this might sound crazy, but I attribute it to that day when I finally stood up for myself."

He went on to say, "I know you're not allowed to give that kind of advice in your talks. It's not politically correct to be advising fighting, but I just wanted to share my story with you because it was such an important experience for me."

And so I share it with you....

Here is another one:

Tyler was in grade six when his mother brought him to see me about being bullied at school. She felt he needed help with his confidence, that he was just being too passive. It turned out Tyler was a very passive kid, one of those nice, shy, polite kids who never get into any trouble. We worked on his body language and his thoughts about himself, and he made a lot of progress. But there were still bad days when other kids, even one of his friends, would push him around unreasonably, as though trying to get a response out of him. Tyler's father was a developer of international properties, so he was gone for long periods. His dad was also a "man's man," found all this bullying news exasperating, and saw the idea of going for counselling as wimpy. He did not spend a lot of time with his son, so when he did, it carried more of an emotional charge.

One day Tyler and his dad were out snowmobiling. They stopped for a break, and Dad sat Tyler down. According to Tyler's report, this is what Dad said: "Son, I'm a bit tired of all this talk about you being bullied. The bottom line is this. You have my permission to hit anybody who hurts you. You might get suspended for it, but that's okay, I won't be mad at you."

When Tyler came to see me the following week, he looked like a different kid. I asked him what had happened, and he told me about this conversation with great enthusiasm. He was amazed by what his father had said, and he was deeply affected by it. It totally changed everything. He was quick to add that he probably never would hit another person, but it was a revelation that he possibly could and that this advice had come from an adult he respected. Tyler's confidence blossomed and the bullying all but disappeared!

A Word on Behalf of the Bully

The bully is not a bad kid. He is hurting. He is afraid and feels weak. He needs love and support more than punishment. Consequences may have their place, but punishment that is shaming only perpetuates the cycle. A kid feels bad about himself and we make him feel worse. Bullies are hard to love; they often haven't been shown a lot of love. Their defenses are always up and they are slow to trust. We have to keep on loving them and find ways of focusing on the positive within them. If they have an emotional hole that they are trying to fill in negative ways, we must help them find positive ways to do so. This can be done by arranging situations where they will feel successful and by creating opportunities for them to practice empathy, like working with animals or younger children. They have a deep need that they don't know how to meet. They need love and acceptance, not contempt and rejection.

PART THREE

The ELECTRONIC WORLD of BOYS

The WORLD of VIDEO GAMES

Video games are now a permanent fixture in our culture. They satisfy those two great loves of the male brain: looking and moving through space. Parents worry about the influence of the extended periods of time boys are spending at screens, especially with video games. Rather than condemn what our children are doing out of fear and ignorance, we would do better to try to understand just what video games are and why they are so attractive. All behaviour is logical, so there has to be some inner logic to the incredible popularity of gaming among both boys and men. These games are not inherently bad, but, like so many other things in life, they become problematic when over-used. We will examine the problems with video games, but we will also look at their positive aspects.

WHY VIDEO GAMES ARE BAD FOR YOU

Video Games Shorten Attention Spans

Video games (and many other on-screen activities) do shorten attention spans. The degree of novelty and the speed of movement all make for constant stimulation. A gamer never has to wait. Watch how fidgety boys can behave while they're waiting for the game to load or re-set or a boy's leg start tapping if a website takes too long to load.

Researchers like Barbara Strauch tell us that the adolescent brain undergoes a huge restructuring process from as early as age ten to the early twenties. The law of brain development is "use it or lose it."

Those parts of the brain that are not exercised tend to atrophy or, in extreme cases, take on another function. There is a part of the brain whose job it is to pay attention. When focusing on a screen, that part is not getting much of a workout, and attention spans shorten.

Video Games Inhibit Verbal Development, Including Reading and Writing

Playing video games exercises the spatial functions of the brain. There is nothing wrong with that in itself. An exercise that develops arm strength is good for you. But we would question an exercise regimen that only required using one's arms. We have an entire body with many parts performing many different functions. We want our whole bodies to be healthy and strong, and the same could be said of the brain. I meet kids in my classroom, who, to use the arm exercise metaphor, have huge biceps, but scrawny little legs. They are working (i.e. playing) very hard at developing one brain function, spatial perception and movement, while neglecting another, logical, linear language processing, including speaking, reading, and writing.

When boys are playing video games, they are not talking, listening, reading, or writing. These last four skills have a payoff at school. Spatial perception and movement do not (unless you have the potential to be an elite athlete). It is a question of balance. If you're going to develop your arm strength, develop your legs too. In fact, if school is a race, then leg strength will have a greater payoff.

"But I'm going to be a game designer. I don't need to read books." The way the educational race is set up, to learn video game design, you have to have a graduation diploma, and you need decent marks. To get those things, you have to be able to read and write.

We are living in an age of "credentialism," where there are few opportunities to simply do what you like — or even what you're good at — without some kind of externally awarded credentials. As the competition for career positions in all areas becomes greater, credentials (marks, diplomas, degrees) have become the currency one uses to gain access to these exclusive programs. You may in fact be a whiz at computer animation, but without the credentials you're not going to go very far. The gatekeepers of our educational and corporate institutions only accept one passport — credentials gained at a lower rung on the ladder. It's ironic, because many video games operate on this same system. You need to earn "life points" or all kinds of equivalently named "credentials" in order to move on to the next "level." Video games are very hierarchical, and they reward the demonstration of technical prowess. It is interesting that so many boys accept and even like this structure in cyberspace, but run into a brick wall in school when they are unable to demonstrate the kinds of technical prowess, reading and writing in particular, that will take them to the next level.

Schools are closely linked to the economic system. The educational system is the sorting room for the social order. Employers at all levels, from small business to multi-national corporations to the civil service, depend on it to sort and label their products. Students take these stickers to employers and cash them in for jobs. Someday the educational and employment landscape may change and it may be possible to specialize in one area at a young age, become highly proficient, and be hired into that career. That time has not arrived. Students are still expected to be generalists almost right up until the end of high school. In courses that require complex language proficiency, boys are falling behind. Grade twelve university preparation classes, especially in the humanities, are predominantly female. College-and-workplace level program enrolments are predominantly male. One of the main characteristics distinguishing these two groups is facility with language demonstrated through speaking, listening, reading, and writing.

Video Games Impede Development of the Imagination

If I ask my grade nine class to write a story and I give no parameters, I will get two kinds: shoot-'em-up or beat-'em-up stories from the boys and relationship stories from the girls. On one level, psychologists

tell us this is predictable and normal. Boys are inherently more competitive, whereas girls are more empathetic. That isn't the problem.
The problem lies in the limited imaginative range of these young
writers. The girls tend to copy the formulas of Hollywood movies,
and the boys the formulas of video games.

The boys' stories centre on the lone male who uses force to achieve
his goal. The "hero" has no particular qualities, and his goal is not an
explicitly honourable one. The story usually concludes with a fight, a
shoot-out, or an explosion of some kind. Many teachers have taken
to prohibiting blood and gore in creative writing assignments. Boys
feel stymied by this restriction. Perhaps a better approach would be
to reintroduce them to other conventions and archetypes. There is
a wealth of story patterns and characters in our collective culture
that boys could be introduced to and encouraged to emulate, such as
the questing hero, the courageous rescuer, the solver of the mystery,
or the perilous journey. Postmodern critics talk about colonization.
Hollywood and video games have colonized the adolescent mind.

Video Games Detract from Real Life Experience, Especially of Nature

Our suburban streets are empty. Sometimes it appears as though
all the children have fled. In a sense, they have. Kids have left real
space and live more and more in cyberspace. They walk through
forests and other landscapes in games, but have seldom experienced
anything close to those landscapes in real life. I was once reading a
story with a boy, and it mentioned the cold feeling of water on the
character's feet as he walked across a stream.

I asked the boy if he had ever put his feet in a stream. He looked
at me blankly. "No." There is a new field called environmental psychology, which studies the importance of contact with nature in the
development of the self. As long as human beings have been around,
we have lived in close proximity to the natural world, so it would
follow that some kind of intimate need is met by nature. The story of

our separation and growing alienation from nature has been a long one. It accelerated noticeably with the Industrial Revolution and has continued with the proliferation of electronic media.

Many children growing up today have minimal contact with nature. If what environmental psychologists say is true, we are going to see the effects of this separation in both current and future generations. To touch dirt, bark, water, and stones. To feel changes in temperature, air pressure, and humidity. To watch, touch, and feed animals. To plant seeds, watch them grow, and eat what they produce. To walk over landscapes of various textures and topography. If these experiences are essential to healthy physical, psychological, and emotional development, then something is going to have to change or kids will feel the effect. Outdoor education programs are disappearing, but most of these involve worksheets on clipboards and not getting dirty. These excursions became more about covering curriculum objectives than free play in nature, which is all but dead. Richard Louv has coined the term "Nature Deficit Disorder." How many of our acting-out kids could be helped by "nature therapy," that is, being in nature, working with animals, plants, or dirt?

Going back to Thom Hartmann's hunter-gatherer theory of ADD, the person who roamed the savannah in search of game for hundreds of thousands of years still exists, and there is simply a huge mismatch between the artificial environments we've created for ourselves, particularly the cinder-block box of school, and the genetic make-up of many of the kids who are forced to exist in these environments. Perhaps our environments have changed at a faster rate than we can keep up with and acclimate ourselves to.

The agricultural revolution is estimated to have occurred around ten thousand years ago. This is not a long time in evolutionary terms. Perhaps there are some *Homo sapiens* who have not yet made the adjustment. What about the Industrial Revolution that took place only about three hundred years ago, when industrial production replaced agriculture? There are certainly kids in my class whose genetic makeup has still not adapted to that change and would be much happier on the farm than in the "factory" of school. A product as simple as the light bulb has changed our sense of time and created a sleep-deprived culture. Adolescents chatting online till one a.m. then getting up for school at six a.m. Hunters and farmers: they sit in our classrooms and try to read and write, and they find it very difficult.

We hear about the devastating effects of modernization on indigenous people all around the world. In Canada, our aboriginal youth are sometimes only one or two generations removed from the nomadic, hunter-gatherer existence of their forbears. This disconnection from the "old ways" can have devastating effects. The only difference between them and us is the rate of change. We've had more generations to "adjust," but not all of us have a nature that has adjusted well.

I spent the better part of my childhood in a maple tree in our backyard. I watched the Apollo astronauts land on the moon while sitting up there looking at the TV through the living room window. There I was, most comfortable sitting in a tree, growing up in a world that not only puts men on the moon but beams live images of it into light-boxes in every home. This is the disconnect that many people (not just the young) continue to feel, consciously or unconsciously, between their essential nature and the artificial environments and lifestyles we've created.

What could we do to reconnect ourselves and our children to the natural world? Things as simple as camping, hiking, going for a walk, or going to the park could go a long way. Why don't we have gardens, perhaps even small fields of crops — even animals — in some of those huge concrete and flat grass expanses we call school playgrounds? Why does this suggestion sound so preposterous? I know of one school where the five hundred or so kids at recess were required to stay on the pavement during the winter months because the administration did not want them throwing snowballs. Another school banned the bringing of any balls or other toys to school to play with at recess, because a kid had been hit in the head by a ball. Why is this not seen as preposterous?

Video Games Detract from Physical Fitness

Rob was not an overweight kid, but he had a case of "gamer's belt," a ring of flab around his waist from sitting and playing so much. When kids are playing video games, they are not running, skateboarding, or playing sports. Video games create the illusion of activity, but they are no substitute for real activity in the real world.

Video Games Take up Huge Amounts of Time

Many kids begin with a couple of hours a day and are soon playing for seven or eight hours. How much time is too much on video games? I tell parents it's a question of balance. If you're going to be sitting for an hour (or two or three), you need to be outside playing for at least the same amount of time. "What kind of parent would I be if I let you sit and eat candy for three hours?" Video games are like visual candy. Millions of dollars have been spent developing them and millions more marketing them. We think we are free, but our freedom is curtailed by media, which conditions us to value certain objects and activities over others.

When I sit down with a child whose parent is concerned about the amount of time spent playing video games, I ask them how many hours the child has free from the time they get home from school until they go to bed. Let's say it's five. I then ask them how many hours they spend on screen time. This includes TV, MSN, Facebook, and video games. I then draw a pie graph showing how much of their discretionary time is being spent on-screen. Sometimes the ratio is huge, other times not. I then ask them about other things they could be doing in the evening and on weekends. It's the same process a dietician might go through with an overweight child. Let's first see what your current eating habits are so we can determine where change is needed. I find this process a good starting point for parents and children in setting reasonable limits on screen time. Once the child sees the issue in a concrete image, like the pie graph, he is better able to talk about the reasonable demand for balance.

Video Games Can Be Addictive

Video games are so appealing to the male brain because they satisfy its two main loves, looking and moving through space. They also provide high levels of excitement through constant novelty, unpredictability, and the possibility of rewards. All of these elements are pleasurable to the male brain and increase the production of the neurotransmitters dopamine and endorphin. Dopamine is associated with reward and motivation. Endorphins are the "feel-good" chemicals of the brain.

In July of 2007, *Discover* magazine, in an article titled "This is Your Brain on Video Games," reported on the long stretches of time gamers are willing to spend.

> The genesis of this reaction [to stick with the game] may lie in the neurotransmitter dopamine. A number of studies have revealed that game playing triggers dopamine release in the brain, a finding that makes sense, given the instrumental role that dopamine plays in how the brain handles both reward and exploration. Jaak Panksepp, a neuroscientist collaborating with the Falk Center for Molecular Therapeutics at Northwestern University, calls the dopamine system the brain's "seeking" circuitry, which propels us to explore new avenues for reward in our environment. The game world is teeming with objects that deliver clearly articulated rewards: more life, access to new levels, new equipment, new spells. Most of the crucial work in game interface design revolves around keeping players notified of potential rewards available to them and how much those rewards are needed. If you create a system in which rewards are both clearly defined and achieved by exploring an environment, you'll find human brains drawn to those systems, even if they're made up of virtual characters and simulated sidewalks.

The important fact about dopamine is that the more its production is stimulated artificially, the less the brain produces it naturally. Hence the need for the "fix." Researchers have suggested that any activity that produces dopamine or endorphins is potentially addictive. "The runner's high" has been well-documented. The "gamer's high" has yet to be.

Vancouver physician Gabor Maté, in his great study of addiction, *In the Realm of Hungry Ghosts*, says the following about addictions,

> All addictions are anaesthetics. They separate us from the distress in our consciousness. We throw off our familiar and tired consciousness to assume another mind state we find more comfortable, at least temporarily. Desperate to be out of our mind and unaware, we surrender to the addiction, to be lulled into a walking sleep.

For heavy "users" of anything, including video games, we might ask ourselves what lies behind the behaviour. Is the behaviour a symptom? Is there a void that needs filling? Some of the heavy gamers I have known were very intelligent kids under-stimulated by school. The type of game a boy chooses might tell us something about him. First-person shooter games may have to do with the feeling of personal efficacy, power, and control. These games certainly put the player in charge of the action. They are also characterized by complex movement through space. Do these kids have spatially-oriented brains that need to get out more often into natural environments?

The virtual environments players prefer might also tell us something. Many first-person role-playing games take place in settings that could be best described as medieval. This is true of most fantasy games. Ever since J.R.R. Tolkien created the norms of modern fantasy in *The Hobbit* and *The Lord of the Rings*, fantasy has taken on this nostalgic aspect, the longing for a simpler time when people lived more in harmony with nature, where roles were not tied to corporate structures but had a more organic quality, and people worked at jobs that suited their nature. The attraction to the fantasy genre, seen in games like *Dungeons and Dragons*, represents a rejection of modern materialistic culture, and the desire to return to a more soulful existence. Many kids are disgusted by the crass consumerism of their own culture. They are fed up with the alienation created by factory schooling, and the corporate machines of society leave them with a "distressed consciousness," to use Maté's term.

Do gamers need more nature, more movement in natural environments? Do they need more authentic human interaction? Do they need to have their essential natures respected more? If all behaviour is logical, what is the logic behind choosing to spend more time in cyberspace than real space? Has real space become so artificial that cyberspace appears more real?

WHY VIDEO GAMES ARE GOOD FOR YOU

Video Games Relieve Stress

While the negative effects of video games are easy to enumerate, we must acknowledge the positive side as well. For many kids these games are a form of stress relief. When a child is playing, he enters another world, and problems and stress disappear. He leaves a world in which he feels buffeted by so many external forces over which he has no control, and enters one where he is seemingly in complete control. He holds the *controller* and the rules are clear. There is a predictable, rational quality to the whole experience, which he does not always feel in real life. There is a specific identifiable task upon which he can focus his whole attention. The rewards and punishments are clear. Failure is possible, but it's not real and not public. If the game is too hard, he can change it to an easier setting. One of the main contributors to stress is feelings of powerlessness. In the world of the video game, he has all the power.

Video Games Create Stress Then Relieve It

Even the boy who is not feeling threatened or aggressive may turn to the game to create and resolve these feelings. The game can provide the kind of creative tension that his real life may lack. There is a kind of "high" or "buzz" associated with the hunt, the chase, the kill-or-be-killed world of the video game. Every sport contains these same tensions — will I win or lose? The tension is immediately created as soon as the game begins. The enemy, the goal, and the rules are clear. Video games are like sports in that they provide a container in which a drama of threat, aggression, fear, perseverance, and victory can be played out. The drama can continue for years in some first-person role playing games or a much shorter time in a sports game, but it reaches a crescendo of some kind, the conflict is resolved, and the same kind of catharsis can occur that Aristotle said should happen in a Greek tragedy — a cleansing feeling of resolution and a return to homeostasis.

Video Games Provide an Outlet for Aggression

Video games also offer an outlet for aggressive feelings. Testosterone feeds aggression, and levels begin to rise noticeably in boys as young as ten. These levels and the resulting aggressive impulses rise when males feel threatened. A boy's life is full of threats, mainly to his masculinity. For the adolescent boy in particular, this can become a daily drama. As he tries to assert his masculine identity, he runs up against peers, teachers, and parents who act to curb or restrain his energy. He feels frustrated and threatened by their power. His aggressive feelings can reach a high pitch. When he returns to the world of the video game, whether he's chasing, shooting, driving, skateboarding, or playing a sport, he is discharging some of those feelings through virtual action. The virtual world of cyberspace allows males to freely express emotions and assert masculine energy.

Video Games Can Have a Social Aspect

One of the most important positive characteristics of video games is their social aspect, but it is a social world more in sync with male than female ways of relating. Boys bond by *doing* things together. When we moved onto a new street, the boys didn't know any of the neighbour kids. One day, one of the boys invited a boy in to play Xbox. They went downstairs and over an hour probably exchanged ten words. When the neighbour boy went home, I asked my son, "Did you have fun?"

"Yeah, he's a great guy!" my son replied.

"What's his name?"

"I don't know."

This is a different way of communicating and bonding, but a valid one. If I described a picture of two boys fishing, we would find that charming and see it as bonding. There would be just as little talking, and yet we see the value because it is a familiar and traditional scene. Playing video games is the new fishing! Males relating shoulder-to-shoulder, talking little, focused on a concrete activity.

Online role-playing games are growing in popularity, especially with a particular type of boy. I'm not sure yet what the common denominator is, but I think these boys are attracted to that kind of closed, controllable world. They are quick to talk about all its levels and landscapes, how big and complex it is, but they find comfort in the outer boundary. This whole world, potentially at least, can be known, understood, and negotiated. There are many boys, and people generally, who do not find this true of the real world. For them it can be a very overwhelming and inconsistent place, not hospitable. For many kids, cyberspace is an alternative world that is, if not friendlier, at least more comprehensible than the real one!

There are boys who have few friends at school, but who have many "friends" online — sometimes from all over the world. It could be argued that these relationships are superficial, but are they any more so than those in the cafeteria or the hallways of our schools? Perhaps in the safe, often anonymous world of the game, kids can feel more comfortable opening up and being who they are. Let's not forget that the kids who play these games make up a self-selected cohort, unlike school, where they are thrown together with all kinds of kids, some of whom they feel an affinity with, others none whatsoever. If you're not comfortable in a video game, you can just exit. If you're not comfortable in school, there is no exit. Well, there are some, but most, like zoning out, getting high or drunk, and causing trouble for kicks, are not productive.

What School Could Learn From Video Games

Phil fell asleep many times in my grade twelve English class. When I pressed him about it, the cause turned out to be *World of Warcraft.* He admitted that he was addicted. "I just can't come off! I know it's ruining me, but I can't stop." Phil did not get all of his grade twelve credits and had to come back for another year. He was very bright, and when he did get off the game, he did very well. Interestingly, after graduation he went on to military school, where he is flourishing. He is taking an engineering degree and wants to become an officer. When he visited me after his first year, he told me that what he loved about military school was the structure and the discipline. He also liked the camaraderie. He found it a very hierarchical world with very clear lines of authority, where rewards were more immediate and goals very concrete and specific. It occurred to me that these were precisely the qualities he valued about *World of Warcraft.* Many young males value these things and find them in video games more than they do at school.

Many kids perceive the hierarchies of school as arbitrary, unfair, and based on illusory criteria. They see the pecking order of administrators, teachers, and students, but they do not always feel that the authority held by administrators and teachers has been earned. They do not understand how they could have progressed through the "levels" (to use gaming terminology) to get where they are. Then there is the whole other pecking order of teen peer culture, where a complex hierarchy has been formed on the flimsiest of criteria — clothing, hair, attitude. For many kids, these two hierarchies are only worthy of ridicule or indifference.

How could the hierarchies of school be more legitimate? Kids will respond to adult leaders they respect and admire — adults who respect students and are themselves motivated by an honourable code. Unfortunately, the ability to lead is sometimes confused with the ability to control. As for the student hierarchy, is true leadership among our brightest and most articulate students encouraged, or is the peer culture ruled by the coolest or the loudest kids? Are students with something significant to say given a voice within the system?

The presence of immediate, concrete, and specific goals and rewards is another positive characteristic of video games that schools might do well to emulate. We have due dates and marks, but these are often quite malleable and subjective. Students perceive, often correctly, much vagueness in the description of "outcomes" and great inconsistency in the way rewards are distributed. "I don't know what she wants." "He's such a hard marker. I wish I had Mrs. so-and-so. She's an easier marker." These kinds of inconsistencies are not found in the land of gaming.

We have talked about the social aspects of video games, but the word Phil used to describe the social world of military school was camaraderie, "a spirit of friendly good-fellowship," says Merriam-Webster. The gaming world is a community, and for many teens it provides a much greater sense of inclusion.

I worked with Peter, a fourteen-year-old who was diagnosed with severe learning disabilities. He was placed in the "lowest" remedial level in grade nine and felt a huge sense of inadequacy and embarrassment after having been part of a "regular" class in grade eight. In one year, he had slid to the bottom of the academic totem pole, and he was feeling the social fallout.

In elementary school, his disabilities had not been so exposed. He spent the majority of his day in his regular class, only occasionally being "withdrawn" for special help. His tests and assignments were modified, but the other kids weren't really aware of it. Now he found himself socially segregated from the majority of kids he had known in grade eight, relegated to small classes where he spent most of his day with the same eight to fifteen kids with similar learning difficulties. He had lost his community and felt like an outcast. For him, high school was no community at all. He felt isolated and labelled.

His main interest outside of school was, of course, gaming, and he belonged to a mostly male cohort in *World of Warcraft* from all over the world. They had formed a "guild," and according to Peter, had accomplished great things in the two years they had been together. He felt a great sense of connection and loyalty to these other guys and that he had really made a significant contribution to their virtual achievements. He could not wait to get home in the afternoon to reconnect — to be accepted into a community that had far more meaning to him than the one at school.

What could school do to create a greater sense of community for all, not just for those students for whom school works? How would schools have to change to create a sense of camaraderie? We talk about "school spirit," a 1950s rah-rah term that seems to have more to do with cheering at pep rallies and sporting events than with meeting the emotional needs of students. Schools will have to become more humane places, organized on a smaller scale, where kids can feel a sense of inclusion, where they are listened to respectfully and spoken to authentically by adults with deep core values. Those are the kinds of things kids need and video games *cannot* provide.

The WORLD of SOCIAL NETWORKING

New Ideas About Intimacy

Social networking sites have changed our notions about intimacy, which always implied physical proximity or contact. This seems to be fading away, and many kids are making their intimate connections online. Some "best friends" have never met in person, and some kids have categories of friends organized according to levels of intimacy. I was surprised to see a girl talking to a particular boy I wouldn't have thought she was acquainted with. When I asked if they were friends, she replied, "Oh, he's just an MSN friend." Some kids have three or four hundred MSN "contacts" or Facebook "friends." Needless to say, this stretches the definition of "friend" to a pretty superficial level.

Girls are particularly susceptible to the allure of online intimacy. They seek connection, and relationships are highly valued. When a girl brings this desire and need to the Internet, she may get burned. New to a school, she wants to make friends and would love to have a boyfriend. A boy comes online and they begin to talk. She relates something personal, and he types two words, "I understand." She reads volumes into these two words and pours out even more. *Finally, someone who understands me!* she thinks. Little does she know that he has four screens going at the same time. Three are online conversations and the fourth is a video game.

Girls have told me, "Sir, I was on MSN with that guy over there for three hours last night, and when I passed him in the hall today, he never even said hi." The technology can trap a girl because it makes it too easy for boys. Adolescent boys are not often good talkers at the best of times and struggle in comparison to girls with all the skills required for good communication, especially reading body language and tone of voice. Boys find online communication easier, because all they have to do is type. The hazard for the girl is that she may project tone into the message that isn't there.

Boys need practice at talking to girls. That is how they develop their speaking and social skills and how they mature. A boy who doesn't get this practice will remain deficient. We hear all kinds of anecdotal reports about boys and young men who can't cope socially and retreat into video games. Some even report preferring Internet pornography to dating because nothing is required of them. I always remember Anthony, who I taught in grade nine. When I met him the following year, I asked him how things were going and whether he had a girlfriend. "No, but I'd like to. The problem is you have to talk," was his mumbled response.

Online communication is very stark. The simplest words are used, as are all kinds of acronyms, symbols, and abbreviations. Along with this pared-down language, there is no tone of voice or body language. As a result, communication is very limited, connections are superficial, and an illusion of intimacy is created. Online social interactions do not provide the practice of interpersonal relationships that will be required for true intimacy in adult life.

The Benefits of Social Networking

On the other hand, there are positive aspects to social networking sites. We all know someone who has dated people they found online, not to mention happily married couples that met that way. Is the Internet any worse than the discos of the Seventies or nightclubs of the Eighties and Nineties? Those venues provided a pretty small sample from which to choose! People unlucky in love were always consoled with the cliché, "There are lots of other fish in the sea." Now single people have a tool for (selectively) trolling through the sea with an efficiency never dreamed of by previous generations.

Many single adults find themselves socially isolated as other networks like church, volunteer organizations, and neighbourhood life have shrunk in importance. Twenty-somethings may find themselves in a workplace with no one their own age. Many of my former students, once they started working, turned to the Internet for their social network, since they found none at work.

Kids do not use the Internet for dating; they spend their days in social environments with hundreds of kids their own age. They do use it for finding kids with similar specific interests. I taught a boy diagnosed with bi-polar disorder in grade ten. He had a very hard time finding the right medication and faced months of mood swings and side effects. He finally found a Facebook group for adolescents who suffered from the condition. He was able to talk freely about his problems and listen to others talk about theirs. He became close with a teenage girl from England, with whom he chatted regularly, and he always said this was a huge help during those years.

Another boy was very isolated socially. He was sensitive and introverted and found the large high school environment overwhelming. He played the guitar very well and was interested in Led Zeppelin in particular. On Facebook, he found a fan group and discovered that one of its members attended his own school. He contacted the other kid, they met, and now they play guitar together once a week. This is a great form of social networking. Ships that would have passed in the night now meet up.

The modern high school can be a daunting place, with student populations in large urban centres often topping out at two thousand students. Many kids feel a great degree of alienation and loneliness. They find online relationships easier to manage, the context more predictable. At school the interactions can be random and very unpredictable, and you can't log off when you've had enough. The social pressures to conform and be cool are intense; the feelings of potential threat, of being bullied, or just not fitting in are huge. In the comfort of one's home, relationships with like-minded, selected friends can take place outside the high-stress social world of school.

Younger kids are also beginning to use social networking sites to develop relationships that begin elsewhere. We ferry our kids from activity to activity, one of the goals being socialization — to meet and interact with other kids. Unfortunately, these organized activities often follow the model of school. There is a directing adult, clipboard in hand, with a very specific agenda. The children are micro-managed and the timelines are very specific. There is little time to just "chill" and enjoy unstructured free play. At swimming lessons there is no swimming for fun. At team sports practice there is little playing just for fun. The changeroom becomes the only unstructured, unmonitored place, and the interactions there are not always positive. But many kids have found a way to subvert the adult agenda of "activities." They slip each other their email, MSN, or Facebook addresses and connect online outside of the activities. Ironically, they have found their own way of socializing despite our efforts at socializing them.

New Ideas About Privacy

Kids today are growing up with a different sense of privacy. They are far more willing to present themselves to the world in a way we would not have — mainly, perhaps, because we didn't have the means. Kids present themselves on social networking sites as though they were mini-celebrities. Scrolling through their online profile and photos is like looking at a model's portfolio. This is who I am. This is what I do. This is my style. Adolescence is all about self-definition and self-display. These sites offer an excellent tool for both of these things.

When Facebook was first getting off the ground, most profiles were open for anyone to browse through. You could see hundreds of pictures and a get a glimpse (sometimes more than that) of a person's private life. Now more kids are putting higher security settings on their profiles. In order to gain access, you have to become a "friend" first, and this is done at the account holder's discretion. This is a positive trend that has grown out of the public discussion about the perils of social networking.

The concept of privacy we grew up with was often closely connected to shame. Privacy was always presented as a lofty value, but it seemed to have something to do with hiding, like we all had something to conceal. Privacy was highly valued because it sheltered us from public judgment and shame. As the boundaries of what is shameful or unusual move further and further out, kids don't seem to have the same desire to hide things. Perhaps young people are leading us toward a world where the perceived need for privacy is replaced by a culture of acceptance or at least tolerance. Our preoccupation with privacy may have aided many shadowy activities — like child abuse, substance abuse, or domestic violence — all those things that went on "behind closed doors" and nobody talked about because they were "private matters." If kids today are more willing to create a society without this notion of "shame" by being more open, is that necessarily a bad thing?

The WORLD of MOVIES and TELEVISION

Media and Trauma

Movies and television is another area of the media landscape that bears discussion. These are not new to parents, but the nature of this landscape has changed considerably in the last twenty years or so. The threshold for what's acceptable in terms of sex and violence has moved in a profound way. Television shows and movies depicting a wide range of sex and violence have moved into prime time, when children of any age can be watching. The evolution of special effects technology has made anything possible. As one director said, "If you can imagine it, you can show it." Alexander Lowen sums up the effect of over-stimulation on a child as "too much too soon."

Here is a definition of psychological trauma from Wikipedia. It raises important issues relating trauma to media. This definition could just as easily be a description of what happens when one is exposed to overwhelming media images.

> A traumatic event involves a single experience, or an enduring or repeating event or events, that completely overwhelm the individual's ability to cope or integrate the ideas and emotions involved with that experience. The sense of being over-whelmed can be delayed by weeks, years, even decades, as the person struggles to cope with the immediate circumstances.

Trauma can be caused by a wide variety of events, but there are a few common aspects. There is frequently a violation of the person's familiar ideas about the world and of their human rights, putting the person in a state of extreme confusion and insecurity. This is also seen when people or institutions, depended on for survival, violate or betray or disillusion the person in some unforeseen way.

Much of the media kids see today overwhelm their central nervous systems. They cannot integrate this information into their "familiar ideas about the world." The result is a feeling of insecurity about the nature of reality, the social contract, and one's own perceptions. The trauma is made worse when it is inflicted by sources that seem to be legitimate, located in places and with people we trust — the TV in our living room, with Mom and Dad present, or at the movies, holding a Coke in a large group who seem to have decided that it is normal to be watching sex, violence, horror, or overwhelming special effects that the child finds extremely scary or shocking. The child attempts to reason these perceptions out: "Since everyone is going along with this, the problem must be with me. My perceptions are not accurate or I am just weak. However, in the immediate moment, I need to insulate myself from this onslaught. I can't cover my eyes because then people will know I'm weak, so I will deal with it inside in a way people can't see. I will turn off my emotions. I will numb myself in order to get through this."

Too many kids I meet today are emotionally numb. A big contributor to this is the overwhelming nature of life, but media in particular has over and over again bombarded kids with images they are unable to process or incorporate into their psychic experience. Desensitization is a real trend that I have seen develop over my three decades in the classroom. In one episode of *The Simpsons*, Bart and Lisa are at a theatre watching a violent and scary movie. Lisa covers her eyes. Bart nudges her and says, "Don't cover your eyes. How else are you going to become desensitized?" It is typical of the dark humour in *The Simpsons*, and like all good satire, it goes to the heart of a social norm that we never question.

Lenore Terr, in her important book, *Too Scared to Cry: Psychic Trauma in Childhood*, includes a final chapter titled "Close Encounters of the Traumatic Kind," in which she talks about the devastating psychological effects of media on children. One of the important facts is the delay that can occur between the traumatic event and its effects. (This was also pointed out in the Wikipedia definition.) People who experience a traumatic episode often revert very quickly to a normal, functioning state in an effort to restore psychic equilibrium, but the feelings have not been discharged. They are stored and come out days, weeks, months, or even years later, sometimes in other forms. I think a lot of the depression in teenage girls and young women, along with the addictive behaviours in teenage boys and young men, could be diagnosed as a delayed response to an overwhelming childhood in which the basic psychological need for a predictable, secure world was disturbed by external forces.

I sometimes raise this issue with my classes. "Can anyone remember seeing a movie when you were a kid that you wish you hadn't seen and took a long time to get over?" Half the hands in the class go up. What follows is a litany of mostly violence and horror, sometimes recounted with great feeling, other times in a flat monotone, but as the discussion continues, the emotional temperature in the room rises and there is what psychologists would call a huge "discharge of affect." I remember a grade twelve boy presenting a seminar on the topic of sex and violence in media, and the class got into one of these collective remembering sessions. The boy who was presenting related that when he was growing up, his parents were quite strict about what he was allowed to see. He said, "At the time I didn't like it, but, listening to you guys right now, I think I'm glad they kept some of that stuff away from me when I was young."

This anecdote shows the important role parents can play as gatekeepers. We don't let just anyone walk into our house; doors allow us to control entry. This metaphor can apply to our regulation of media as well. Sometimes we have to close the door and not let certain things in. Especially when children are young and not developmentally ready for certain experiences, it is our job to protect them. I counselled a ten-year-old boy, and we got onto the topic of movies. One night, he was babysat by a seventeen-year-old cousin who brought over a very violent, scary horror movie. The teenager allowed him to watch it. The boy described a horrific scene of a decapitation. He closed his eyes, and shaking his head said in a tone of frustration and sadness, "I just can't get that picture out of my head. No matter how hard I try to forget it, I can't." This is a form of child abuse and should not be permitted. In this particular case, it is hard to say if the parents should be held accountable for something the teenage cousin did, but the point is to show the necessity for vigilance about what children see.

HOW to DEAL with the ELECTRONIC WORLD

In addition to TV and movies, the Internet, video games, and social networking sites are now a part of life. They are not going to go away; in fact, they will become more pervasive and more sophisticated. These technologies are not evil, nor are they value-free. They are not inherently destructive in the same sense as alcohol, sugar, and salt are not destructive in themselves. It always comes back to how these things are used and whether we exercise moderation and balance.

To speak in terms of a "solution" to media implies that there is a problem. It is not that black-and-white. Various media have simply become part of the physical, mental, and social landscape. These should be understood and the issues they raise discussed. Media literacy is becoming a larger part of school curricula, and the discussions taking place in classrooms need to happen at the dinner table as well. For reasons mentioned earlier, children and teenagers in this new kind of world do not respond well to decrees from above. They expect to be included in the discussion, and so they should. As Barbara Coloroso says, our job as parents is to teach our kids *how* to think, not *what* to think. This is especially true of media, the influence of which can be very hard to detect.

While discussion, debate, and compromise should be the norm in a democratic family, there are times when, of necessity, it must turn into a dictatorship. Sometimes it is appropriate for parents to "pull rank" and restrict access to or the length of use of particular media. The maxim again applies, "I will allow you to control yourself, but if you cannot control yourself, then I will control you for you." There are times at the video store where we have to lay down the law and say, "No, you are ten years old and you're not renting that 14A movie" or "You are fourteen and you're not renting that 18A movie." There are many websites that rate movies for parents, in categories like sex, violence, and profanity. Some websites have specific suggestions on the age-appropriateness of movies.

Another response is to watch together as a family and talk about what you're seeing. That way, we teach our kids to be critical viewers, not just passively letting everything wash over them. To talk about something is to become more aware of it. Media is so ubiquitous and the effects so subtle that we are not always even conscious that it is influencing us. To illustrate the power of advertising, I hold up two identical hats. One has the Nike swoosh on it while the other has a logo the students have never seen before. When I ask which hat they would choose, most pick the Nike one. Why do you make that choice? I ask them. What has influenced you to value that little symbol? If advertising had the power to make you think that way about a logo, what other values and ways of thinking do you have that have been influenced or even created by external forces? This also raises general questions about freedom of choice. Are we free or are we programmed to value certain things over others? Has our free will been altered by advertising? Are some of our responses now automatic?

When it comes to video games, parents should at least watch some of them, if not play them with their children, to see what they really are. Some are not as scary as they appear. Some are scarier than they seem. Before I would allow my boys to buy *Halo* for their Xbox, they had to show me what it was. We played at the house of a neighbour and I discovered that it was pretty tame. On the other hand, I had some of my students show me *Grand Theft Auto*, and I was not impressed. This is not a game I would allow young children to play. Killing prostitutes and policemen and driving while drunk puts the user in the position of a criminal. There are no heroes in some of these games — the whole theme and tone is about life outside of social constraints. It feeds into the desensitization process. Watch together, play together, and talk about what you're seeing.

We should model for our kids that we are not afraid of this new environment, to learn about it ourselves, and know what we are talking about. If we simply shut it out, nothing is learned, since we are not really engaging with it. We must teach ourselves and our kids that the environment created by media is artificial but does have a value system and influences people's thinking. Kids will say, "Ah, it's just a game. Why is everyone so worried? I know it's not real. I'm not going to become a serial killer because of a game!" While this may be true, we cannot deny the subtle and long-term effects of any media. As Marshall McLuhan famously said, "The medium is the message." Kids are just as much affected by the form as by the content, and the form is predominantly a passive one that requires very little critical thinking on the part of the user.

In very practical terms, one way of cutting down on screen time and to monitor its use is to have one family computer in a high-traffic area. It has to be shared, automatically cutting down the amount of time available to each user. When it is in a high-traffic area, kids are less likely to be lured into some of the darker corners of the Internet. A number of parental controls and filters are also available, but these seem to be used less and less. Most computers allow an administrator to monitor search history, but sometimes the parents know so little about computers that the kids are easily able to turn off the filters or even make themselves administrators!

In the end, it all comes down to awareness, moderation, and balance. Parents have to be role models, mediators, and sometimes police officers. What is our relationship with media? Are we heavy or uncritical users? How can we be responsible gatekeepers, mediating between children and the "outside world"? Do we have the fortitude to simply say "no" when all the forces of peer pressure are brought to bear against *us*? We don't want our kids to grow up in a bubble, unprepared to make the kinds of judgments that will be required of them when we are not around. Nor do we want them to lose their

souls to a corporate machine bigger and better funded than any institution in history. People question intrusive government and authoritarian institutional religions, but all too often, we not only accept but
even seek out and welcome corporate influence. Corporate capitalist
consumerism is a "Big Brother" many have learned to love.

PART FOUR

A
NEW KIND
of
PARENT

PARENTING in a NEW KIND of WORLD

Put On Your Own Oxygen Mask First

"I just want my kids to be happy."

Then *you* get happy.

"I just want my children to be well-adjusted."

Then *you* get well-adjusted.

"I just want my children to have strong self-esteem."

Then *you* work on your self-esteem.

We cannot take our children somewhere we have never been ourselves. So often I have seen students develop to a certain level and then stop. When I meet the parents, I see why. The kids are not able to evolve beyond the point their parents have.

Parenting presents us with the opportunity to work on our "stuff": our emotional baggage, our intellectual interests, our own dreams and goals. As we think about what we want for our children, the corollary becomes what do I want for myself? Thinking about our child's potential and how that can be realized leads to the topic of our own potential and whether we are living up to it. There is a fine balancing act here. Some parents focus on their own dreams and goals, to the exclusion and detriment of the child, who is left alone and behind while the parents are off "doing their own thing" or "fulfilling themselves."

At the other end of the spectrum is the parent who puts his life on hold and stops working on any personal dreams or goals to live "for" the child. This is the "martyr complex" and does not serve the child's deeper need for a fulfilled adult role model. The child of a martyr may end up copying the parent and martyring himself to the cause of someone else's life — usually a spouse or child. Putting yourself second becomes the unconscious lesson.

Once, when my children were very small, we were out walking in newly fallen snow over a foot deep. I was leading the way, and when I looked back I saw my four children following slowly and deliberately behind me, lifting their legs high and setting them down in the holes I had made with my boots. This image is a metaphor for parenting. Your kids will not remember your lectures; they won't even remember a lot of the things you did. But they will remember how you lived, and they will copy you. They will "follow in your footsteps." This is a very sobering thought because it raises questions like: "Am I living well?" and "Am I living in a way I would like my kids to live?"

These are deep questions, but can be a wonderful opportunity to renovate our own lives. When flight attendants demonstrate emergency procedures, they tell you to put on your oxygen mask first before you help anyone else with theirs. You are no good to them if you die before them. This is good advice for life generally. You are more help to your kids when you are healthy, strong, and whole. Take care of yourself both for your benefit and your kids', to help them and you become who you were meant to be.

Take Care of Your Relationship

The Merriam-Webster dictionary defines "matrix" as "something within or from which something else originates, develops, or takes form." It is connected to an Old English root for "womb." The relationship between Mom and Dad is the matrix out of which children grow. They begin their lives in the mother's womb and continue their development in the womb of the parental relationship. In this new kind of world, this matrix relationship may not involve the child's two biological parents. That is the optimal situation, but whoever the caregivers are, the model of a loving relationship with another adult is fundamentally important. One of the greatest gifts we can give our children is a matrix relationship that is strong, healthy, and loving. This requires effort and sacrifice.

At a time when approximately half of all marriages eventually end in separation or divorce, this is a hard topic to write about. Many single parents feel a sense of failure and anxiety about the effects of their break-up. These feelings are not helpful. At the same time, if half of all marriages are ending that way, how many others are just being held together "for the sake of the kids," for social appearances, or for economic reasons? If we saw the truth behind the façade of the modern family, we would probably find a pretty disturbing picture of the "institution" of marriage. How many kids are growing up without the daily model of a loving relationship? Where will they learn how to love? Parents must take care of their relationship for their own sake as well as their children's.

Conscious Parenting Versus Auto-Pilot

There are two kinds of parents: conscious and unconscious. Unconscious parents simply do what was done to them, which is their default mechanism in any situation. They are flying on "automatic pilot." They never evolve beyond the level of their own parents, and their kids may never evolve any further either.

Conscious parents reflect on their own parenting. They look back on their upbringing and ask themselves which aspects they would like to retain and which they would like to let go of. What did my parents do that I respect, admire, and benefited from? What did they do that was not helpful and that I would rather not pass on? These are important questions. They are not about passing judgment; they are about making choices for the future.

One of Alice Miller's great contributions to psychology was the way she exposed the blind spot we have toward our own parents and the parenting we received from them. In her treatment of patients, she found great resistance to any kind of questioning of parental decisions or styles. Those topics were off limits. She found that the fifth commandment, "Honour thy mother and father," is deeply embedded in Western consciousness. She shows how this admonition can present a roadblock to the personal transformation that might come from being liberated from the effects of poor parenting. The belief that we must never question our own parenting, and that the very act of questioning is perceived as an act of criticism, is not helpful. The line, "They did the best they could" puts an end to all further analysis. It may be true, but with all we know today about child psychology and child development, could we do better?

Programmed Children: Nature Versus Nurture

Are our children the product of inborn characteristics that eventually reveal themselves (nature), or are they the product of all our efforts (nurture)? Our culture has become steadily more mechanistic and deterministic. Things happen as the result of processes that are externally imposed, and the outcomes can be determined with relative certainty. In our technological world, we have become very good at acting on objects and manipulating things to get the outcomes we want. Parenting has been very much influenced by this attitude. Parents of young children, in particular, fall into the trap of seeing their offspring as objects to be acted upon; we can program the child to be what we would like him to be. We have come to like the word "program." We put our children in programs. School implements them, and we feel that by subjecting our children to a particular program or process, they will become better products.

A colleague, a kindergarten teacher at the time, told the story of a parent-teacher interview where the father of a four-year-old said, "My daughter is going to be a lawyer, and I would like you to show me what's in the curriculum that is going to help her achieve that goal." While this may sound extreme, it reveals a mindset held by many. I remember the mother who enrolled her eight-year-old son in dance classes because she felt he was very clumsy. She wanted to cure him of this shortcoming, and the way to achieve that was through the imposition of a program. Of course, he hated the classes, felt like a terrible failure, and eventually quit. Lessons and programs are fine, but they should complement the child's nature, not attempt to alter or determine it. Children are who they are. Our job is to discover this mysterious inner nature, work with it, and encourage it, not to turn our children into "something." We must help them realize their latent potential.

As the father of four, this was one of the hardest things for me to learn. As I began to carve and chisel away at my kids' identities, I could not ignore the startling reality that there was already a person there. This realization was reinforced when I began to see how different each of them was. My greatest challenge was to step back and let them be. My role was to provide a nurturing environment to allow them to become what they were meant to be. As Gabor Maté says, "The relationship with the parents is the earth, the rain, the sun, and the shade in which the child's mental development must blossom."

We all know that the nature versus nurture debate is not an either/or proposition. Both forces are at work. What I do find, however, is a lack of regard for the importance of nature in determining who a child will become. What I call the organic approach to rearing children is currently out of vogue. I work with two kinds of kids, those who have been highly programmed and those who have been given greater freedom to explore their possibilities. I find the highly programmed kids often "show well," but there is something missing, a groundedness or authenticity. They don't seem to know who they really are. They always know what they "should" be doing, but if you take the external expectations away, they seem confused and disoriented. They have lived according to the program, and a part of them has not had the chance to fully develop. They are like flowers raised in a hothouse, and when they encounter the unpredictable weather of the real world, they find it hard to cope.

Their behaviour is highly conventional. They value conformity in themselves and choose friends who value social conventions, since these are the ultimate yardstick by which value is measured. In contrast, I find children who have been raised in a more organic way much more interesting. They are "free range" children whose essential natures are respected, who have been given greater freedom to follow and develop their own inclinations. They are far more open-minded and much more comfortable with ambiguity. They are more willing to take risks and are more tolerant of other points of view and ways of living.

The Lunatic Asylum: What is Normal?

In society, there is often a blatant disregard for the nature of the child and an unwillingness to allow for differences — especially when those stray too far from the norm. We place a high value on normalcy. From the time our children are born, we want to know what percentile they fall in. We start by weighing and measuring the newborn, and this continues, in various forms, all through childhood. We want nothing more than for our child to be normal. We have great suspicion about anything that is unique or different.

Among the most over-used and toxic words of the past few decades are disorder, dysfunction, and disability. All of these terms imply a standard against which someone does not measure up. One of Mel Levine's great contributions to educational theory (and parenting) is the notion that these words simply imply differences, and these differences do not always require cures, drugs, or therapies. They need to be understood, accommodated, and even celebrated. There is a movement among those diagnosed with autism and their parents to see it as just another way of being instead of some kind of disease. We must broaden our conception of what is normal, and one of the ways we can do that is through the language we use.

I have a reproduction of a map of Toronto from 1872. When you look along Queen Street, you can see a building that is still at 999

Queen Street West today. Today it is called "The Centre for Addiction and Mental Health." On my map of 1872, the building is labelled "Lunatic Asylum." This simple detail shows how our language changes as our understanding changes. People used to believe that "madness" was influenced by the moon (*luna* in Latin). Hence, the name "lunatic." Today we have a much more complex understanding of mental health and would never use such an archaic term, the product of a time when understanding was limited. Perhaps we could show the same humility about the labels and categories we use today. Future generations may look back with shock and disbelief at all the disorders, dysfunctions, and disabilities we have identified and tried to cure. I hope a day will come when children who don't fit into the widest part of the bell curve will be proud of their unique qualities, not made to feel deficient.

In order to create a wider spectrum of "normal," one of the institutions that will have to change is school. With its "one size fits all" approach, it is quite efficient at delivering its program to the largest group, the middle. In the past thirty of forty years, we have seen huge growth in special education, but rather than expanding the concept of normal to include a wider range of children, it has become a kind of side industry that depends on diagnosing and labelling to ensure its own continuation. It becomes a place where round pegs are helped to fit themselves into those square holes. Special education has very little to say about the squareness of the hole; the problem is more the roundness of the peg.

Special education departments within schools have helped to ease some of the pressure classroom teachers feel as they are required to deliver a prescribed curriculum to a group of students who span a huge spectrum of ability. To break down the distinction between "regular" classes and "special education" classes, our notions about prescribed curriculum and singular methods of delivery are going to have to change, not to mention our concept of the learner — each one unique.

In Greek mythology, we find mention of a bandit named Procrustes, a host who, according to the *Encyclopedia of Greek Mythology*, adjusted his guests to their bed. Procrustes, whose name means 'he who stretches' kept a house by the side of the road where he offered hospitality to passing strangers, who were invited in for a pleasant meal and a night's rest in his very special bed. Procrustes described it as having the unique property that its length exactly matched whomsoever lay down upon it. What Procrustes didn't volunteer was the method by which this "one-size-fits-all" was achieved, namely as soon as the guest lay down Procrustes went to work upon him, stretching him on the rack if he was too short for the bed and chopping off his legs if he was too long. Theseus turned the tables on Procrustes, fatally adjusting him to fit his own bed.

Schools can become "procrustean beds" when we become obsessed with measuring and calibrating students and their performances. The ideology that dominates education today is "outcomes." To measure these outcomes we use "rubrics." The "performance tasks" are held up to these rubrics and measured in order to see if the outcomes have been achieved. While none of this is done maliciously, it does disturbingly remind one of the procrustean bed. Procrusteus is put out of business by the questing hero, Theseus, who puts him on his own bed and fatally subjects him to the "one-size-fits-all" process. If our students were ever to turn their yardsticks on us, how would we measure up?

King Lear's Mistake: Living Through Your Children

We all have roads we didn't go down, things we never finished — courses we dropped, projects we abandoned, dreams we let fade away. And then God gives us a "Mini-Me"! We say to ourselves and then to our children: "I didn't finish grade three conservatory piano.

You're going to finish all the grades!" Or, "I never made the honour roll. You are going to make it!" The list goes on.

I remember sitting with Andrew, who was a nervous wreck by the time he was in grade twelve. He loved soccer and was a good player, but it was May and he had not yet been offered the soccer scholarship to an American university that he and his father had assumed would come quickly and easily. He broke down crying in my office. "I can't live my dad's dream any more!" His father had risen quite far up the ranks of European soccer as a young man, but had never been able to make a career of it. He was determined that his son would go further. Luckily, Andrew loved soccer too, so the years he had devoted to it were not a sacrifice of his own talents for some other goal. But still, he felt that he was chasing someone else's dream.

He had to cut that cord and make the dream his own, and during this crisis, he mustered the courage to talk to his dad and tell him about the pressure he felt to get this scholarship, not just for himself but for his father. After a few conversations with me sorting out his feelings, he was able to face his dad, telling him straight out, "I can't live your dream." Surprisingly, his dad accepted this. They both cried, as though some kind of spell had been broken. Their relationship was better, and a few weeks later, Andrew was offered the expected scholarship. He went on to great success at that college, and the success was his own. Could the father be proud of his son? Of course. Did the father play a part in the son's success? Of course. Our job is to support the dreams of our children and do what we can to help them come to fruition. If we have any unfulfilled dreams, we have two choices: go and follow them or let them go.

In the opening scene of *King Lear*, Lear has decided to retire and divide his kingdom among his three daughters, Goneril, Regan, and Cordelia. He tells them that they will each receive a third in proportion to how much they say they love him. Goneril speaks first and pours out a false speech of flattering words. She gets her third. Regan does the same, claiming that her love is even greater than Goneril's.

She gets her third. Then he turns to Cordelia, his favourite, and asks her to join in this game of what kids today would call "sucking up." Her response is, "Nothing, my lord."

> *Lear: Nothing will come of nothing. Speak again.*

> *Cordelia: Unhappy that I am, I cannot heave my heart into my mouth. I love your majesty according to my bond, no more nor less.*

A few minutes later, Lear exclaims, "Better thou hadst not been born than not to have pleased me better." At this point in our reading, I ask my grade twelves, "Is it your job to *please* your parents?" Silence always follows. They are very confused. They almost seem to feel it's a trick question. In this moment of silence, I see these seventeen-year-olds standing at a crossroads in their lives: "Do I live for myself and follow my own path, or do I live for my parents and follow the path they expect of me?" I let them off the hook of this moral dilemma by telling them, "According to Shakespeare, the answer is 'no.' It is not your job to please your parents. Your job is to live your own life. Cordelia was right. In refusing to give King Lear what he was asking for, she chose to live her own life and follow her own path. Her sisters chose to remain enmeshed in their relationship with their father while their husbands stood dumbly by." As Cordelia pointed out to them,

> *Haply, when I shall wed that lord whose hand must take my plight shall carry half my love with him, half my care and duty. Sure I shall never marry like my sisters, to love my father all.*

This is a stinging comment! Are there adults who marry but whose primary attachment is still to the parent? It does happen, and it's a sad thing to witness when it does. As A.S. Neill put it, "The function of the child is to live his own life — not the life that his anxious parents think he should live."

If you have unfulfilled dreams, follow them. If you have unfinished business, finish it. We could say it's never too late, and perhaps that's true, but it's also okay to let dreams fade away, to let unfinished business go. For some things, it *is* too late. We can be at peace with the decisions we've made, the roads we've taken. We are a "just so story," to use Rudyard Kipling's phrase. To live is to make choices, one path over another. We are the product of the choices we've made, and choices have many aspects — the thing we did and the things we could have done but didn't. It's okay. We did what we did.

I have always been bothered by the cliché, "I have no regrets." How can one get through life without them? It is natural. Letting them consume the present is the problem. We regret certain decisions, but there is nothing we can do about them now. People say, "If I had my life to live over again, I would not do one thing differently." This is denial and rationalization. Surely we learned enough that if we had to live our lives again, we would do things differently, but we can't, and this brings us back to our Mini-Me.

The unlived life of a parent can be a great burden to a child. Own your own unlived life and deal with it. Whatever you don't deal with, you will pass on. Your children will have their own unlived lives. As soon as they start making choices, they end up going down particular roads and leaving other roads not taken. This is how life works. If we have regrets, we can either go back and repair them, try to understand them, or just let them go and move on. This is how we become wise. Our kids need wise parents, not ones who are "working things out" through their children.

Conditional Love: I Will Love You If ...

I was handing out report cards to my grade nine class. Sylvia was the smartest kid in the class and her marks had been in the nineties all through school. She sat wide-eyed and tense waiting for this piece of paper. When she got it, she scanned it intensely then held it to her chest and proclaimed in a heart-felt tone, "Yes! My mother will love me!"

Sylvia grew up in a home where love was conditional on her performance in school, or at least that's how she perceived it, and that's how she behaved. For many kids, their parents' love is something they feel they have to earn. "I will love you if you live out the script I have planned for you, if you behave in ways I like, if your values and opinions are the same as mine." The great challenge for many parents, particularly those who experienced conditional love themselves, is to love unconditionally. "I will love you no matter what you do. I will love you if you come home pregnant. I will love you if you come home in a police car." Can we say this?

We do not need to like some of the things our children do, but we must always love who they are. Our children are more than their actions and the choices they make. Some of us were raised in homes where love operated almost like an economic system; it was earned and lost in a kind of invisible stock market where our share value seemed to fluctuate from day to day. When we were compliant and successful, we shone in our parents' eyes, and our value seemed to increase. When we were oppositional or failed at something, we felt tarnished and our value fell. The sadistic withdrawal of attention or affection was a common way of communicating this fall. The Amish and Mennonites of my own ancestry had an extreme ritualized form of this withdrawal of attention called "shunning," which involved ignoring a person until they repented and were accepted back into the fold. A lot of low-level shunning is still practiced in our homes and schools.

Bad actions are done by bad people and good actions by the good. This is an unconscious moral equation that we seem to live by. The truth is that good kids can do bad things, and that doesn't make them bad kids. The problem is that good kids who are told enough that they are bad end up stuck in that role and, in a sense, *become* bad kids. People become what they are perceived to be. We have to remember to "hate the sin and love the sinner," and this love must be unconditional.

Holding Close Versus Letting Go

The process of raising a child is one of letting go. When they are infants, we have complete control over every aspect of their lives. We stick our hands down their pants to see if their diaper is wet. We cart them here and there like luggage. Very seldom do we have to ask them what they would like. We make most of the decisions and have most of the control. And then come the "terrible twos!" But who are they terrible for? They are terrible for us because we begin to lose control. The child discovers he has a will of his own and he can use it. Before, we shoved their arms and legs into that snowsuit with little resistance. After two, the child discovers he has the power to fight back! It's not necessary to passively accept the actions of the parents, and thus the battle of wills begins. It is a battle that, in some families, will continue until the literal reading of the will! Over the years, I have acted as referee between so many parents and children where the essential issue boiled down to the need for power and control.

When I talk about "letting go," I don't mean relinquishing responsibility for the child. I mean letting go of the need for total power and control over a child's life. Every child's gain in these things does not have to be felt as a loss for the parent. In the battle of wills, the parent must eventually be the "loser," but this is a good thing, because we are not raising submissive robots. We are raising adults.

Children become adults as they gain more control, autonomy, and independence. The parent is the one who needs to let go in order for this to happen. There is no other way. If we keep holding on, we may create an obedient and passive "adult child" who has never learned to think or act on his own and will also be full of resentment. The ranks of adult children seem to be growing as the ethos that a good parent is a strict, controlling one gains ground. A current term, "helicopter parenting," captures the idea of this need to micro-manage the child's life. We used to talk about the "suffocating parent." The metaphors are different, but the idea is the same: the inability to let go.

We Teach Responsibility Through Freedom

In the conflict situation, it is often the parent who needs to take a step back. The child wants independence and the parent wants the child to do the responsible thing. Our first impulse is to tell them the responsible thing to do. But we do not teach responsibility through sermons or lectures, we teach it through freedom. However, before we can give freedom, there has to be trust. Such a circle! How can I learn to be responsible if I'm never given the freedom to choose (even if I screw up)? How can I gain my parents' trust unless they give me responsibility? All three of these things go hand in hand: freedom, responsibility, and trust.

The fly in the ointment is failure. When it happens, we want to pull back from the freedom; we interpret it as a lack of responsibility, and our trust is shaken. We only have one choice: to trust again. The child who is never allowed to take his first steps because he might fall will never learn to walk. Children learn how to walk by trial and error. If we never failed at anything, would this be good? The answer is obviously "no," and yet we have so much fear of failure. It's a cliché, but failure is an uncomfortable but necessary part of life.

Kids complain about the dilemma of getting their first job. "They say I need experience, but how am I supposed to get experience if no one will hire me?" This is a reasonable question. The first employer's decision to hire the young person is based on trust. The parent must do the same. I was helping to facilitate a student council retreat and the discussion turned to trust. One girl's comment struck me. "When an adult trusts me, I make better decisions, because I don't want to lose the trust of the person I respect."

This is very important information for adults. Children will rise to our expectations of them. People become what they are perceived to be, and children who are assumed to be irresponsible are more likely to be so. When they are assumed to be responsible, they are more likely to make responsible choices.

There are voices in our society that say things like, "The problem with kids today is they don't have enough rules. They're given too much freedom. What kids need are more rules and firmer boundaries (and maybe a good slap now and then)." This is external locus of control and teaches very little. It teaches kids obedience to authority based on fear of punishment or hope of reward.

The alternative is to trust kids' judgment, but, as Barbara Coloroso says, it has to start when kids are young and the stakes are low. For example, your son or daughter doesn't want to go to a sleepover. You feel it would be a good chance for some socialization, to connect with some nice kids. But maybe you don't know the whole picture. Maybe one of the kids has been bullying your child. Maybe they're going to be watching a scary movie that your child is afraid of watching.

Let the child make the final decision. One statement that is worth more than gold is, "I trust your judgment." When we say this, we are giving the child freedom to take responsibility for the situation, and we are allowing her to trust her own perceptions.

Fast-forward in time to the driveway at a party when the same girl is seventeen and the boy who drove her there is drunk and insists on taking her home. The girl who was raised with "I trust your judgment" will be in a better position to trust her own perceptions. "No, you're too drunk. I'll drive or we can call for a ride." The girl who was raised on external control, obedience to rules and the voice of authority, will experience the same situation differently. "Get in the car! I brought you. I'll take you home. Get in now!" She was never taught to trust her own judgment; she was raised in a home where you just did what you were told. She will have a harder time acting responsibly in this moment of free choice, because she was never trusted to make decisions when the stakes were low. Now they are high, and there is no authoritarian parent to tell her what to do. The most "authoritative" voice is the one of the drunk driver.

In our schools we fall into this trap of over-controlling kids. There is something about the "tight ship" school that we like. It sounds like the boundaries are very clear and there is little tolerance for misbehaviour. In my experience, the tight ship school is usually one based on external controls and fear. Kids "behave" not out of a sense of responsibility, but for fear of being caught doing otherwise. I fear we turn out many graduates who seem unable to accept the responsibilities of adulthood, because they never had the chance to practice them in school. They have been treated like children for so long that they never develop beyond the level of a child.

I saw a quote attributed to *Mad* magazine: "Teenagers are people who act like babies if you don't treat them like adults." I have seen this over and over again. Senior students who are cajoled and nagged and pushed to perform the simplest task are less likely to take responsibility for themselves than those who are left to feel the natural consequences of their behaviour. The mother of one of my grade ten students used to call several times a week to ask what her son's homework was. She would write it all down, but he never did it anyway. She was taking responsibility for his commitments. When I suggested that she needed to pull back and let him take responsibility, she exclaimed, "But if I don't keep on him, he's going to fail!"

Perhaps failure would be the best lesson in this case — natural consequences, as Barbara Coloroso calls them. He was being shielded from the natural consequences of his choices. The mother was, as psychologists would say, enabling her son's dysfunctional behaviour. Dysfunction occurs when you are functioning, but in a way that prevents you from achieving your stated goals. Another teacher made it his duty every morning to clear the senior hallway in time for the playing of "O Canada." He would strut up and down the halls yelling, "Get to class! Clear the halls!" This all appeared very dutiful, and he had the air of a responsible disciplinarian. The problem was he was taking all the responsibility on himself. What he never saw was the mornings he was not there — how these seventeen-year-olds would be even later for class without his cajoling. He had not trained them to be responsible. When he was absent, they took no responsibility for their own actions.

We read in the news all the time about the university "Animal House" syndrome, where first year students, away from Mom and Dad for the first time, are unable to impose any kinds of limits on themselves and spend too much time drinking and partying. They are so used to having limits imposed externally that when these are absent, they behave irresponsibly. We teach responsibility through freedom, and this has to begin at a young age, when the stakes are low. The process must continue through each of the developmental stages. We learn to walk by being treated like someone who can. We learn to become adults by being treated like one.

Trust

Trust is one of those catch-22 situations parents face. It has to be earned before it can be given, but it has to be given before it can be earned. The first person to "give" has to be the adult. "But I have no evidence that he can be trusted." That's what trust *is*: going ahead with something even when the outcome is uncertain. We will trust our kids, and they will violate our trust, and we will have no choice but to trust them again. When a child is trusted, it sends a message: you are a responsible person. When it is violated and the child feels his lack of responsibility, it's not a good feeling for anyone. It is not a feeling that he will want to repeat, not just because he fears punishment, but because he wants to be seen as a responsible person. The danger comes if we do not push the reset button on trust, and we fall into automatically thinking that he cannot be trusted. This becomes a self-fulfilling prophecy.

I counselled a boy who was having all kinds of trouble with his mother. He had violated her trust so many times that she had given up on him. He was at a point where he found it better to lie about what he was doing or not tell her, because she never believed him regardless. Instead, he decided he would just tell her whatever sounded best or got him into the least amount of trouble. One common scenario becoming exacerbated now with cellphones is the teenager who does not answer when he sees it is his parent on call display.

"Why don't you answer her calls?" I asked Mario.

"What's the point? She won't believe anything I say anyway, so why have a conversation at all?"

When trust is gone, communication goes too, because neither side feels they are having a real conversation. Lack of trust leads to lying. In the end, if parents want to keep the lines of communication open, they have to assume trust. If it turns out the child is lying, then consequences can be imposed, but the "trust button" has to be reset. This is the only way the child will learn responsibility. When our toddlers were learning to walk and fell down, we didn't set them in a chair and say, "I'm never trusting you to do that again." We knew falling over was the only way they'd learn, and we knew that they would get it eventually. The same is true with responsibility. Even when the teenager "falls," we have to let them get up and try again.

Worrying

There is only one thing to say about worrying: it serves little purpose. It is wasted energy unless we act on it. There are only two possible responses: we can either do something about it or we can't. If we can do something to change a situation for the better, then do it, but if we can't, then let it go. The familiar old prayer is very relevant for worrying parents: "God grant me the serenity to accept the things I cannot change, the courage to change the things I can, and the wisdom to know the difference."

Worrying is ultimately a control issue. We want so badly to be able to control the outcome, but it is not always in our power. Worrying can be a call to action — stop fretting, get in there, and

do something constructive. More often, it is the result of a realization of helplessness. It is as though all the energy we would put into
doing something goes into worrying, and it becomes a substitute
for effective action by creating the illusion that we're doing something! It is not only fruitless but exhausting. We have to learn to let
go of situations we can't control.

Guilt

Guilt too serves no purpose in itself. It is wasted energy unless it
is used as a call to action. If we feel guilty about something we've
said or done, then we can act on that guilt by making some kind of
amends. If that is not possible, then we must let the guilt go.

Guilt has the added dimension of morality: we have done something wrong. Is that really the case? Have I done something wrong,
or do I just wish I'd handled a situation differently? If a moral code
was violated, then we can seek forgiveness from the person we've
harmed. More often, we are simply punishing ourselves for a bad
decision, and we should forgive ourselves as we would a child.

Guilt may originate in a moral code, but it also might just be
the product of a critical inner voice. "How could you be so stupid?"
"What were you thinking?" "You're such a failure." We should talk
back to that voice and erase some of the programs that create
unwarranted guilt.

Daily Family Life and Family Memories

Someday your children will be grown up and gone. In fact, they will
only spend about 20 percent of their lifetime under your roof. My
wife always used to say, "We're not raising kids; we're raising adults."
Keep the end in mind. When your children have children and return
for family gatherings, one of the most precious things you will have
given them is memories to talk about and pass on. These memories
will be about the big events, but they will also be about daily family
life and the little unexpected moments.

Sometimes we get so caught up in the day-to-day blur of activity, we never stop to ask ourselves, what is our lifestyle? Is this what we want? We can end up falling into patterns by default rather than choice. An interesting, and scary, question is: "If I could choose how our daily family life was going to be, what would it be like?" Possible simple answers include: "I'd take the kids to the park more often. I'd take them to more cultural events. I would just sit and be with them."

What kinds of memories are you creating for your children? What are the family rituals that they will imitate or talk about when they are older? What are your positive practices around Christmas, birthdays, and summer holidays? What little traditions are unique to your family? How will your kids finish these sentences: "I remember the time we went to … I remember how our family always used to … I remember how Mom/Dad used to say …"

Funny and interesting things are more likely to happen if we get outside the box. In our conformist, safety-obsessed culture, parents explore a very narrow range of activities. They gravitate toward things that are offered as "programs." If everyone's doing it, this must be good. I see few kids out with Mom or Dad exploring the local stream, the local farmer's market. How many Saturdays are spent trying to bake or make jam together?

There are several memories my kids like to go back over. One year I decided that I would try to bake all the family bread. I did this for about two years! Every Sunday afternoon I would get out the big mixing bowl and start the lengthy process. The kids would sit on the counter and help with the various stages. When I put the yeast in the mixture, it would start to bubble and the kids would all gather round to see "The Yeast Monster" coming to life. They still speak fondly of the Yeast Monster. It was a simple event, but the memory of Dad making bread is cherished.

Another time, we had gone to what was called a "Fur and Feather" show. It was a place where people could bring animals to sell both for farm use and as pets. There were so many different, fascinating kinds of animals. There was a goat that turned out to be a (male) African Pygmy Goat. I was hooked. I had to have this goat. For the low price of fifty dollars, it was soon mine. At the time, we owned a one-acre lot in the country with a shed. This would be perfect, I thought. We loaded the kids into the van and then the African Pygmy Goat with his huge curly horns and all. The goat stayed with us for about a month, butting its horns on the shed wall until we took it out for "walks." We ended up giving it to a local exotic animal farm. Buying that goat was a crazy thing to do, but it sure made a great memory. My kids love to tell the story of the African Pygmy Goat, and I'm sure it will get passed down.

The WILL to POWER

You're Not the Boss of Me!

According to the German philosopher Friedrich Nietzsche, the "will to power" is one of the strongest motivating forces in our lives — the need to feel we have some degree of control over ourselves and the external world. Having raised four children and taught hundreds of teenagers, I completely agree with him. I have come to believe that the will to power is a very positive thing. Such a feeling gives a sense of well-being and personal efficacy, also called "individual agency." Whatever name we give it, this feeling that we are in control of our lives is essential for human happiness. This is best demonstrated by what happens when it is taken away. The feeling of powerlessness leads to frustration and anger.

When the individual no longer feels in control, a phenomenon sometimes called "counterwill" takes over. I first saw this term quoted in Gabor Maté's book *Scattered Minds*. There he attributes it to Vancouver psychologist Gordon Neufeld and notes that it was originally coined by psychoanalyst Otto Rank. This is one of the most powerful forces at work in children and teens, especially those who live under a lot of external controls and whose will to power is constantly being suppressed. When kids feel powerless, one of the ways they react is by doing the exact opposite of what the controlling authority figure wants. I have seen kids whose refusal to do homework was in direct proportion to the parent's insistence that they do it. Through their refusal, they regain a sense of power.

Unfortunately, this use of power might benefit them psycho-logically and emotionally but often sabotages other goals. I have seen kids fail their high school English credit because of Mom or Dad's constant badgering. In so many of my counselling situations with parents and children, my advice to the parent is "back off." Maté quotes a telling line from one mother: "But how will I teach my son self-discipline if I don't make him do his homework?" This line perfectly illustrates the problem of the conflict between the parent's and child's wills — one or the other must surrender, and in order for the child to triumph, it is the parent who must pull back. No parent wants to be told they are over-controlling, invasive, or coercive, but many are. Again, some inner work is necessary here. Why do I feel such a strong need to control my children? What am I afraid of? Are these fears realistic? Am I helping my child learn independence by being so controlling?

One of Aesop's fables illustrates this dynamic:

> The Wind and the Sun were disputing which was the stronger. Suddenly they saw a traveller coming down the road, and the Sun said: "I see a way to decide our dispute. Whichever of us can cause that traveller to take off his cloak shall be regarded as the stronger. You begin." So the Sun retired behind a cloud, and the Wind began to blow as hard as it could upon the traveller. But the harder he blew the more closely did the traveller wrap his cloak round him, till at last the Wind had to give up in despair. Then the Sun came out and shone in all his glory upon the traveller, who soon found it too hot to walk with his cloak on.

When dealing with kids, we often adopt the approach of the wind and use external force to achieve our goal. Note that the goal of the story is simply to prove who is stronger — sometimes that is our goal too! We get much further with kids when we create the conditions for what we would like to see happen. The man could just as easily have decided to keep his coat on in the hot sun. The decision was his, but he did what was logical, natural, and right. That's what we want to teach our kids, and we do it by letting go.

There are three developmental stages where the will to power and the phenomenon of counterwill can escalate drastically, causing major conflict: the so-called "terrible twos," adolescence, and midlife.

"The Terrible Twos"

We have already talked about the terrible twos, when the child first discovers he has a will of his own and begins to use it. During this stage, all kinds of conflicts and complications arise, but parents are usually the winners. We are bigger and stronger. In the end, we have all the power. In the old days they talked about "breaking" the will of the child and, back then, to be a "wilful" child was a negative thing. If we didn't curb his will, he would end up "spoiled." This kind of language reveals the importance previous generations gave to power and control over children. The obedient, submissive child was the ideal. This attitude was a by-product of patriarchy. There had to be a pecking order, and young children were certainly kept at the bottom.

With the cultural revolution of the 1960s, there emerged a philosophy of child-rearing that often appeared to be at the other end of the spectrum — allowing the child to actualize his potential from the youngest age possible through total freedom. A.S. Neill of the famous Summerhill school was one of the leaders of this movement. By 1966, he felt the need to address American parents about their misinterpretation of a liberal child-rearing philosophy. He wrote a book specifically for the American market called, *Freedom — Not License!* in which he tried to explain that the purpose of freedom in child-rearing is to teach what he called "self-regulation." He had been raised in the patriarchal world of external control mechanisms that kept everyone in their place. He rejected this paradigm in favour of a vision of a world where people lived freely according to their own natures but also in harmony with others.

In *Freedom — Not License!* he quotes from his 1960 revolutionary best-seller *Summerhill: A Radical Approach To Child-Rearing*: "In the disciplined home, the children have *no* rights. In the spoiled home, they have *all* the rights. The proper home is one in which children and adults have *equal* rights." Even in our present age, with the United Nations ratification of the Convention on the Rights of the Child, we still seem unsure about this idea that children have "rights and freedoms." This lack of faith in children is a legacy of our authoritarian past, a fear-based patriarchal culture that produced the Hitler Youth and McCarthyism.

Rebels With a Cause: The Will to Power in Adolescence

At no other developmental stage is the will to power as strong as during adolescence. During this period, kids are in the process of completely re-creating themselves. I love working with this age group because of the incredible dynamism. The individual identity of the child is in a state of total flux. The child has lived for eleven or twelve years more or less as the product of the mirroring provided by parents. "This is who you are. This is who I would like you to be. This is what a good boy/ bad boy is." The degree of parental definition is huge during these early years. The lessons we teach are both explicit and implicit. We teach them by what we say, by what we don't say, by what we do, and what we don't do. In adolescence, kids begin the project of self-definition. "Who am I apart from who my parents told me I am?" The only way to find this out is to turn to other mirrors.

The main mirrors teens turn to are peers and popular culture. Peers provide real life interactive feedback and media simply downloads messages into kids' hard drives.

Whatever the effects of this project, the project itself is extremely important. Kids define themselves by questioning previous identities and roles, sometimes rejecting them outright. This process goes by the name "rebellion." Rebellion against parents is an essential stage in human development and must be understood and honoured as such. Kids who rebel are not bad, defiant, or oppositional. They are perfectly normal. Imagine being forty years old and making all your decisions based on the criteria of what Mom and Dad would approve of. If an adult were still living by his parents' definition of them, we would describe that adult as suffering from arrested development.

Some parents will have an easy ride. The teen rebellion may simply take the form of an infuriated "Shut up!" For others, the ride will be a little bumpier, with piercings, tattoos, wild hair, wild clothes, wild music. For some the ride will be a disturbing one — drugs, police, failed courses at school. It is a great mystery to me why some kids go through adolescence fairly calmly and others very dramatically. Sometimes the intensity of the rebellion is in direct proportion to the degree of control and externally imposed definitions of the self in childhood. I also think there are essentially two kinds of teen personality profiles — conservative, cautious teens and liberal, risk-taking ones. The second group are the experimenters, those who prefer to learn from experience and are not adverse to high-risk behaviour. The parents of these kids have more grey hair.

Midlife: The Will to Power's Last Stand

The first half of life is spent performing, achieving, and acquiring. At midlife we experience a kind of plateau. We take a step back and ask ourselves if we are where we want to be. Often the answer is, "not really." In the daily grind that makes up the first half of life, we sometimes make choices based on expediency rather than what is best for our souls. In the hurly-burly, we don't always feel we have time to honour our souls. We do what is practical, what makes sense, what we're influenced by others to do, and we often end up following paths not completely our own or living in roles that do not satisfy.

At midlife, when we begin to listen to the deeper voices, we might find they are cranky. "This is not where I want to be. I can do better than this. This is not what I had planned for myself." The will to power has been subverted. Many people fall into a kind of *ennui* or depression because they feel they have crawled into a box they can't get out of. This situation is jokingly referred to as the "midlife crisis" and is usually mocked in popular culture. There are all kinds of stereotypes associated with it, like the middle-aged man who leaves his wife for the perky nymphette or the conservative secretary who buys the yellow Corvette. The person in the throes of a midlife crisis is depicted as pathetic and confused.

Instead of ridiculing and demeaning the midlife experience, our culture would do well to embrace and celebrate it. Individuals have so much to gain from this experience — mainly, the opportunity to redefine themselves. Like a second adolescence, we can take stock and ask ourselves, "Am I just the role I have come to play? Do my accomplishments and possessions define me or am I something other, something more, than these?" These are extremely important questions. So many people lose the opportunity presented by midlife, simply rejecting the old role and adopting another equally shallow one or ignoring the questions altogether, losing their essential selves in the process. The cynical, jaded older adult is often one who missed the opportunity of midlife and remains stuck in a role he can't get out of. He settles for the limited horizon of possibilities and visits those limitations on everyone else by becoming the cynical naysayer.

I began teaching right out of university. I was twenty-three and still an adolescent myself when I went into the classroom to teach other adolescents. I remember standing outside the staff-room. Directly across the hall was the student cafeteria. I distinctly remember standing there, holding my lunch, wishing I could go and sit among the students instead. I did not feel like an adult, and I was unready to enter their world. I quickly donned the role of "Mr. Reist." Teachers have very defined roles, so I was able to put that on like a costume. I didn't feel confident in the role, but I faked it and eventually it began to fit. One of the occupational hazards of having an occupation is that you can end up becoming the role you play. Mr. Reist becomes a persona, a mask you can end up wearing for the rest of your life. You become a kind of caricature and all your responses are rote.

At midlife, I was lucky enough to find a book by the Jungian analyst James Hollis called *The Middle Passage*. This was a book that described what was going on and presented the "crisis" as a golden opportunity for growth and transformation. The will to power re-awakens and says, "I want more." Not more accomplishments and status and things. One demands more depth, more meaning. As we head down the other side of the mountain, we become aware of our mortality and can ask, "What has my life been for?" Relationships become more important than possessions. Wisdom becomes more important than knowledge. Sharing oneself with the world becomes more important than rising up in it. Love becomes more important than competition.

In all three of these stages, the terrible twos, adolescence, and midlife, the will to power is at work. In each case it is a very positive force that pushes us on to the next stage. Complications occur when this will to power meets an opposing force. For the two-year-old, this is the parents. For the adolescent it can be any authority figure, but most often it is parents and teachers. For the person at midlife, it can be a spouse, a boss, or the world in general. Ironically, in many homes, the teenager's will to power awakens at the same time as a midlife parent's, and that can be a volatile mix! When the will to power runs up against an obstacle, the result is a feeling of power-lessness, and that leads to anger.

ANGER

If You Don't Have Your Feelings, They Will Have You

One of the most important emotions to understand is anger. When I was in grade two, we were preparing for our first confession. The nun who was preparing us put a list of possible sins up on the board to choose from — in case we couldn't think of any ourselves! I distinctly remember that one of the sins was anger, and it's funny how that stayed with me. On some level, my seven-year-old mind got snagged on that idea. I must have had questions about its truth, but I would dutifully go into the confessional and confess that I had gotten mad five times (we were supposed to report the frequency of our sins as well), and the priest would absolve me.

As an adult, I see that anger is not a sin but an emotion. In fact, it is a very valuable one. Anger is a message from the soul that some boundary has been violated or an expectation has not been met. The phone rings, Mother answers, "Yes … Yes … Okay… No problem … Talk to you later." She hangs up and announces to the child that the much-anticipated sleepover has been cancelled. The child flies into a fury, which is a perfectly reasonable response. An expectation was not realized and, on a deeper level, the child's will to power has been obstructed by forces beyond her control. She feels as though a boundary has been violated.

It is important to understand these feelings so they can be better accepted and accommodated. All feelings are important and should be at least acknowledged, if not expressed. Psychologists talk about the "discharge of affect," which means having your feelings — getting them out. I heard it said once that if you don't have your feelings, your feelings will have you. Many of us grew up in families where feelings were not expressed, or only the positive sun-shiny variety were allowed. The dark end of the spectrum was inhibited or denied altogether by lines like, "You have no right to be angry." "Nice people don't talk like that." "If you can't say anything nice, don't say anything at all." Sometimes feelings were given other names: "Oh, you're just tired."

Repressed anger will come out in other ways. In adolescent males, it can come out as addiction and high-risk behaviour. In adolescent girls it can come out as depression. Boys act out. Girls act in.

We must allow feelings in the home and encourage the discharge of affect. This may involve reflection on the way feelings, anger in particular, were handled in one's family. If we come from a family where feelings were denied, we are more likely to have trouble accepting their spontaneous expression in our children. Feelings are closely associated with control. One of the reasons we fear them is that we feel they may overwhelm us. When we talk about "losing it," the "it" we are referring to is control over our feelings. We sometimes feel like walking Pandora's boxes, that, if opened, would unleash terrible forces impossible to control, so we keep our emotions under control, only to have them come out in other ways. Very often, when a child expresses strong feelings, this can act as a trigger that unleashes our own strong, but repressed feelings. If we have a lot of pent-up anger, and our child "loses it," we may find ourselves losing it too. It's almost a sympathetic reaction. When one tuning fork is tapped, another across the room will begin to vibrate as well.

When a child screams in anger or runs into his room slamming the door and yelling profanities, should this behaviour be punished? The behaviour has not hurt anyone else. If the expression takes the form of hitting or verbally abusing, or damaging property, then we're in a different area. You are free to express your feelings, but your freedom ends where the rights of others begin. You have a right to be mad about the sleepover being cancelled, but it doesn't give you the right to hit your brother, break something, or call me names.

Expressing feelings is part of the larger topic of communication. If we create an environment of open communication, then the expression of feelings will follow naturally and the discharge of anger will be allowed.

COMMUNICATION

Stop Talking!

Ryan, seventeen, and his mother were fighting a lot. His mother was a teacher and his father was quite removed from the emotional life of the family (as are many fathers). Ryan's mother asked me to speak to him and find out what could be done to stop the fighting. I asked him a simple question: "If you could tell your mother one thing, what would it be?" His answer: "Stop talking." Whether it was objectively true, Ryan *felt* that his mother was doing all the talking, that the communication was largely one-way and he felt overwhelmed by her.

I have seen this scenario so many times, the non-verbal adolescent male with the verbal adult female. It is a match that does not always work very smoothly. Many males, particularly in adolescence when testosterone levels are high, can have poor receptive and expressive language capacity. The boy feels frustrated, overwhelmed, and incompetent in the face of all this language. He can also feel threatened, and when a male feels this way, his testosterone level rises even further. A stressed male does not want to talk. He acts on his most primitive drives: fight or flight. He might choose the fight response — hitting Mom physically or verbally or hitting a wall instead. He is more likely to choose the flight response — leaving the room or, if he stays, going silent. Many parents have come to me for help when their last straw was the hole in the drywall or the door. We might be surprised at the number of people looking for small, patch-sized pieces of drywall at Home Depot.

What Ryan needed was to be listened to, like so many adolescents. I asked my grade twelve class about parents and listening, and here are some of the things they said: "She starts giving advice." "He tries to solve my problem." "She turns it into a lesson." "They start telling stories from when they were young." One of the hardest things for adults, it seems, is to remain quiet when their children begin to talk. Psychologists talk about "active listening." In the conflict situation, we take what the other person says and use it to line up our next volley. We are always waiting to speak, and most importantly, we take the other person's words and immediately assess their weaknesses so that we can disprove or undercut, thereby strengthening our own position.

One of the hardest things while listening is to suspend our own point of view and enter into that of the other person. When we do this, we discover that there is a deeper level. "I want to drop this course," on a deeper level is about "I'm afraid of looking stupid. I'm afraid of failing, or I need some help." In another situation, "I want to go to that concert in Toronto," is really about, "I want more independence. I want to be treated like an adult. I want to broaden the horizons of my experience. I feel I'm ready for more."

In the conflict situation, these deeper, legitimate thoughts and feelings are not dealt with. The argument focuses on the surface statements with lots of nitpicking about the details. It isn't long before the child feels overwhelmed by the adult's superior language processing ability, not to mention reasoning ability and broader life experience. The child is clearly at a disadvantage. They feel this and are quick to jump on the defensive.

The listening side of communication would be so much more fruitful if adults could practice greater empathy. As one of my grade twelve students said: "Sir, it's as if my mom's forgotten what it was like to be seventeen. She talks to me as though I'm forty, too! I know she did the same kinds of things when she was young that I want to do now, but when we're talking, it's as though she has totally forgotten that!"

The other common theme expressed by the students was the feeling they get that their parents are trying to "fix" them somehow. Often, we begin with the assumption that the child cannot solve his own problems, that he is helpless without us. Imagine taking the approach that he is capable of figuring out how to handle the situation. How does that change your role? You are no longer the dispenser of wisdom or authority. You are the midwife trying to help the child draw out the best choice in a given situation. Try these responses:

Tell me more.

Continue.

And then …

And if you don't?

And if you do?

Another strategy when a talker stalls is to restart the thought processes by using the last sentence and restarting it, but not finishing it:

… and you don't like him because …

… and what you really wish you could say is …

… and what you'd really like to do is …

One of the greatest gifts we can give our kids is that of listening. It is a precious gift for two main reasons. First, it requires time, something kids love to be given! Second, it involves focusing on the speaker. Children and adolescents are naturally egocentric. It is appropriate for them at this stage. Let them have the spotlight, the microphone, your ear! I meet so many kids who have not been listened to enough. They talk over each other. They talk at me. They are not good listeners themselves because they've never had it modeled. You can spot kids who've been listened to — they don't seem to have this same hunger for attention. They are also better at the give and take of conversation. They realize, from experience, that communication involves two — a speaker and a listener. We can easily model the speaker role for our kids, but we also need to model the listener role.

Learning to Talk by Talking

If we teach our children to listen by listening ourselves, it would seem to follow naturally that we teach them to talk by talking. That is certainly true. Children who grow up in a rich language environment have a greater chance themselves of being proficient in language production and reception. Adults are important role models for speech production. We learn by watching and listening, but we cannot learn without doing. This is especially true for talking. One of the most important places we practice talking early is in social situations in the real world. Parents sometimes fall into the trap of talking over the child, talking for them, and coaching them in the social situation. We should allow for practice, and sometimes that means saying nothing.

The Things We Don't Say

Sometimes our most powerful messages are conveyed by what we don't say. I remember leaving my counselling room one evening carrying a large box with both hands. I asked the boy I had just been working with to turn off the light. Just as his finger was poised over the switch, his mother said, "Push it down." There is a profound form of communication going on here. The message sent is, "You are not capable of handling simple situations alone." At the same time, there was something else going on, the insecurity that so many parents feel. We all feel we are being judged at times, and this feeling seems to magnify around our children. In his book *The Soul's Code*, James Hillman talks about "The Parenting Fallacy" — the idea that we make our children into who they are. This idea leads to the corollary: if my kids look bad, I look bad. If my kids fail, I fail. A lot of our parenting behaviour originates in this myth.

Sometimes saying nothing sends the best possible message. "You can handle this on your own. I have confidence in you. You will know what to do." These are powerful and affirming messages communicated by saying nothing at all! People become what they are perceived to be, and we communicate how we perceive them by what we say as well as what we don't.

My youngest son, Luke, was an avid tree climber. He would climb as close to the top as he could. I used to stand below and call up, "Be careful." My other three kids would laugh. "Do you think he's not being careful? Does he really need to be reminded of that?" And then they would add quite rightly, "You're causing more of a problem by distracting him." Sometimes when I called up, "Be careful," Luke, as an ironic joke, would pretend to lose his balance, as though he was going to fall. It became the family joke that Luke was safe as long as I wasn't around calling out "Be careful" down below.

Researchers studied mothers watching their children on a jungle gym, recording the number of bumps, scrapes, falls, and arguments that occurred, once with the mothers watching and once with them absent. The study found that the children were much more likely to hurt themselves with their mothers present. The mothers watched their children closely and called out directions and cautions like my "Be careful." The children were experiencing an external locus of control and did not feel they had to take control themselves. When the mothers were gone, they were forced to adopt an internal locus of control and make decisions on their own.

Speaking Between the Lines

Some of the things we say to our children have no meaning or mean something else.

"What's the matter with you?"

"What's gotten in to you?"

"You used to be so …"

"[Insert name of peer or sibling] doesn't act like this."

"If everybody jumped off a cliff …"

All of these sentences are critical, disapproving, shaming, and are destructive to a child's self-esteem. When tempted to use these kinds of sentences, we should pull back and ask ourselves what we are really feeling and thinking. These sentences are often motivated more by our feelings of anger and frustration, our feelings about the child not behaving in the way we want them to, and on a deeper level, not being the person we would like them to be. This is pretty strong stuff, and, for the child on the receiving end, the message received is one of rejection — either for my behaviour or, more deeply, for who I am as a person.

Our language often betrays our deepest assumptions, and one of those might be that we can mould our children. When they do something counter to our plan, we use language of rejection. We fall into the fallacy of thinking we have total control over them, even down to the choices they themselves make. When this doesn't work, we reject what we cannot control.

Sometimes we have to stop and ask ourselves what we are really feeling or thinking *before* we speak. This is especially true when overwhelmed by negative emotions. One of the best communication skills we can learn as parents is saying what we really think and feel, but before we can, we have to know ourselves. We may discover that some of these things have more to do with us and our own unrealistic expectations and perceptions than they do with the child. By gaining perspective on our own emotions, we're in a better position to avoid making hurtful comments. A key way to avoid using critical shaming language is to use "I messages." Start your sentences with the word "I" and stick to what is going on inside of you. "I don't understand why you won't do your homework." "I wish you and your sister would get along better." "I see a big change in your behaviour lately." These kinds of sentences might lead to discussion of the issues.

SELF-ESTEEM

Praise

Praise is essential for the development of a child's self-esteem. We need to emphasize the positive with our kids. We have so many worries and fears that it is easy to get bogged down in negative thinking. We need to be just as much on the look-out for positives, and when we see them, name them.

We should also be realistic about praise. False praise can be a corrosive force in a child's life. When we praise things disproportionately, we send a confusing message. Children, especially older ones, know when something is good. To have something called "awesome" that really is only mediocre sends a message: "This is the best I think you could do. This is amazing *for you*. This is the most I would expect from you." The parent who goes on about how great something is might end up sounding like he's trying to convince himself or the child. I've had many kids say to me, "Oh, she's just saying that because she's my mother," or "She always says stuff like that." Too much praise comes to lose its meaning. It must always be tied to real accomplishment, or our words become hollow.

If praise can be destructive when it's hollow, it can also be so when it means too much. In this case, it can lead to performance-based esteem, positive self-regard based on one's performance and the need for external affirmation. Our self-esteem ends up being tied to our accomplishments and, secondarily, the display of those accomplishments before others. This dynamic develops when the only positive regard we get seems to come from external public accomplishments. The term "trophy child" describes this extreme version of performance-based esteem, when the child becomes a trophy to be displayed. He feels this and comes to believe that he is only as good as his last report card or hockey game. These children can become "praise junkies," always looking for their next "fix."

One of the "boogie men" in all parents' lives is fear. Fear that I'm not giving my child enough praise, that he will have low self-esteem, or, in the case of the trophy child syndrome, that others will judge me on his performance.

Praise is essential to the development of a child's self-esteem, but it must always have its roots in love, not psychological manipulation. If we are praising our kids in order to *try* to make them feel better about themselves, they will know this. When we simply love them and let this love express itself authentically, praise will come naturally.

Encourage Competence in One Area

I have seen kids who showed genuine talent in one area, only to have that interest and ability used as a bargaining chip for doing better in areas where they didn't excel. "If you don't bring up your grades, no more hockey." One of the greatest contributors to core self-esteem is the feeling of competence in one area. For some kids this may be video games. I told the story of Peter, who was not experiencing much success in school but felt a great sense of accomplishment about his standings in the game *World of Warcraft*. The self-esteem he derived from this accomplishment was completely legitimate.

Some parents lament, "My child doesn't seem to have any special gifts or competencies in one area. How do I get him to be interested in something?" This can be taken in two directions. If you've been pushing him to try a number of different things and he has shown no interest, the problem may be that it's coming from you. It seems that you want it more than he does. This is when the counterwill dynamic can set in and, "I'm not going to do anything that you want me to." In this situation, it is best to back off and wait. Unfortunately, his passive-resistant stance may have become an ingrained habit. Some kids who are pushed too hard in childhood become completely unmotivated in adolescence.

If this difficult dynamic has not set in and the child is still open to trying new things, then the fundamental rule is to take your lead from him. Beware of signing him up for things that *you* are interested in or *you* think would be good for him. Let him decide what interests him, even if it's not something that appeals to you. I mentioned the story of the mother who enrolled her "clumsy" son in dance class to cure him of this tendency. After much resistance and argument, he chose fencing classes and went on to compete at the national level.

We would do well to encourage existing interests. Sometimes we have to listen carefully to find out what those are. If all he does is play Lego, is that an interest in other kinds of building like woodworking or electronics? If all he does is play *Warhammer*, is that an interest in the Middle Ages, and might it be a good fit with military re-enactment clubs? I have seen many kids who liked Lego and *Star Wars* move on to stop-motion movies made with the little plastic characters, which they post on YouTube.

Support Decisions Already Made

When a child decides on a project or a course of action, we may see the pitfalls and problems better than they do. Unless these potential problems are dangerous, it is best to let them proceed. Experience is the best teacher, and when we support decisions already made, we are demonstrating confidence in our child. When they come up with an idea or a plan, we might be tempted to list all the reasons why this will not work or shouldn't be done. We want to protect our child from feelings of failure, but the problem-solving involved in the task and the perseverance required are just as important as the end itself. We would do better to support and facilitate the project. We might be surprised! And what might appear as a relative success to us may be a great triumph in the eyes of the child.

Negative Self-Talk

Cognitive behavioural therapy is based on the premise that what we think influences how we feel and act. Cognitive behavioural therapists talk about "automatic thoughts" which are activated in particular situations. We all have this inner voice, this self-talk that can empower us or disable us. "I'm so stupid." "I can't write." "I'm a terrible public speaker." "I'll never find a girlfriend." These self-critical recordings that play in our heads become self-fulfilling prophecies. We are dictating our own life script as we play it out.

Where do these thoughts originate? They come mainly from external experience, not so much from actual failure, but from pre-dictions of failure or emphasis on it by significant people in our lives. These automatic thoughts become ingrained in childhood, and they can be very difficult to expel. Negative thoughts are communicated in several ways: by actual words, by tone, and by behaviour. Lines like, "What were you thinking?" and "How could you do that?" send a strong message of shame and incompetence. The second person "you" gets transformed into the first person "I." "I'm so stupid." "I can't do anything right."

Tone can send just as strong a message. Sometimes the parent just has to say the child's name in a shaming, disappointed tone and the same message is received: "Joh-shu-ahh!" Negative self-talk is instilled through the behaviour of those we love, especially when that love is withdrawn. The silent treatment, being ignored, or simply having the loved one look away in apparent disgust can be devastating for a young child and teaches a powerful message that is translated into negative self-talk.

Negative comments from caregivers carry more emotional weight than praise. Criticism is felt on a deeper level. It is felt as a threat. The primary caregiver is our most important protector and nurturer. If she rejects us, our very survival could be at stake. Though praise does not guarantee survival, rejection threatens it.

The other origin of these automatic negative thoughts is institutional religion, particularly the Judeo-Christian tradition. Matthew Fox wrote a book called *Original Blessing* in which he tried to suggest an antidote to the teaching of Original Sin — the idea that people are born sinful, are prone to sin, and that our default mode is to do wrong. Is this teaching a description of human nature or has it become a prescription for it? The idea that we are all weak sinners cannot be much help to our self-esteem.

The other place this negative self-talk originates is in school. It is a place of judgment, and those are not always positive. Judgments are felt in the actions, words, and tone of voice of teachers and peers, and perhaps most of all, in the supposedly objective technology of marks. It could be argued that school implicitly teaches that you can never be good enough. As soon as the concrete measuring stick called "marks" comes into the equation, we are all at a loss.

All grading is based on a scale, usually a letter or a percentage. If the medium is the message, then what is the one sent by marks? You will never be good enough. A hundred percent is seldom if ever achieved, even though you might have given it 100 percent or what you just did far surpasses your previous attempt. Your efforts are always held up against a yardstick that will always show them to be lacking. The spectrum moves from adjectives like excellent to very good to good to average to satisfactory to fair to poor. There are some kids who go through school never achieving a mark higher than 65 percent, which equates to words like "average" or perhaps "satisfactory." What does this do to one's self-perception? What conclusions does a child draw? What kind of negative self-talk does this create?

As parents, there are two pieces of inner work for us here. One is to examine the voice in our own heads and talk back to it when we hear negative condemnations. Some of us have to literally reprogram ourselves to emphasize the positive over the negative. The other thing is not to pass on our own negative self-talk to our children or create these automatic negative thoughts in them. This requires a conscious effort and listening to oneself.

DISCIPLINE

Discipline is one of the areas that requires the most conscious parent-ing. When we are in a disciplining situation, we are usually agitated, and we are more likely to fall back on unconscious patterns, what I called earlier "automatic pilot." We will re-create our parents and do what was done to us.

To avoid this, it may help to pause and consider these questions, if you can, in the heat of the moment:

- Is the child tired or hungry?
- Are you tired or hungry?
- Are you worried about what the neighbours will think?
- Are you worried about what your mother (mother-in-law) would think?
- Is the child's behaviour expressing some feeling (anger, frustration, excitement)?
- Are you frustrated by other things unrelated to this particular situation?
- Does this situation push a button from your own childhood?

If the answer to any of these questions is "yes," then you should give yourself a time-out, and calm down, rest, eat, or think your feelings through. In the discipline situation, when emotions are running high, we tend to say and do things we regret later. Our best self is not in control of the situation.

THE FOUR F'S: FEW, FAIR, FAST, AND FIRM

Few

When it comes to rules, less is more. It can be a very helpful exercise to sit down and ask yourself, "What are the most important rules in this house? What are the battles I am willing to fight?" First do this with yourself, then have your spouse do the same separately and compare notes. Then have the discussion with your kids. Ask them the same questions. The key is to keep the list as short as possible. Once you have it, the next topic to submit to the same process is consequences. "What will the penalties be for infractions of these rules?" Get input from all parties then try to arrive at consensus about both the rules and consequences. These lists should be made when everyone is calm and feeling good, never in the heat of a conflict. The rules should be posted somewhere in the house. After a week or two, you may want to revisit it as a family to discuss whether the rules are realistic. Situations may have arisen that you feel strongly about, but had not been included. Similarly, you might realize that something on the list is either unenforceable or just too vague.

Here is a sample list of rules.

- No hitting
- No swearing
- Pick your toys up off the floor before bed
- Pick your clothes up off the floor before bed
- Put your dirty clothes in the hamper
- Put your dishes in the dishwasher
- Homework must be done before supper
- Homework must be done before any screen time after supper

Here is a sample list of consequences.

- Time out (sitting in your room for ten minutes)
- Time out (sitting on a chair for ten minutes)
- No computer time for the rest of the day
- No video games for the rest of the day
- No TV for the rest of the day
- No going outside for the rest of the day

Examples of rules that are too vague and unenforceable:

- Be polite
- No rude talk
- Share your toys
- Be respectful
- No talking back
- Do what you're told
- Co-operate
- Keep things neat

Fair

A healthy family is a democratic one in which all members, including the children, have a voice. In our radically interconnected world, everyone wants their voice to be heard. This is not always possible at the macro level of general society, but it is on the micro level of the family. We prepare our children for life in a democracy by giving them a say in matters of importance to their lives. Authoritarian top-down structures are an anachronism. Parents do have veto power; they are still the ultimate authority in the home, but if children are at an age where they can participate and where the issues are relevant to them, they should be given as much opportunity as possible to participate in the decision-making process.

In John Irving's novel, *The Cider House Rules*, the main character ends up working for a time with some migrant farm workers. In the bunkhouse where they sleep (the Cider House) is a list of rules that none of the illiterate workers can read. The main character finally reads the rules to the others, and one of the workers says to burn them because they were written by people who never lived in the Cider House. The message here is you don't have to follow rules that you didn't help make. This is a basic tenet of democracy.

The Thirteen Colonies broke from Britain over the issue of taxation without representation. The colonists were faced with many rules that they had no say in making. Benjamin Franklin fought hard to convince the British parliament to let the colonies have a seat in the House of Commons, where they would have a voice. This was denied, and the colonies rebelled. This is what our kids do, too. One of the sources of teen rebellion is the feeling of having no voice. It is interesting to read the history of the American Revolution and see the paternalistic (from the Latin *pater* meaning father) attitude of the British lords toward the colonists. They saw them as ignorant children who must be controlled at all costs, and were incapable of making their own decisions. They also saw any gain in the power of the colonists as a loss of power for themselves. It is interesting the extent to which these attitudes still persist in the parent-child relationship.

Fast

Dr. Sam Goldstein put it best when he wrote, "Act, don't yak." So many parents will launch into a tirade or long sermon when a rule is violated. You've already discussed the relevance of the rule and the reasonableness of the consequences. Your job now is to do what you all agreed on. This is where actions speak louder than words. Your son hits his sister. You say nothing. You pick him up, take him to his room, and close the door.

Your son's curfew is eleven p.m. He comes in at 11:45 without having called. You show that you've noted it by saying. "It's 11:45.

You were supposed to be home by eleven." The next evening, if that acknowledgement hasn't been enough and he's heading out the door, you say, "You were forty-five minutes late last night. You're in tonight. That was the deal." If you have to use words, keep it short and simple.

Firm

Consistency is one of the hardest areas in disciplining kids. As mentioned earlier, Barbara Coloroso uses three metaphors to describe consistency in families: the Brick Wall Family, the Jelly Fish Family, and the Backbone Family. The Brick Wall family is not interested in considering grey areas, in discussing extenuating circumstances, or listening to reasons. For the Jelly Fish Family, every area is grey. There are no certainties. Everything is made up as we go along. In contrast to these two, the Backbone Family is consistent.

There are a couple of reasons for inconsistency. The first is exhaustion. Sometimes parents are just too tired to follow through. You fall into bed knowing the toys never got picked up. After a long, frustrating day at work, the prospect of spending an evening with your angry grounded teen is just too much to bear, so you let him go out. One solution is to get more sleep.

The other cause of inconsistency is guilt. I find this particularly strong in parents who are both working long hours. They feel guilty about the limited time they have with their kids, and the last thing they want to do with that time is play the "heavy" and turn it into negative time. The solution lies in what was said earlier about guilt — either do something to change the situation (work fewer hours), do something to make amends (explain why you are doing this and allot extra time on the weekends), or let the guilt go.

At its core, inconsistency is based on fear of losing the child's love. If we grew up in a home where love was conditional: "I will love you if you behave," "I will love you if you do as I say," "I will love you as long as you don't make me angry," then we may end up applying this same logic to our relationship with our children. We tell ourselves: "They will love me if I behave" (i.e. I am a fun, nice parent), "They will love me if I do what they say" (i.e. I don't impose or enforce too many rules), "They will love me as long as I don't make them angry" (by imposing consequences). The solution is to take some time for reflection on the nature of love. What is unconditional love and what would it look like? If my kids are mad at me or say they hate me, is that real? Can I deal with it?

PART FIVE

RAISING BOYS with CHARACTER

WHAT MEDIA TEACHES ABOUT CHARACTER

School used to be the first curriculum. According to Neil Postman, media has now replaced it as the primary source of learning and information. Has it replaced the family? I suppose it depends on the family. There are still families so immersed in a set of values that they are passed on to the children almost unconsciously, and there are still some that make a conscious effort to instil particular values. For a growing number of kids in North America, however, it could be argued that their primary authority on values is media. If this is the case, just what are the values communicated?

Being Good is for Geeks and Nerds.

Lisa Simpson wins the award again as one of the few characters on TV who stands behind any kind of moral code. She is totally alone in her attempts to make the world a better place or critique her society. She is a victim of the postmodern age, when any truth-system is seen as relative and therefore open to ridicule. Since "the good" and "the true" can no longer be defined, only geeks and nerds would hold on to these antiquated notions. If being good is for them, then it follows that being bad must be for "cool" people.

Sadly, this is often the message. It is interesting that while there are no longer any valid definitions of goodness, badness is relatively easy to define. It sometimes seems as though the culture is still in rebellion against all forms of "should" from previous generations. Many of these "shoulds" (moral imperatives) were, in fact, arbitrary and sometimes just plain wrong, but the baby, it seems, has been thrown out with the bathwater. In an attempt to eradicate the silly and pointless "shoulds," all moral imperatives seem to have gone out the window. Western culture is engaged in a long process of redefining morality. All the juries are out, leaving young people with no moral compass to follow. What is right and what is wrong? These are profound moral questions for which the media has no answer.

Civil law has replaced moral law. We may not know the difference between right and wrong, but we do know the difference between legal and illegal. Police shows are reassuring to viewers in that the good guys and the bad guys, as defined by the law, are still identifiable. Larger questions about how to conduct one's life and the meaning of moral integrity have lost all their salience. I find teenagers extremely knowledgeable about the laws that apply to their age group. Senior high school law classes are very popular with students who want to know the rules.

Moral questions cannot be raised or debated without the spectre of religion raising its head — and religion, according to the media, is the ultimate comedy. Organized religion has become the antithesis of the liberal media. It is automatically seen as conservative or regressive, the refuge for those geeks and nerds still holding onto their fossilized ideologies of good and bad.

Everybody Is Secretly Bad

According to the media, there is a skeleton in every closet. Every public figure, from TV and movie stars to politicians, is fair game in the hunt for scandal. Media searches out a person's weaknesses and magnifies them out of all proportion to the person's strengths. Many great political leaders of the past would never have survived the harsh scrutiny of modern media. The private lives of all public figures have become fodder for entertainment.

If there is one thing kids need, it is people to look up to, on whom they can model themselves. I have heard it said that there is no such thing as learning; there is only copying. The process of growing up is in many ways one of copying the behaviour of those just ahead of you. While in the past it may have been unrealistic to put certain people on a pedestal, some kind of moral integrity or virtue usually led to their elevation. In current media, anyone, even the morally questionable, can be raised up for public adulation — or at least public attention. Fame is a kind of virtue. The parallel logic is found in capitalism, where wealth is associated with virtue. To be rich is to be good.

So, if everyone is secretly bad, then whatever I might not like in my own behaviour, I should embrace. It's cool to be bad and, apparently, there's really no need to change it.

What Gives You the Right to Judge?

This question is the default response for any kind of critique of mass media or popular culture. There are no moral yardsticks in this new world order. Every kind of behaviour is okay to somebody. One of the key words in the sentence, "What gives you the right to judge?" is *you*. What gives *you*, of all people, the right to judge? You are just one person, and surely your perceptions cannot be accurate. The term "mass media" implies something consumed by the masses and approved by them. If it's watched or consumed by millions, it must be right, and normal is whatever the majority believes it to be.

George Orwell claimed, "Sanity is not statistical," but in Media Land it is. The indirect message is, "Don't trust your own perceptions. Just accept the constructions of media and popular culture as they are." Learn to love Big Brother. Those who continue to question or judge what happens in media are simply seen as eccentric or conservative. In *Nineteen Eighty-Four*, Orwell wrote, "Being in a minority, even a minority of one, did not make you mad." Mass media has no interest in minority views unless they are being held up for ridicule. One of the most pervasive teachings of media is the directive to fit in. Whatever you do, don't stick out — people will think you are crazy.

Living in Media Land

Media studies classes in high school and post-secondary institutions used to be primarily about critiquing and "deconstructing" media. Today they are more about learning how it works and imitating its constructs. Students used to be interested in exposing the manipulations and biases; today, they simply accept them. Any attempts to "burst the bubble" created by corporate media are met with derision, even by the young people who are being manipulated.

The project of deconstructing media implied that there was a truer reality not being represented. For young people today, the distinction between Media Land and the real world has become blurred. The made-up world is in fact the real one in which most people spend their lives. One of the reasons environmental degradation continues apace is that young people have so little experience of nature. They are not sure what they would be losing. In Media Land there is no natural environment to harm. Nature happens outside. Politics happens outside (unless there's a juicy scandal). Media Land does not include anything too complex.

Viewer Discretion Advised

"Viewer discretion advised" does not mean exercise caution and possibly leave. It means what you are about to see will push some social or moral boundary, and you don't want to miss that because it's cool. One of the characteristics of addictive behaviour is that over time, it can take more and more of the mood-altering substance to create the same effect. This seems to be the case with media: more and more violence, more and more explicit sex, and more and more profanity. One wonders how far the boundary will move.

WHAT Is CHARACTER?

Jung talked about the process of "individuation." Abraham Maslow popularized the term "self-actualization." Both terms attempt to describe the process of becoming an individual, separate from the herd. It seems we start off life as individuals with no reference to the herd, and the process of growing up often means the process of conforming to it. Having character, then, means holding on to what is unique in yourself — not conforming completely. Conforming to social norms is an essential part of growing up, and the first half of life is often about achieving external definitions of success, but there comes a time when each person must ask himself whether he has remained true to himself. In *Hamlet*, Polonius admonishes his son, "To thine own self be true." The person with character is one who has remained true to himself. He has managed the balancing act between conforming to society and remaining a unique individual.

On my classroom wall, I have a quotation from e.e. cummings that I have carried with me since my first year of teaching. "To be nobody but yourself — in a world which is doing its best, night and day, to make you everybody else — means to fight the hardest battle which any human being can fight — and never stop fighting." I copied it when I began to realize how prone teachers were to the pressures of conformity. After all, we are in the "business" of getting kids to conform. While school claims to be developing the "whole person" and helping each student "realize his or her unique potential," this ideal is often sacrificed for the more pragmatic goal of getting everyone "on the same page" and coercing kids to "get with the program."

Teachers are particularly vulnerable to the pressure to conform. It is a very conservative profession. If we look into it, we find that school itself played a big part in making teachers that way. They are usually adults who liked school as children and readily conformed. It is important for teachers to be aware of this bias toward conformity, both for their own development as individuals, but also for the benefit of those kids who are not so willing to conform, those who don't fit in as well at school, who push back against our attempts to homogenize them.

The person with character is aware of the battle for selfhood, considers it worth fighting and fights it. He has a significant degree of self-knowledge and self-acceptance. He knows who he is and accepts it, but is also in the continual process of revising these perceptions. This person is open, not closed, alive, not dead, is in the process of becoming. Bob Dylan said, "He who is not busy being born is busy dying." The person with character is busy being born. He lives by a set of self-chosen principles, consciously or unconsciously. Some people are able to articulate their values and principles, others just live them. Both are legitimate and require inner work — reflection on experience.

The person with character is not afraid of being different, standing out in a crowd. He has looked into the mirror of his own soul and seen his inner truth, the good and the bad, conventional and unconventional. He is willing to own both, even though he might risk social rejection. For him, being true to oneself is more important than being accepted by others.

There are "standard procedures" for almost everything we do today — the right way, the cool way, the legal or "appropriate" way. The person with character knows what to do when there are no rules, policies, or procedures. Many people spend their entire lives living "by the book" without ever really questioning who wrote the rules or whether they make sense. The person with character examines the rules, questions their validity, discards some, and keeps others.

People can be motivated by fear of punishment or hope of reward. This is called "extrinsic motivation," doing or not doing things depending on outside forces. At other times, we can be motivated from within, knowing that a certain course of action is appropriate simply because it is right, and doing the right thing is its own reward. This is called "intrinsic motivation." The person with character is more likely to be motivated by inner imperatives rather than external coercion. In other words, he is harder to control. He has an internal locus of control. He believes he has personal agency, that what he does makes a difference in the world.

Many others believe that they are subjects of an external locus of control. They feel that the world around them has more power, and they are more passive in the face of external forces. "What can *I* do? That's just the way it is." These people are easier to control — they actually welcome it. When we put the responsibility for our lives "out there," it lets us off the hook. We no longer have to make hard personal choices. "That's just the way it is," leads to, "You can't do anything about it," and the sad motto, "Why bother?" People with character are bothered by things and set out to change them, even when the chances of success look slim. The attempt is just as important as the achievement; the journey is as important as the destination.

CAN CHARACTER BE TAUGHT?

Character Can Be Taught by Precept

There is much accumulated wisdom in the world about what constitutes character and how it can be achieved. I fear that this wisdom is not as widely disseminated as it perhaps once was. Institutional religions have always been the main purveyors of wisdom. The other main source of wisdom in Western culture is our literature, in which I include the great works of philosophy and, later, political philosophy and psychology. The oldest and most profound source, however, is our stories. Before the ancient philosophers, storytellers transmitted culture, including its wisdom.

One thing the most ancient stories share is the character of the hero who faces obstacles and overcomes them. The hero is the paradigm of the person with character. He draws on inner resources and welcomes external aids to accomplish a noble goal. He perseveres in the face of adversity, feeling fear and self-doubt but overcoming them. He is motivated from within by moral fortitude, and from without by a vision of right or good. The hero is our model for the person with character.

Kids need heroes. Several years ago I taught a young man in grade twelve, Aidan, who fell into a major depression just as he was heading off to university. It had been building for a while, but it was precisely at the moment he had to set off on his solitary quest — leaving a protective, close-knit family — that he found himself unable to cope. Aidan would sit in his basement and watch

David Lean's *Lawrence of Arabia* over and over again. He read *The Lord of the Rings* many times through. His room was piled high with books about medieval knights and the Crusades and fantasy novels of all kinds. The common denominator in all of them was the hero's quest.

Aidan revered Tolkien, and we read some of his literary theories together, particularly his 1936 essay, "The Monsters and the Critics." Here Tolkien talks about the northern concept of the hero as the one who perseveres even though he knows he is doomed. This idea provided the impetus for much discussion about Aidan's predicament. He could not "get motivated." He felt life was pointless, yet despite this apparent nihilism, he devoted himself to the study of these great heroic works. I believe Aidan was suffering from the malaise that afflicts many young males today: the loss of meaning. Viktor Frankl said that our suffering must have a meaning. Jung said it is meant to take us somewhere — perhaps to a new level of consciousness. Young people today suffer just as much as in past generations, but I think their suffering is exacerbated by its apparent pointlessness.

The hero who perseveres even though he knows he is doomed is motivated by a vision of right and good. He does what he *must* do. There is both an internal imperative to be faithful to his self and an external obligation to protect the common good. In the past, the matrix of family, religion, government, and culture all echoed this idea. The first sentence I learned to type in grade nine typing class has stuck with me all my life. I think it was used because it included lots of newly-learned letters: "Now is the time for all good men to come to the aid of the party." We typed this sentence over and over again.

Would such a sentence be used today? The situation was completely mundane, but this simple sentence points to a kind of social web where the reinforcement of particular ideas once existed. You can call it patriarchal, hierarchical, sexist, and manipulative, but it implied a worldview that permeated society: individual responsibility for the common good.

I do a lesson on art history in my grade twelve English class, and we look at one of the many images of St. George (or St. Michael) slaying the dragon. I tell the males that this image is as valid now as ever. We need brave young men who are willing to get up on their white horses and go out and slay the dragon. In the particular image I show, there is a woman kneeling and praying in the immediate background and a walled city in the distant background. "Why must the young man do this?" I ask. "For the sake of the woman and for the benefit of society."

While this may sound very old-fashioned, conservative, or even sexist, it is not in the least. The boys listen with rapt attention and a few giggle nervously. Why? Because they feel the frisson of truth. What is the modern truth that this image conveys? Young men need to be brave and strong and accept their responsibilities as citizens. They must prepare themselves for life in the modern world. That is the knight part. They must equip themselves with knowledge and skills that will be of use to the world and with which they can support themselves and a family. That is the white horse part.

They should honour the feminine principle within themselves (their feeling and emotional lives) and be responsible and respectful to the females in their lives. They should show commitment to the woman they take as a partner. That is the damsel part. Finally, they should work for the good of the whole community, not just their own self-interest. That is the city in the background part. What about the dragon? In the beginning it is fear and self-doubt and the vacuum of meaning. At each stage of life, the dragon changes. In youth it is slain every time a fear is faced and overcome. Ideally, the mature male is called to slay the dragons that plague us all — poverty, injustice, environmental degradation. There is no shortage of dragons, but there does seem to be a shortage of knights. Boys and young men need to be taught about their knightly potential.

Aidan needed to slay his first dragon, his fear and self-doubt. But first he needed to accept his role as questing hero. To do that, he needed to understand and feel that his life had a purpose beyond himself, and that others depended on him to "get his act together" and "go for it."

It took him another year or so to start moving forward. In the interim he read voraciously and kept watching *Lawrence of Arabia*. That was his process of preparation. One could call him lazy, but there is a mysterious alchemy in our lives that must be respected. It was a "stage" he had to go through, and none of us will ever know what inner dramas were played out. Perhaps there were some demons that needed to be slain first, the ones that hold us all back from being what we could be. I do believe, however, that in Aidan's particular case, it was the great stories that saved him, giving him signposts pointing out of the dark forest. I worry about the kids today who, instead of being raised on the great stories, are raised on a Walt Disney diet where suffering always leads to victory, triumphant music, and a standing ovation at the end. The northern hero described by Tolkien seldom gets his standing ovation. He sometimes dies in obscurity. His reward lies not in the adulation of the crowd but in the knowledge that he did the right thing, that he fought the good fight.

Character Is Taught by Example

Talk is cheap. Actions speak louder than words. The problem with precepts is they can just remain precepts — quotable quotes. Truth, wisdom, and goodness are most profoundly communicated when they are incarnated in the behaviour of an individual.

We do not reveal ourselves so much by what we say as by what we do. Humans are great imitators. It is a mystery to me why some will imitate the buffoon while others will copy the wise man. It must begin in youth with the first models we imitate, our parents. If they have character, if they are seeking to be better people living better lives, coming closer to the truth, then I think their children will pick up that pattern. People with character believe in the existence of an objective truth beyond our understanding that we are always striving to better understand.

Some people live according to a relative finite truth. They live in a moral bubble of their own making, and once the mental furniture is arranged, it never changes. We must provide our children with a dynamic model of life, not a fossilized one. What is the metaphor for our lives, a road we travel or a destination we reach? A problem to be solved or a mystery to be lived out? A series of hardships to be endured, or a fortifying process leading to greater challenges? The list could go on. For the person with character, the metaphor will always be an open system, not closed. It is this *process* that is conveyed or "taught."

Finally, the person with character is often "a character." We use this term tongue-in-cheek, with a bit of a smile, because we find these characters endearing. Why are we attracted to characters? Because they have a kind of freedom we envy. They seem to have transcended social norms and live according to their own nature, however eccentric that may be. The etymology of the word "eccentric" means "outside the centre." The centre represents what is "normal." The periphery represents what we call eccentric. We spend our lives rushing toward the middle of the circle, trying so hard to appear normal, and along the way we meet these individuals who have no interest in that goal, known in modern parlance as "the rat race." They are content to stand where they are and be who they are.

Bob Dylan once said, "All I can do is be me, whoever that is." The person with character follows the thread of who he or she is. When we meet these people, they make us stop in our tracks. They represent an alternative way of living. T.S. Eliot once wrote, "In a world of fugitives, the person taking the opposite direction will appear to be running away." I have always been interested in the fringe dwellers, the hermits, the recluses, and the oddballs. I see them in my school and in my town. They are important witnesses to the fact that there really is no one way to live. There are many ways of being a character and many ways of having character.

Father Mattice

I am very lucky in that I have been exposed to people with character. As a young boy, I used to go over to the school playground in the evening to ride my bike. Right next to the school was the parish rectory where Father Mattice lived. He would come out in the evening with his breviary, a thick prayer book containing what is called the Divine Office, a regimen of daily prayers and readings. He wore sandals with socks, drove a Volkswagen Beetle, and had a cottage outside of town where rumour had it he would lie in a hammock listening to Leonard Cohen songs through speakers he had hung in the trees.

I would watch him walk slowly back and forth with the book open in one hand in front of him. He seemed lost to this world, his attention focused on something profound. The image made a deep impression on me, a man devoting himself to things I could not see or understand. I wanted to see what he saw, to know what he was thinking about. I wanted to be like him. He was a man whose "lifestyle" included both the staid Catholic church he presided over and his own earthy personal existence. What made him impressive was the fact that he did not fit into any single category. He seemed to have created his own, one into which he fit quite nicely, not in a selfish way, but in one that benefited the whole community.

Father Mattice was much-loved by his congregation, not because he adhered to prescribed norms, but because he lived his life authentically. Even more powerful was the fact that he was able to do this in a "job" traditionally thought of as one of the most prescribed existences. One day Father Mattice pulled his Beetle off to the side of the road and died of a heart attack. His death was a huge loss to thousands. The community had lost a person with character who *was* a character. People with character tend to live on in the memory of those who learned from them.

Miss Patterson

Teachers, our stand-in parents, play one of the biggest roles in our young lives. If we are lucky, we might have one or two really memorable teachers, people who make a deep and lasting impression on us, who mould us and become models of behaviour that we imitate in future life.

One such teacher for me was Miss Patterson, my grade thirteen English teacher. She was very short and stocky and shuffled around the school in Wallabees. She always wore pants and a blouse covered by a patterned woollen crew neck sweater. She looked round and cuddly like a little teddy bear, but that effect ended with her face, which always wore a stern expression of grim indifference to her surroundings. Once in class, however, this persona disappeared completely. She became a relaxed, intelligent, articulate woman who had a passion for what she was talking about and for conveying it to young people. She had a comfort with great literature that I found so attractive. I wanted to feel what she felt and know what she knew, to see through her eyes when she looked at art or the world around her.

She was one of the first people in my life to raise the issue of consciousness. Watching her, I came to realize that people have different levels of consciousness, and there seemed to be some connection between that and education. The more you know, the more you realize how much you don't. Education teaches you confidence and humility at the same time. That is what Miss Patterson had, confidence and humility. I think she was a very shy person. She lived with her mother and had never married. Externally, her life was quite plain. But when she spoke, she revealed a very rich inner world.

Like Father Mattice looking into his breviary, when Sheila Patterson looked into the novel in her hand, she was seeing something beyond the literal meaning of the text. I wanted to see what Father Mattice and Miss Patterson were looking at or perhaps searching for. Neither was very interested in the material world; possessions, status, and power were not important to these two.

Sheila Patterson was a person with character. I don't remember any particular words she said, I just remember her *way* of being.

Jean Vanier

When I was sixteen and bored with grade eleven, I read Jean Vanier's book *Eruption to Hope*. This was one of those books that came at just the right time. I felt like the world had opened up, and someone was finally addressing the bigger issues of life. I read about his work at L'Arche, a community in France where volunteers live and work with the developmentally disabled. I decided to take a step outside the small box that my family, school, church, and town had become. I wrote a letter to Vanier in France asking if I could visit his community and see it first-hand. To my great surprise, I received a response from the director in Troly-Breuil. She told me Jean had passed my letter on to her, and I was welcome to come. What I saw at L'Arche changed me forever.

We live in a society that ranks everyone according to intelligence, income, appearances, and power. At L'Arche I saw a community where people made a sincere effort to avoid all such distinctions. There was a real attempt being made among the people there to relate as equals. There was a radical atmosphere of acceptance. What made this possible, I think, was the presence of the developmentally disabled, who stood as a constant challenge to societal yardsticks of respectability and normalcy. The developmentally disabled people I met there were incapable of social pretense. They had to be accepted just as they were, and they accepted you in the same way. They were not interested in the yardsticks one might use to measure a person, except perhaps one: "Is this person kind? Is this person capable of showing love and receiving love?" This was one of the most profound experiences of radical love that I have ever had before or since.

The community revolved around the charisma of Jean Vanier, who lived this radical acceptance every moment. He had such a peaceful and loving manner that one could not help but be drawn to him. Part of the attraction lay in a desire to receive some of that peace and love. The other part was the desire to pick up his resonance, his frequency, just by being in his presence, to see things the way he sees them. To experience something of his *way of being*.

Vanier had the added gift of being a beautiful speaker. He was able to articulate and convey his vision through words. He taught character by example and by precept — words of wisdom. Once a week he would hold a talk for all the volunteers and staff of L'Arche. I remember being in a large room with everyone mingling and talking. There was a great sense of excitement and anticipation. Jean was simply one of those in the crowd. Then he went and sat on a stool in the middle of the room, and everyone slowly went quiet. We sat down and settled ourselves to listen. In our modern, cynical age, this might sound cultish or Hollywood. Having been there and seen it for myself, I can only say this was not the cult of personality. Whatever the focus was, it was not Jean Vanier. There was something deeper. As Father Mattice and Miss Patterson looked beyond this world to a deeper reality, so did Vanier. He had done the lonely work of tending his inner garden, and the fruit was his way of being and his words. He wasn't talking about himself; he related what he had learned and was still learning from his way of being, from his experiment of L'Arche, and from the people he met in the community. He was speaking as a person with character.

Vanier talks a lot about our woundedness and weakness, and about the strength that comes from an acknowledgement of these two things. People with character are often those who have been wounded themselves, but have not let it debilitate them. They almost always have great weaknesses that make them more empathetic to the weaknesses of others and more willing to reach out to the wounded or weak. A person with character is often a wounded healer.

The NATURE of CHARACTER

Integrity

As we go through life, we wear many faces. In adolescence, in particular, we try on many different identities. This is phase-appropriate. We are in the process of becoming the person we would like to be, apart from the identity of childhood, which was, for the most part, quite unselfconscious. One of the goals of life is to get the number of faces back down to one. We have an expression for people who are phoney or insincere; "two-faced." Some people are five-faced or ten-faced.

In *To Kill a Mockingbird*, Miss Maudie tells Atticus's two children, Scout and Jem, that what makes Atticus so unique is that he is the same person on the streets as he is in the house. The person with one face has integrity. All of the character traits that make up that person have been *integrated*. "What you see is what you get. I am who I am. I am comfortable with myself, and I don't *need* you to like me. Being true to myself comes before social acceptance or external approval."

When a person lives with integrity, there is no discrepancy between what they say and do. The person has *integrated* their values so completely that they are incapable of insincerity. Again, in *To Kill a Mockingbird*, Atticus's sister, Aunt Alexandra, asks him to speak to the children about their behaviour, especially their association with a poor boy. She wants him to remind the children that they come from superior stock and it is unseemly for them to be behaving so liberally and associating with the lower classes. Atticus tries to have this conversation with the children. They become nervous because they know this is not their father speaking. Finally, Atticus is unable to sustain this false face and tells the kids to forget everything he just said. When a person has integrity, false words stick in their throat. In *Fugitive Pieces*, Anne Michaels pays tribute to the people who helped Jews during the Holocaust. "Again and again they give us the same explanation for their heroism: 'What choice did I have?'" For the person with integrity, there is no choice. One must act according to one's values.

Our kids need to be exposed to people with integrity and see that it is possible to have one face, especially teenagers who worry that their identity might always be as fragmented as it is now. Teenagers are not moved by sermons, but they do notice ways of being. They are keenly aware of the hypocritical adult because they are so aware of their own hypocrisy, a necessary and natural state that comes from being so fragmented, so confused about identity and values. They want to know that this confusion will pass, that it is possible to live an integrated life with their actions equalling their words.

Empathy

The person with character is able to leave his own point of view and put himself in that of another. This leads to a greater understanding, and, if taken all the way, it means feeling what the other person feels. Empathy is not just an intellectual exercise; it is emotional. It is experienced not in the head but in the heart. It creates an invisible bond. The one empathizing feels a connection, and the one being empathized with feels that the other person understands on more than just an intellectual level. Empathy is communicated beyond words. One can say, "I understand how you're feeling," or, "I feel for you," but the person on the receiving end may not feel an authentic connection at all.

Everyone's spirit vibrates at a certain frequency. Empathy is the ability to synchronize your own frequency with that of another person. When this kind of simpatico happens, communication takes place beyond words. It is one of the most healing forms of communication: to be seen, listened to, and understood.

Moderation

We live in a culture of excess. This is a by-product of a consumer culture. Our economy is based on buying things. The wealth and health of a country is measured by GDP (Gross Domestic Product) or, in other words, how much "stuff" is made. Individuals measure their own wealth and success by how much of this stuff they have and the quality of it — well, not really the quality, just the perceived quality of the brand names and the prestige that they bring. We are heavily influenced by marketing and advertising to believe certain objects carry more value than others. It is all an illusion; one we all buy into. Many people define themselves by externals like what they own and where they live. As a result, their inner life withers. Every stone used to build the exterior castle is one taken from the interior castle. In addition to material immoderation, we can also lack moderation in our activities — working, drinking, and eating to excess.

We are taught by advertisers to believe that more, bigger, and more expensive are better. There is no voice in our culture advocating moderation. The ancient Greek philosophers and the theologians of the Middle Ages taught the importance of moderation, which implies self-control or self-regulation. We decide how much of some thing or some activity is good for us. How do we decide how much is too much? Does it get in the way of our health, the clarity of our thinking, or our freedom? Does it damage the quality of our relationships? If the answer to any of these questions is "yes," then perhaps we are not practicing moderation in a certain area.

The person with character practices moderation. He is not controlled by his passions and appetites — he has control over them. We are still recovering from centuries of religious repression of the passions and appetites, so any talk of controlling them is seen as regressive. The maxims, "If it feels good, do it," or, "Just do it," have replaced teachings about moderation. We will have to develop a new ethos around moderation based on criteria like physical and mental health rather than the outmoded concept of whether it pleases or angers a patriarchal God.

Respect

Respect is at the opposite end of the spectrum from bullying. Bullying demonstrates a total lack of respect for the other person and is always motivated by a desire to make the bully feel more powerful and more in control. Bullying is all about *me*. Respect, on the other hand, is characterized by a willingness to acknowledge the value and integrity of the other person. Respect is an attitude that sees other points of view, indeed their very existence, as equal in value to one's own. It can be clearly felt by the person on the receiving end. In my experience with young people, respect is one of the most powerful ways of forming a personal connection. It is closely related to empathy, but then there must be an added element of deep regard for the feelings of others.

I see a lot of false respect between adults and children. Teenagers, in particular, are very good at showing it to adults. They have learned that this is what adults like, that it feeds their egos and, most importantly, it will get the teen what he wants or help him avoid getting what he doesn't. Kids learn this hypocrisy (as with most things) from adults who do the same thing. In reality, it is not true respect but rather a sort of "lip service," and they use it when it suits them. When a teacher says, "You need to take off that hat, please. [pause] Thank you," the words please and thank you are often emphasized as the all-important currency that will buy compliance. If the young person shows any resistance, the adult can fall back on the claim, "I asked you nicely." Respect then becomes a kind of false dance in which each party is playing a role to achieve their private ends. The difference between respect and this type of lip service is so subtle that it does not reveal itself in words but in tone.

If respect is based on the idea that "we are equal," or "we have equal value," this can be a difficult concept for adults dealing with children. There is still something in the hard drive of Western culture that says children are lesser beings. Teenagers are included, and the attitude is directed perhaps even more strongly toward them. The notion of respecting a teenager as of equal value can be a difficult pill for some adults to swallow. As teens will easily testify, their demographic is one of the most discriminated against.

When we talk about "equal," we do not mean "the same as," nor do we mean having the same status in the social pecking order. In that sense a student is not equal to a teacher or a principal. But when we are talking about respect, it is the existential level of being where the value of your existence is equal to mine. Kids can feel when they are respected and, in my experience, they rise to higher levels of behaviour. Respect is given when it is shown.

Love

Jesus said, "Love your neighbour as you love yourself." He makes a huge assumption in this sentence: that people love themselves. I see so many people who do not. Why is self-hatred and self-contempt so prevalent? It comes out in the voices in peoples' heads: "How could you be so stupid?" "You're such an idiot!"

Where does this programming come from? From parents and school mainly, from judgmental authority figures we've encountered who may not have spoken these exact sentences, but these were the messages conveyed by their tone. These voices and attitudes became embedded in our consciousness, and they make it hard for us to love ourselves.

The person with character has silenced those voices and has a degree of self-acceptance. "I am who I am. I accept who I am. I love who I am." It is reassuring to be around someone like this, because we see that such a condition is possible. Self-contempt and insecurity are not the only possibility, and it is possible to love one's own self.

The Greeks had several words for love: *eros*, having an erotic aspect, *philia*, which meant friendship, and *agape*. Thomas Cahill translates *agape* as "affectionate kindness." He notes that *agape* was the word early Jewish translators chose for the Hebrew *ahava* when translating the line, "Love your neighbour as yourself." Kindness is a great synonym for love. Love has more to do with feeling, whereas kindness is a word that conjures up actions: "Be kind to yourself. Be kind to others." It is something that is shown.

"The greatest wisdom is kindness." This saying has been attributed to the Talmud and to the Greek Stoic philosopher Epictetus. It has probably been uttered intuitively by many wise people over the centuries. If there is one common denominator in people with character, it is kindness. There is always a sense of love and respect for the individual apart from anything that person may have said or done.

Our boys need to be taught and shown this kind of love. They are growing up in a culture where the concept of love has become almost completely sexualized. Following close behind is the idea that love and sex are related to power and control. One uses sex to get love and uses love to get sex. They become "capital" in relationships. The notion of love as self-sacrifice, giving of oneself to another, is seen as putting oneself in a position of weakness. Love and sex have nothing to do with vulnerability or with opening oneself up to another in trust.

Love, as a concept, has also become feminized. In popular culture, women are depicted as obsessed with love and men as obsessed with sex. Males reject thoughts and words of love as soft or weak or feminine.

Boys first learn how to love from their mothers. The nurturing and caring they receive will become a template for all future capacity to love and nurture. Boys who have been generously loved in childhood will be better lovers in adulthood. When they reach adolescence, they learn how to love from other men. During this time of transition from attachment to the mother and attempting to define oneself as a man, boys look to other men as role models. They want to see how it's done. The way Dad shows love toward Mom and his children will become the next template the boy applies to his own relationships. In addition to the father, the boy will look for other male role models — relatives, neighbours, friends of his parents, and teachers. The most powerful models he will encounter may be those presented in media.

When our children are young, we can control their media diet to a great extent. We can ensure that they see images of love that emphasize commitment and self-giving. As they grow older, we lose this control, and images of male love that emphasize dominance and control and sex as the singular expression of love begin to take over. We have to silently trust that the foundational template laid down in infancy and childhood will persist and that this foundation will reassert itself in the young man's life.

We also have to talk to our sons about the one-dimensional, stereo-typical images they see in media. This is a particularly important role for men. When a boy is learning how to be a man, he is much more likely to listen to another man, especially one he respects. I worked with a nine-year-old who had accidentally seen some pornographic images on the Internet. Of course, they made a deep impression on his young psyche. He was a particularly intelligent and articulate boy, and when he told me what had happened, he asked very calmly and clearly, "What is the connection between sex and love?"

He was able to intuit that the images had nothing to do with love. At a very young age, he had articulated a question many boys have. They need our help deconstructing this hyper-sexualized culture. Sexual images are very concrete, and love is much harder to depict visually. Boys learn love from being loved by their mothers, fathers, sisters, and brothers, and by extended family. Later they learn it from friends and other adults. Eventually a boy will turn to a particular person with thoughts of sexual love, and he will know how to connect sex and love to the extent that he has been loved.

Humility

Before we can truly love others, we have to love ourselves. Again, this sentence smacks of vanity or arrogance — self-love is seen as narcissistic. Many of us were raised with a notion of false humility, that the virtuous person, the humble person, is someone who speaks in negative terms about himself. "Oh, I'm not very good at that. Oh, I could have done better."

Thomas Merton said, "Humility is truth." This is a much healthier definition. We all have shortcomings, and we are better off when we know what they are and acknowledge them, but we also have gifts and positive attributes, and we are richer and wiser and better people when we live them out with confidence. Denying or downplaying our gifts does no one any good, least of all ourselves.

Acceptance

One of my greatest lessons in acceptance came when my son, Justin, wanted to get his hair cut into a "mohawk." Justin is one of the most intelligent, principled, grounded kids I know. I trust and respect him completely. He was about sixteen at the time and had done a fair bit of research on the punk movement of the 1970s. Whatever his reasons were for wanting the cut, he asked me if it was okay to get it, and I said sure, never believing he would actually go through with it. I thought he just wanted to gauge my reaction. One day I came home from work, and there it was, a razor-thin ridge of hair right down the middle of his scalp and each side shaved bald to the skin. I was shocked! My immediate response was, "Good for you, Justin. I'm amazed you have the confidence to go out in public like that." I didn't mean this sarcastically. Justin was not attention-seeking or disturbed in some way. He wanted to do this on principle. It was his way of subverting the conformity of his culture, and I was proud of him for having the courage to go against the herd, especially when he knew that this haircut held negative associations for many people.

The lesson about judgment came when I saw how people responded to him. We were at a mall one day, and I was shocked by the looks of disgust and horror and fear on the faces of those we passed. Some even seemed to convey hatred. Here was my wonderful son, who suddenly, because of a haircut, had become the object of other people's negative judgments.

Listen to people's conversations and ask yourself how much time is being given to statements of judgment. We spend so much time judging things that don't need to be judged and any judgment we do pass makes no difference. If we were to take all of the energy we spend on judging and put it into acceptance, our lives would open up.

Children and teenagers, while they may be extremely judgmental themselves, respond incredibly to acceptance. Young people deal with so many judgments from parents, teachers, and peers, but most of all from themselves. They live under the constant threat of not measuring up or not conforming to some unwritten rule of fashion or behaviour. When they feel they are not being judged, they will let their guard down and reveal themselves. I work with many kids who have been diagnosed with some kind of learning disability or exceptionality. They feel very judged as a result. In our sessions, I like to think I accept them as they are and do not try to change them into something their parents or the school system would like them to be.

Children must have their true selves mirrored and affirmed and their true voices listened to. We all have a vision of how we would like our children to be, and sometimes it is totally out of sync with who they actually are. I have seen this over and over again in parents who have either an idealized vision of their child or a corrupted one. We need to do the soul-searching it takes for us let go of our own judgments, which are more about ourselves than our children.

Involvement

The person with character is not detached from the world, standing aloof from it. He knows what is going on locally, nationally, and internationally. This is such an important stance for our kids to witness, and later copy. Being involved in the world means being aware and actively participating in public affairs. This teaches children a sense of communal belonging. In our narcissistic culture, it is easy to retreat inside our sterile little bubble and not concern ourselves about the affairs of the world. This egocentric stance is not the one we want to pass on. It is in others that we are complete. Engagement in the world enriches who we are as individuals.

Mass media has made this task much more difficult. Today we suffer from information overload, and many people simply shut out the world because the problems just seem too overwhelming. "What can I do? It's all too depressing." People stop following the news and don't want their children exposed to it. We cannot shield our kids completely from the harsh realities of the world, but we can act as a filter for what does get in, and some things *should*. Kids need to know both the good and the bad, but unfortunately the media tends to emphasize the bad.

We used to take our kids to Dr. Simone's Canadian Food for Children warehouse. Here they would help load shipping containers headed for developing countries. My father used to make up the Christmas hampers for the St. Vincent de Paul Society in our parish. We would help divide up the donated food into boxes. These are the kinds of projects that can help a child understand the problems in the world in a positive way. That sounds like a contradiction, but it's not. Kids know that suffering exists. What they need is a channel to react to that knowledge, to do something about it; otherwise, they feel helpless, and helplessness leads to feelings of passivity and despair.

Hope

This leads to the next characteristic of the person with character. He has hope. Our kids do not need to hear that the world is going to the dogs, that things are much worse now than they were before. In some ways this may be true, but in many ways it's not at all. It's the only world our kids have, and to tell them it's doomed is a terrible disservice. They need to see the future in positive terms, because it's their only future. They need to believe in the possibilities of the future because they are the ones who will make those possibilities come true.

Orwell, in *Nineteen Eighty-Four*, made a great effort to demonstrate the importance of knowing history. This was not because of some conservative agenda to make kids aware of the accomplishments of their elders. Rather, Orwell believed that all history taught one great lesson: things change. The way things are now is not the way they've always been and not the way they need to be in the future. Change has occurred and will again because of the efforts of individuals who took it upon themselves to work for social change. This is a very hopeful message. In the novel, the Party (Orwell's embodiment of all systems of control) indoctrinated its citizens with the idea that the way things are now is the way they've always been. They have never been better and cannot get better. You live at the pinnacle of history, and the status quo must be preserved at all cost. We live in an eternal present where the Party is always right.

In the system of social control under which we live, the Party is corporate capitalism. It is our given, the water in which we swim. Participation in such a culture requires unconsciousness. The person who is engaged in the world, who works for social change, is a conscious one who is motivated by hope.

Courage

In addition to having hope, the person who is involved in the world must have the courage to persevere in the face of adversity. Doing the right thing is not always easy. There are powerful forces at work that do not want to see social change, and these forces benefit from the status quo. To stand up to them requires strength and conviction. In *To Kill a Mockingbird*, the Finch children see their father, Atticus, as a weak man. He's just a lawyer who does a lot of talking every day in the courthouse. One day a rabid dog appears on the street, and surprisingly, Atticus is able to kill it with one shot. Jem, Atticus's son, is particularly impressed. Later in the novel, Atticus has Jem read to a Mrs. Dubose, who is near death and wants to die free of her morphine addiction. After Mrs. Dubose's death, Jem asks why his dad made him do that. Atticus responds, "I wanted you to see what real courage is, instead of getting the idea that courage is a man with a gun in his hand." For many boys, the image of a man with a gun has become the picture of courage. This is a sad state of affairs.

Our modern word "courage" comes from a Latin root, *cor*, meaning heart. *Corage* was an Old French word originating in the twelfth or thirteenth century before it became the English word courage, a synonym for bravery. Today, we equate the heart with love, not bravery. But we still believe the heart to be the place where strong feelings originate. It is the source of emotion. It is our deep core, the origin of profound conviction. The man with courage is a man with heart. This connection between courage and feeling has to be revived. The word first came into use during the time of the chivalrous knight, the male hero we talked about earlier, who mounted his horse to ride off in defence of the kingdom or the damsel in distress. Today the kingdom needs defending more than ever, and it's not just damsels who are in distress. The courageous knight, the man with heart, is steadfast in the face of adversity because he is motivated by the most powerful emotion he possesses: love.

On BEING a "GOOD PARENT"

My mother used to say, "No one sets out to be a bad parent. We all think that what we are doing is the best thing." What complicates the picture is that the world keeps changing. Our children are growing up in a very different world. We must make an imaginative leap into their world and see things from their point of view. What is it like to grow up online? To grow up without nature? To grow up in a sexualized culture? These are the kinds of questions this book has attempted to answer. Their world is not better or worse than the world we grew up in. It is just different: a new kind of world. Some things have gotten worse; some have gotten better. We should be thankful for the things that are better and help them to deal with the things that are worse.

We cannot change the world, at least not tomorrow, and we cannot change who our children are. The one thing we *can* change is ourselves, and that includes the way we raise our children. This change will not come about through the external application of tricks and tips. There are simply too many possible situations. Changes in parenting practices come about as a result of understanding. The more we understand about this new kind of world and the influence it is having on our kids, the better able we will be to respond to particular situations. A good parent is one who knows what to do when there are no rules!

ADVICE
to
FATHERS

One of the saddest things I have witnessed in the past twenty or thirty years is the loss of the father in North American culture. On more occasions than I would like to admit, I have had to say, "I am embarrassed for my gender." I have watched boys grow up in single-mother homes and get into all kinds of trouble while Dad did almost nothing to help. I have watched these mothers trying to raise sons on their own, only to be abused and later abandoned by those same sons. I fear for the future of fathering, as there are so few men modelling what a good father should be.

If you had good modelling from your own father, then copy it. If you didn't, then ask yourself what kind of father you wish you'd had, and *be* that kind of father. What did you need? Give your son that. What kinds of things do you wish your dad had done with you or for you? Do those things. We can learn as much from poor modelling as we can from good.

If you don't know what to do or how to act or what to say, just sit down on the floor. The kids will take care of the rest. The most important thing is just to be there.

BIBLIOGRAPHY

Amen, Daniel. *Healing ADD: The Breakthrough Program that Allows You to See and Heal the 6 Types of Attention Deficit Disorder.* New York: Berkley Books, 2001.

Aron, Elaine. *The Highly Sensitive Person.* New York: Broadway Books, 1996.

Barkley, Russell and Arthur Robin. *Your Defiant Teen.* New York: Guilford Press, 2008.

Barkley, Russell and Christine Benton. *Your Defiant Child.* New York: Guilford Press, 1998.

Baron-Cohen, Simon. *The Essential Difference: Male and Female Brains and the Truth About Autism.* New York: Basic Books, 2003.

Bly, Robert. *Iron John: A Book About Men.* New York: Vintage Press, 1992.

Brizendine, Louann. *The Male Brain.* New York: Three Rivers Press, 2010.

Coloroso, Barbara. *The Bully, the Bullied and the Bystander: From Pre-School to High School — How Parents and Teachers Can Help Break the Cycle of Violence.* Toronto: Harper Collins, 2002.

Coloroso, Barbara. *Kids Are Worth It! Giving Your Child the Gift of Inner Discipline*. Toronto: Penguin Books, 2001.

Corneau, Guy. *Absent Fathers, Lost Sons*. Boston: Shambhala, 1991.

Crenshaw, Dave. *The Myth of Multitasking: How "Doing It All" Gets Nothing Done*. San Francisco: Jossey Bass, 2008.

Diamond, Jed. *The Irritable Male Syndrome*. Emmaus, PA: Rodale, 2005.

Dodes, Lance. *The Heart of Addiction: A New Approach to Understanding and Managing Alcoholism and Other Addictive Behaviours*. New York: HarperCollins, 2002.

Faludi, Susan. *Backlash: The Undeclared War Against American Women*. New York: Three Rivers Press, 2006.

Fox, Matthew. *Original Blessing*. New York: Tarcher/Putnam, 2000.

Frankl, Viktor. *Man's Search for Meaning*. Boston: Beacon Press, 2006.

Freire, Paulo. *Pedagogy of the Oppressed*. New York: Continuum, 1984.

Green, Ross. *The Explosive Child*. New York: HarperCollins, 2005.

Gurian, Michael. *Boys and Girls Learn Differently: A Guide for Teachers and Parents*. New York: Jossey-Bass, 2001.

Gurian, Michael. *The Boys and Girls Learn Differently Action Guide for Teachers*. San Francisco: Jossey-Bass, 2003.

Gurian, Michael. *The Minds of Boys: Saving Our Sons from Falling Behind in School and Life*. New York: Jossey-Bass, 2005.

Gurian, Michael. *The Wonder of Boys: What Parents, Mentors and Educators Can Do To Shape Boys Into Exceptional Men*. New York: Tarcher/Putnam, 1997.

Gurian, Michael. *A Fine Young Man*. New York: Tarcher/Putnam, 1999.

Hallowell, Edward and John Ratey. *Delivered From Distraction: Getting the Most out of Life with Attention Deficit Disorder*. New York: Ballantine Books, 2006.

Hallowell, Edward and John Ratey. *Driven to Distraction: Recognizing and Coping with Attention Deficit Disorder from Childhood through Adulthood*. New York: Simon and Schuster, 1995.

Hartmann, Thom. *Attention Deficit Disorder: A Different Perception*. Grass Valley, CA: Underwood Books, 1997.

Hillman, James. *The Soul's Code: In Search of Character and Calling*. New York: Warner Books, 1997.

Hollis, James. *Castration and Male Rage: The Phallic Wound*. Toronto: Inner City Books, 1991.

Hollis, James. *The Middle Passage: From Misery to Meaning in Midlife*. Toronto: Inner City Books, 1993.

Hollis, James. *Under Saturn's Shadow: The Wounding and Healing of Men*. Toronto: Inner City Books, 1994.

Holt, John. *How Children Fail*. Toronto: Pitman Publishing, 1968.

Ignatieff, Michael. *The Rights Revolution*. Toronto: House of Anansi Press, 2007.

Illich, Ivan. *Deschooling Society*. New York: Penguin, 1973.

Jackson, Graham. *The Living Room Mysteries: Patterns of Male Intimacy Book 2*. Toronto: Inner City Books, 1993.

Jackson, Graham. *The Secret Lore of Gardening: Patterns of Male Intimacy*. Toronto: Inner City Books, 1991.

Johnson, Robert. *He: Understanding Masculine Psychology.* Toronto: Harper and Row, 1989.

Johnson, Steven. "This Is Your Brain On Video Games." *Discover.* July 9, 2007.

Levine, Mel. *A Mind At a Time.* New York: Simon and Schuster, 2002.

Levy, Ariel. *Female Chauvinist Pigs: Women and the Rise of Raunch Culture.* New York: Simon and Schuster, 2005.

Louv, Richard. *Last Child in the Woods: Saving Our Children from Nature-Deficit Disorder.* New York: Workman Publishing, 2008.

Lowen, Alexander. *Narcissism: Denial of the True Self.* New York: Touchstone, 1997.

Mallinger, Allan and Jeannette DeWyze. *Too Perfect: When Being in Control Gets Out of Control.* New York: Fawcett Columbine, 1992.

Maté, Gabor. *In The Realm of Hungry Ghosts: Close Encounters with Addiction.* Toronto: Knopf Canada, 2008.

Maté, Gabor. *Scattered Minds: A New Look at the Origins and Healing of Attention Deficit Disorder* .Toronto: Vintage Canada, 2000.

Meade, Michael. *Men and the Water of Life: Initiation and the Tempering of Men.* Toronto: HarperCollins, 1993.

Miller, Alice. *For Your Own Good: Hidden Cruelty in Child-Rearing and the Roots of Violence.* New York: Farrar, Straus and Giroux, 2000.

Miller, Alice. *The Body Never Lies: The Lingering Effects of Cruel Parenting.* New York: W.W. Norton and Company, 2005.

Miller, Alice. *The Drama of the Gifted Child: The Search for the True Self.* New York: Basic Books, 1997.

Miller, Alice. *The Truth Will Set You Free: Overcoming Emotional Blindness and Finding Your True Adult Self*. New York: Basic Books, 2001.

Miller, Alice. *The Untouched Key: Tracing Childhood Trauma in Creativity and Destructiveness*. Toronto: Anchor Books, 1991.

Miller, Alice. *Thou Shalt Not Be Aware: Society's Betrayal of the Child*. New York: Meridian, 1990.

Montessori, Maria. *The Secret of Childhood*. New York: Ballantine, 1966.

Neill, A.S. *Freedom, Not License!* New York: Hart Publishing, 1966.

Neill, A.S. *Summerhill: A Radical Approach to Child Rearing*. New York: Hart Publishing, 1964.

Ontario Ministry of Education. *Me Read? No Way!* Toronto: Queen's Printer for Ontario, 2004.

Parsons, Les. *Bullied Teacher: Bullied Student*. Markham: Pembroke, 2005.

Pollack, William. *Real Boys: Rescuing Our Sons from the Myths of Boyhood*. Toronto: Random House, 1998.

Pollack, William. *Real Boys' Voices*. Toronto: Penguin, 2000.

Pollack, William. *Real Boys Workbook: The Definitive Guide to Understanding and Interacting with Boys of All Ages*. Toronto: Random House, 2001.

Postman, Neil. *The Disappearance of Childhood*. New York: Vintage Books, 1994.

Postman, Neil and Charles Weingartner. *Teaching As a Subversive Activity*. New York: Dell Publishing, 1969.

Postman, Neil. *Teaching As a Conserving Activity*. New York: Dell Publishing, 1979.

Rao, Anthony. *The Way of Boys: Raising Healthy Boys in a Challenging and Complex World*. New York: HarperCollins, 2009.

Real, Terrence. *I Don't Want to Talk About It: Overcoming the Secret Legacy of Male Depression*. Toronto: Scribner, 2003.

Reist, Michael. *The Dysfunctional School*. Philadelphia: Xlibris Books, 2007.

Sax, Leonard. *Boys Adrift: The Five Factors Driving the Growing Epidemic of Unmotivated Boys and Underachieving Young Men*. New York: Basic Books, 2007.

Sax, Leonard. *Why Gender Matters: What Parents and Teachers Need to Know About the Emerging Science of Sex Differences*. Toronto: Doubleday, 2005.

Spence, Christopher. *The Joys of Teaching Boys*. Markham: Pembroke Publishers, 2008.

Stein, Janice Gross. *The Cult of Efficiency*. Toronto: House of Anansi Press, 2002.

Strauch, Barbara. *The Primal Teen: What the New Discoveries About the Teenage Brain Tell Us About Our Kids*. Toronto: Doubleday, 2003.

Taffel, Ron. *Getting Through to Difficult Kids and Parents: Uncommon Sense for Child Professionals*. New York: Guilford Press, 2001.

Terr, Lenore. *Too Scared To Cry: How Trauma Affects Children and Ultimately Us All*. New York: Basic Books, 1990.

Wolf, Naomi. *The Beauty Myth: How Images of Beauty are Used Against Women*. New York: HarperCollins, 2002.

INDEX

abstract thinking, 57–58

ADD, 28–30, 55, 63–64, 78–79, 87–102, 103, 183

Aesop, 234

age-mixing, 39, 51–52

"aggression nurturance," 75

alcohol, 96–97, 132, 144, 147–48, 205, 227, 285

"Alexithymia," 146

American Pediatric Association, 139

"Animal House" syndrome, 227

Aron, Elaine, 136

attention span, 23, 28–30, 63, 93, 179–80

"automatic thoughts," 254

Baby Boom, 34, 88

Backlash: The Undeclared War Against Women, 19–20, 140

Bart Simpson Syndrome, 140–41

Beauty Myth, The, 140

Bly, Robert, 142

boundaries, 36–37, 48, 56–57, 76, 134, 135, 138, 171, 199, 225, 226

Boys Adrift, 50

Boys and Girls Learn Differently, 66–67, 73

bullying as peer initiation, 132–33

Cahill, Thomas, 288

Campbell, Joseph, 29

Canadian Food for Children, 292

"chunking," 83

Cider House Rules, The, 260

cognitive behavioural therapy, 254

Coloroso, Barbara, 48, 82, 129, 205, 225, 226, 261

competition, 34, 52, 69, 106–07, 114, 153–54, 180–81, 239

conditional love, 221–23

conscious parents, 213–14

Convention on the Rights of the Child, 236

corpus callosum, 77

credentialism, 180–82

Crenshaw, Dave, 31

cueing, 74

Cult of Efficiency, 37–38

cursive writing, 53, 122

cutting, 144, 146–47

cyberbullying, 160–61

Danish cartoonist, 15

December babies, 51

Delivered From Distraction, 63

Disappearance of Childhood, 16–18

disciplining a boy, 69–70

distractibility, 85, 87, 88–89, 98–100, 115

dopamine and video games, 103, 186–87

Dylan, Bob, 270, 277

Dysfunctional School, The, 41

Eliot, T.S., 277

empathy, 42, 121–22, 150–51, 175, 246, 284–85, 286

EQAO, 58–60

Eruption to Hope, 280
evolutionary biologists, 61, 73
exercise, 103–04, 113–14, 180
expressive language, 65–66, 125–26, 245
external locus of control, 225, 249, 271
extrovert, 136, 137
eye contact, 55, 65, 71, 74, 75, 84–85,
    107, 127, 149, 169, 170

Facebook, 25, 33, 160, 185, 195, 197,
    198–99
factory school, 34, 88, 141, 165, 188
Faludi, Susan, 19, 140
Family Guy, 14–16
"father hunger," 135
"feeling stones," 101–02
Female Chauvinist Pigs, 140
Fine Young Man, A, 143
Fox, Matthew, 255
Frankl, Viktor, 27, 274
"free range" children, 216
Freedom — Not License!, 235, 236
From Me to We, 151
Fugitive Pieces, 284

Gaia Hypothesis, 22
Girl Power, 141
God, new images of, 14–16, 18–22
Goldstein, Sam, 260
Grand Theft Auto, 206
graphomotor skills, 53, 103, 123–24
guilt, 229, 261
Gurian, Michael, 66–67, 73, 75, 143
Gutenberg, 24, 87–88

Hallowell, Edward, 63, 94
Halo, 206
Hamlet, 269
Hartmann, Thom, 87, 183
"helicopter parenting," 224
Highly Sensitive Person, The, 136
high-risk behaviour, 16, 132, 237, 242
Hillman, James, 248
Hollis, James, 21, 142, 239
homework, 81, 83, 91, 103–06, 107, 129,
    226, 233, 234, 250, 259
hunter-gatherer, 61, 87–88, 183, 184

hyperfocusing, 29, 78–79, 89
hyper-masculinity, 144

Ignatieff, Michael, 38
impulse control, impulsivity, 54–55, 57,
    63, 87, 88–89, 91–92, 96, 97, 98, 100,
    103, 108, 109
In The Realm of Hungry Ghosts, 187
Industrial Revolution, 88, 133, 182–83
initiation, 131–35, 144, 154
internal locus of control, 249, 271
introvert, 136–38, 197
Irving, John, 260

Jesus, 14–16, 18–20, 40, 287
Jung, Carl G., 21, 136, 239, 269, 274

Kielburger, Craig, 151
Kids Are Worth It, 82, 129
King Lear, 218–21

L'Arche, 280–81
Lawrence of Arabia, 273–74, 276
"learned helplessness," 104
Levine, Mel, 38, 84, 122, 216
Levy, Ariel, 140
Locus of control, 225, 249, 271
Lord of the Rings, The, 187–88, 273–74
Louv, Richard, 183
Lowen, Alexander, 201
Luther, Martin, 24

Mad magazine, 226
marijuana, 96–97, 147
Maslow, Abraham, 269
Maté, Gabor, 84, 94, 187–188, 215, 233,
    234
McLuhan, Marshall, 24, 207
Media Awareness Network, 160–61
Medication for ADD, 94–98, 100
Merton, Thomas, 290
Michaels, Anne, 284
Middle Passage, The, 239
Miller, Alice, 213–14
Mind at a Time, 38
mirroring, 108–09, 236
Montessori, Maria, 110, 111–12

MSN, 33, 160, 185, 195–96, 198
multi-tasking, 77
Myth of Multitasking, 31

"Nature Deficit Disorder," 183
Neill, A.S., 40, 42, 220–21, 235–236
Neufeld, Gordon, 233
Nietzsche, Friedrich, 233
Nineteen Eighty-Four, 30, 267, 293
noise, foreground and background, 112,
    115, 127, 128–29

Obama, Barack, 26, 141
Office, The, 163–64
Original Blessing, 255
Original Sin, 255
Orwell, George, 30, 267, 293

"Parenting Fallacy, The," 248
Piercing, 132, 237
Pollack, William, 47, 67, 126, 143, 148
Postman, Neil, 16, 23, 29, 121–22, 265
postmodernism, 14–15
"prepared environment," 110
Primal Teen, 57
Procrustes, 217–18

Rank, Otto, 233
reading trauma, 120–21
Real Boys, 143
realpolitik, 98
receptive language, 65–66, 99, 125–26
redirecting, 112–13
repetition and memory, 106
Rights Revolution, 38
Romeo and Juliet, 16–18

Sax, Leonard, 29, 50
Scattered Minds, 233
Schulz, Charles, 128–29
Schwarzenegger, Arnold, 20
Seating in the classroom, 114–15, 12
Second World War, 88
self-harming, 144, 146–47
self-medication, 147
self-regulation, 54, 95, 108, 235, 285
sex-role stereotyping, 139–41, 142

"shunning," 222
Simpsons, The, 140, 202–03, 265
single-mother home, 133, 297
Soul's Code, The, 248
Stallone, Sylvester, 20
Stein, Janice, 37–38
Strauch, Barbara, 57, 179–80
stress and language, 66–67, 69–70
Summerhill, 40, 236

Terr, Lenore, 203
testosterone and language, 30, 68–69,
    71–72, 245
"tight ship" school, 226
To Kill a Mockingbird, 58, 283, 293
Tolkien, J.R.R., 187, 274, 276
tone of voice, 32, 33, 85–86, 127, 196,
    255
*Too Scared to Cry: Psychic Trauma in
    Childhood*, 203
transitioning, 78–79, 81–82
trauma, 120–21, 138–39, 168, 201–04
trust, 135, 171, 175, 202, 224–25, 227–
    28, 288
Twain, Mark, 30

*Under Saturn's Shadow: The Wounding
    and Healing of Men*, 142
Unstructured time, 54, 109–10

Vanier, Jean, 280–81

Walt Disney, 276
Warhammer, 253
"War on Terror," 159
White, T.H., 14
Williams, Robin, 29
Wolf, Naomi, 140
World of Warcraft, 191, 193, 252
worrying, 228–29
writing, 30, 32, 33, 35–36, 53, 59, 62–63,
    80, 88–89, 103, 105, 117–29, 140–
    41, 145, 180–81, 182

zen of boyhood, 82–84
"zoning out," 73–74, 191

OF RELATED INTEREST

To Be a Friend

The Key to Friendship in Our Lives
by David E. Hunt
978-1554887514
$14.99

In today's busy world, we may fail to realize that our need for friendship is as vital and important as our basic needs for food, air, and water. However, thanks to the high-stress environments people currently live in, they are now starting to realize how important friendship is to a healthy and full life.

This book shows readers how to open the flow of friendship in their lives by learning to be friends. It offers activities that have proven helpful to participants in the author's workshops, exercises that prompt readers to examine their personal beliefs about friendship and apply them in daily life. By following these activities, readers discover how to be friends with themselves, how to be friends with others, and how to strengthen existing friendships. Author David Hunt also describes his experiences with learning how to be a friend, including his successes and failures.

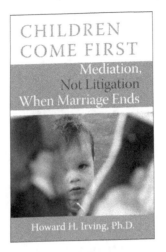

Children Come First

Mediation, Not Litigation When Marriage Ends
by Howard H. Irving
978-1554887958
$24.99

For three decades Dr. Howard H. Irving has championed the use of divorce mediation outside the adversarial court system to save couples and their children from the bitter legacy of legal wrangling and winner-takes-all custody battles. Now, calling on his vast experience mediating more than 2,000 cases, Irving has written this book directly for couples contemplating or undergoing divorce.

In this book the author takes a tripartite approach that points out: the dangers of the adversarial approach to divorce; the benefits of divorce mediation; and how parents can put their children first during and after their divorce.

Ultimately, this book takes parents through the process of building a shared parenting plan that places their children's interests uppermost while still addressing the parents' unique situations and needs.

Available at your favourite bookseller.

DUNDURN
www.dundurn.com

What did you think of this book?
Visit *www.dundurn.com* for reviews, videos, updates, and more!